olser ed on
corpus

THE KNIGHT'S TALE

D0369504

THE KNIGHT'S TALE

FROM THE CANTERBURY TALES

BY

GEOFFREY CHAUCER

*Revised Edition edited with Introduction,
Notes and Glossary by*

A. C. SPEARING

CAMBRIDGE
UNIVERSITY PRESS

Published by the Press Syndicate of the University of Cambridge
The Pitt Building, Trumpington Street, Cambridge CB2 1RP
40 West 20th Street, New York, NY 10011–4211, USA
10 Stamford Road, Oakleigh, Melbourne 3166, Australia

© Cambridge University Press 1966, 1995

Library of Congress cataloguing in publication data
Chaucer, Geoffrey, d. 1400.
[Knight's tale]
The knight's tale, from the Canterbury tales / by Geoffrey Chaucer. – Rev.
ed. / edited with introduction, notes, and glossary by A. C. Spearing.
p.   cm.
I. Spearing, A. C.   II. Title
PR1868.K6S6   1995
821'.1–dc20   94–44398   CIP

ISBN 0 521 49912 7

First published 1966
Seventeenth printing 1993
Revised edition 1995

Printed in Great Britain at the
University Press, Cambridge

The cover illustration shows a manuscript illumination depicting
Geoffrey Chaucer, reproduced by permission of The Huntington Library,
San Marino, California

CONTENTS

PREFACE

This edition of *The Knight's Tale* was first published in 1966; some corrections were made in 1974, but after that it was reprinted without further change. Chaucer studies, and studies of this Tale, have developed considerably since then, throwing new light on such matters as medieval warfare, medieval conceptions of love, and Chaucer's interest in the pagan past, while feminism and other forms of theory have taught us to ask new questions about past cultures and their literature. As a result of these developments and of my own work on the Tale, my view of it has changed in important ways. For this revised edition, the Introduction has been completely rewritten, the Notes have been thoroughly reconsidered, and some corrections have been made in the Glossary. The text of the Tale remains unaltered except for a few changes in punctuation.

I am greatly indebted to my wife for her detailed collaboration in composing both the original edition and this revised version.

Much of the further reading that I think likely to be useful is mentioned in footnotes to the Introduction, but I would also recommend the following:

Kathleen A. Blake, 'Order and the Noble Life in Chaucer's *Knight's Tale?*', *Modern Language Quarterly* 34 (1973)
Giovanni Boccaccio, *The Book of Theseus*, trans. Bernadette Marie McCoy (Medieval Text Association, 1974) (a complete translation of the *Teseida*)
Susan Crane, *Gender and Romance in Chaucer's Canterbury Tales* (Princeton University Press, 1994)

N. R. Havely, *Chaucer's Boccaccio* (D. S. Brewer, 1980)

Ronald B. Herzman, 'The Paradox of Form: *The Knight's Tale* and Chaucerian Aesthetics', *Papers on Language and Literature* 10 (1974)

Maurice Keen, *Chivalry* (Yale University Press, 1984)

A. J. Minnis, *Chaucer and Pagan Antiquity* (D. S. Brewer, 1982)

Elizabeth Salter, *Chaucer: The Knight's Tale and The Clerk's Tale* (Edward Arnold, 1962)

Joseph Westlund, 'The *Knight's Tale* as an Impetus for Pilgrimage', *Philological Quarterly* 43 (1964)

A.C.S.

Wattlefield, Norfolk
August 1994

INTRODUCTION

ORIGINS

Like most of Chaucer's poetry, and indeed like most medieval literature, *The Knight's Tale* is not original in its story. It was not the habit of medieval writers to invent their own stories; on the contrary, they were pleased to be able to claim the authority of age for the tales they told, and to begin:

> Whilom, as olde stories tellen us . . .

The Knight's Tale is derived from a specific written source, though Chaucer does not anywhere say what it is. It is in fact the *Teseida* of Giovanni Boccaccio, an Italian poet who was an older contemporary of Chaucer, and from whose work he translated the whole or part of a number of his own poems. Notably, Chaucer's longest single work, *Troilus and Criseyde*, is essentially a translation of Boccaccio's *Filostrato*, while Chaucer borrows from the *Teseida* not only in *The Knight's Tale* but also in *The House of Fame*, *The Parliament of Fowls*, *The Franklin's Tale*, the *Troilus* again, and in an unfinished poem called *Anelida and Arcite*. The last appears to be a first attempt at a self-contained translation from the *Teseida*, though in it Chaucer shows more interest in the 'epic' style of Boccaccio's poem than in its story.

The *Teseida* was written in 1339–40. It too had an 'old history' as its source, the *Thebaid* of Statius, a Latin epic completed in AD 92. (Chaucer also made some direct use of the *Thebaid* in *The Knight's Tale*; in many *Canterbury Tales* manuscripts this tale is prefaced by a brief quotation from Statius, possibly placed there by Chaucer himself.) Boccaccio's aim in the *Teseida* was characteristic of the early Renaissance—to produce an equivalent to classical epic poetry in a modern vernacular language. His poem has the same number of books and even the same number of lines as Virgil's *Aeneid*, and he was careful to present it in the form in which classical epics were read in the medieval schools—accompanied by a prose commentary interpreting the meaning of its fiction in moral and allegorical terms. (Whether Chaucer knew this commentary is uncertain; if he did, he probably made little use of it.) Boccaccio claimed that the *Teseida* was the first vernacular poem to match the classics in treating the predominant epic subject of war. An additional part of his fiction was that the *Teseida* was addressed to Maria d'Aquino, allegedly his mistress, in order to regain her favour. The part of the story that concerns Palemone (Chaucer's Palamon) and Arcita (Arcite) was probably invented by Boccaccio himself, and Emilia (Emelye) was intended to stand for Maria, while Arcita, the unrecognized lover who is compelled by his lady's attraction to return to the danger of Athens and who eventually suffers death in his pursuit of her, represented Boccaccio. This level of personal allusion is, so far as we know, completely absent from Chaucer's poem, and in general his 'translation' from Boccaccio is very different from the literal rendering that we understand by the word in modern times. He transmutes his source, to an extent which is most obvious in the fact that he reduces its length from nearly 10,000 lines to 2250. He makes in effect a new poem, a reinterpretation of the old story which is thoroughly and unmistakably Chaucerian.

The work of the great Italian poets of the fourteenth century, Dante, Petrarch and Boccaccio, was not familiar in Chaucer's England. These poets meant much to Chaucer himself, for they gave him a sense of the heights attainable by poetry in a vernacular language that he could not have gained from reading the French courtly poets who were fashionable in England during his lifetime, still less from the mainly anonymous English writings likely to have been known to him, beautiful though some of these are. The Italian poets offered models for a poetry of elevated style and learned substance, emulating the great Latin writers of classical antiquity, but employing the living and changing flexibility of a modern language. But these models were available only to those few Englishmen who could visit Italy to encounter them directly, and Chaucer is the only English poet we know of before the sixteenth century who was in this position. Chaucer was employed as a diplomat and trade negotiator, and he was sent to Italy on royal business in 1372–3 (to Genoa and Florence) and again in 1378 (to Milan). Then as later, French was the language of diplomacy, and in this Chaucer was fluent, but presumably he was chosen for these trips in part because, as an apt linguist, he also knew some Italian, which he could have learned from the Italian merchants and bankers resident in London in his time. Both Boccaccio and Petrarch would have been in Florence in the early 1370s; there is no telling whether Chaucer had a chance to meet them, but we can be sure that while in Italy he acquired manuscripts of Italian poetry, including copies of Boccaccio's *Filostrato* and *Teseida*, which he brought back to England with him.

These manuscripts were a basis for the creative borrowing that inspired the works listed above.

Beyond their general value as models for a new, more serious and learned type of vernacular poetry, capable of handling large political, moral, and philosophical issues, the *Teseida* and *Filostrato* are likely to have interested Chaucer in several ways. Perhaps more than anything else, he was attracted by their imaginative reconstruction of the pagan past; this aspect of *The Knight's Tale* will be discussed below. The sheer energy and scope of Boccaccio's narrative power must have appealed greatly to Chaucer; and it has rightly been suggested that Chaucer found stimulus to the development of his own work in the Italian poet's freedom from doctrinal narrowness, his 'intimation of many legitimately held attitudes towards the life of man at war, man in love, man faced by the working of Fate and the Gods'[1]. It would be a mistake, though, to suppose that Chaucer's public were in a position, like modern scholars, to measure his achievement against Boccaccio's. Neither in *The Knight's Tale* nor anywhere else in his work does Chaucer mention Boccaccio's name, and there is no reason to think that it would have meant anything to his readers if he had done so. The *Teseida* and even its story were completely unknown in England, and Chaucer's pretence throughout *The Knight's Tale* is that he is translating from authentic classical sources, presumably in Latin: 'Stace of Thebes [the *Thebaid* of Statius] and thise bookes olde' (1436), as he vaguely puts it in describing Emelye's rites in the temple of Diana. If Chaucer's intentions had emerged only from a comparison of his poem with its Italian source, he would

[1] Elizabeth Salter, *Fourteenth-Century English Poetry: Contexts and Readings* (Clarendon Press, 1983).

4

have failed. I shall therefore refer to the *Teseida* only when comparison seems to clarify specific points, rather than using it as a permanent guiding star.

In the *General Prologue* to *The Canterbury Tales*, the group of pilgrims (including an 'I' who is apparently Geoffrey Chaucer) who are about to set out from the Tabard Inn in Southwark for the shrine of St Thomas à Becket at Canterbury agree to the suggestion of Harry Bailly, landlord of the Tabard, that they should pass the time on their journey by telling stories to each other. On the morning when they depart, Harry proposes that they should draw lots to decide who is to tell the first story. They do so, and, 'Were it by aventure, or sort, or cas' (Whether by chance, or fate, or accident), the lot falls to the Knight. This is highly appropriate, for the Knight is the person of highest secular rank among the pilgrims and was the first of them to be described in the *General Prologue*, and questions of 'aventure, or sort, or cas' will be of central interest in his tale. The Knight immediately agrees to begin, and the tale he tells is the poem with which we are concerned in this book.

But the poem we call *The Knight's Tale* did not begin life as the first of *The Canterbury Tales*. In another poem, dating from about 1386–8, the Prologue to *The Legend of Good Women*, Chaucer dreams that he is being defended by Alcestis against the charge that, in writing about unfaithful women, he has committed heresy against the God of Love. Alcestis lists the works he has written in praise of love, and includes among them:

> al the love of Palamon and Arcite
> Of Thebes, thogh the story is knowen lite.

This poem, 'little known' in the late 1380s perhaps because it had only recently been written, and since then completely unknown, must be an earlier version of *The Knight's Tale*. We have no way of telling how it may have differed from the poem that survives, but there is little to indicate that Chaucer made many changes. Lines 27–34 are clearly inserted to connect the story with its new context in the pilgrims' tale-telling competition; the final couplet may have the same purpose; lines 1252–8 could be read as an insertion addressed by the Knight to his fellow-pilgrims, inviting them to share a military man's enthusiastic transposition of the ancient tournament to the English present. Apart from these brief passages, there is nothing in *The Knight's Tale* that could not have belonged to a separate version of the *Teseida*, composed before Chaucer had begun to compile *The Canterbury Tales*. Occasionally, indeed, he fails to alter turns of phrase that are inappropriate to the fiction of oral tale-telling, and that recall the written nature of the text before us:

> What sholde I al day of his wo endite? (522)
>
> Of this bataille I wol namoore endite,
> But speke of Palamon and of Arcite. (1883–4)

There are similar moments, though, in other *Canterbury Tales*, many of which are also likely to have had an earlier existence as separate poems. (One of them, later to become *The Second Nun's Tale*, is also mentioned in the Prologue to *The Legend of Good Women*.) Writing, as he was, on the border between an age in which storytelling had been oral and communal and one in which private reading was to become the norm, Chaucer frequently plays on the double existence of his works, as scores for performance and as texts for study. *The Canterbury Tales* itself, after all, survives as a written fiction of oral delivery and reception.

Why did Chaucer choose 'the love of Palamon and Arcite' as the story for the Knight to tell? As described in the *General Prologue*, the Knight has devoted his life to warfare governed by the chivalric values of 'Trouthe and honour, fredom and curtesie'. His career is a list of battles extending over some thirty years, and in that sense *The Knight's Tale*, which contains more descriptions of fighting than any of Chaucer's other poems (more, it has been suggested, than all his other poems put together), has an obvious appropriateness to its teller. The battles in which the Knight has served have all been far from England, part of that crusading activity that was still a living and valid ideal for fourteenth-century Englishmen of knightly rank, though it was rare for any to be so totally devoted to the ideal in reality. It has kept him far distant from the public life of administration and business in which many English knights of Chaucer's time were engaged, and in that way too the remote setting of the tale he tells is suitable to him. Few would dispute that *The Knight's Tale* is a knightly tale.[1] In other ways, though, there is a marked gap between the tale and the teller to whom it is attributed. The Knight's battles have nearly all been fought on behalf of Christianity against the heathen; unlike the Squire, his son, he has taken no part in the Hundred Years War between England and France, that struggle among Christian nations that had

---

[1] A few twentieth-century scholars have taken a different view, seeing the Knight as a brutal mercenary and the Tale as an account of Theseus's hypocritical tyranny. For an extreme example of this interpretation, in my opinion based on misunderstanding both of fourteenth-century England and of Chaucer's poetry, see Terry Jones, *Chaucer's Knight: The Portrait of a Medieval Mercenary* (Weidenfeld and Nicolson, 1980).

begun shortly before Chaucer's birth and was by far the commonest field of activity for English soldiers during his lifetime. (Chaucer himself had seen service in France as a young squire, and had been captured by the French and ransomed by King Edward III.) The conspicuously Christian motivation of the Knight's career makes the exclusively pagan setting of the tale he tells seem extremely surprising. Moreover, that pagan setting is associated, as we shall see, with a learned probing of fundamental philosophical issues, of a kind also found in other poems by Chaucer set in pagan times, such as *Troilus and Criseyde* and *The Franklin's Tale*; and it is hard to see how this could have any connection with the man who has spent his life riding from one battle to another and who joins the Canterbury pilgrimage still wearing a tunic rust-stained from his mail-coat.

Determined attempts have been made to show that *The Knight's Tale* expresses the specific character or consciousness of its teller, but in my view these have been unconvincing.[1] In *The Canterbury Tales* generally, Chaucer was content to establish generic relationships between tales and their tellers: pilgrims of low rank such as the Miller and Reeve tell comic tales about their social equals, nuns tell religious tales about miracles, and so on. He was often careless about narratorial detail (as when in describing the temples of Mars and of Diana in *The Knight's Tale* he repeatedly writes 'Ther saugh I . . .', even though the Knight cannot conceivably have seen these buildings). In

[1] Among the most important recent attempts are those of H. Marshall Leicester, *The Disenchanted Self: Representing the Subject in the Canterbury Tales* (University of California Press, 1990), Part III, and Lee Patterson, *Chaucer and the Subject of History* (University of Wisconsin Press, 1991), ch.3.

some cases he did not even get round to creating generic links (the Shipman, for example, tells a tale evidently intended for a woman), while in a few extremely interesting cases, such as those of the Pardoner and the Wife of Bath, he seems to have gone beyond the merely generic, devising tales that are in some sense dramatic monologues, and that reveal more about their tellers than the tellers realize. *The Knight's Tale* is a tale appropriate in many ways to a knight, but it tells us more about Chaucer and his interests than about the idealized Knight who is among the Canterbury pilgrims. I shall normally refer to the teller of *The Knight's Tale* simply as Chaucer, because even phrases such as 'the teller' or 'the narrator' tend to imply the existence of a distinct and consistent narratorial persona, of a kind that I do not believe Chaucer ever imagined. 'Narration', as we shall see, is a central part of our experience in reading the tale; 'the narrator' is not. For a medieval man, Chaucer was unusually sensitive to the ways in which tales can reveal the preconceptions and prejudices of those who tell them, but he largely shared his contemporaries' assumption that stories have a life of their own, larger and more fruitful of meaning than any individual consciousness. Can we be sure that he was wrong?

THE KNIGHT'S TALE AS CHIVALRIC ROMANCE

Chivalric romances

The 'knightly tale' attributed to the Knight is of a kind that modern scholars would define as chivalric romance. The term 'romance' is commonly used in medieval languages (*roman* in French, *romaunt* or *romaunce* in English), but it does not have a very precise meaning. It may indicate no more than a narrative in a vernacular language, as opposed to Latin (we still speak of 'Romance languages', meaning those descended from Latin, such as French and Italian); or, in an age when Latin was the language of serious thought and learning, it may imply the kind of material that would be supposed characteristic of vernacular narrative—fictional, fanciful, extravagant, lacking in intellectual seriousness. Modern scholars recognize a large group of narratives, in many vernacular languages, as belonging to a somewhat more precise category of 'chivalric romances' or 'courtly romances'. These narratives have certain fundamental features in common, but rather than a precisely delimited genre they form an extended family, with many variant branches. The most important thing they have in common, and the feature that makes it especially appropriate that one of them should be told by Chaucer's Knight, is that they are stories of aristocratic life—stories of kings and queens, dukes and duchesses, knights and ladies. The normal medieval assumption is that social rank, conveyed by birth for men and by birth or marriage for women, is a fundamental and permanent human category. Terms such as *cherl* or *vileyn* (peasant) and *gentil* (noble) have ethical as well as social meanings: a peasant, it is assumed, will behave *cherlisshly*, while a nobleman or gentleman will behave *gentilly*. (Everyone knew, of course, that this assumption might sometimes not be fulfilled, and Chaucer himself in other poems, such as the tales of the Wife of Bath and the Franklin, is anxious to argue that true *gentillesse* is a matter of conduct, not of social origin.) And the basic structure of medieval literary genres is an offshoot of this ideology: vulgar, comic stories (fabliaux) are about *cherles*; romances, idealizing stories, are about those of *gentil* birth.

Idealization is an essential feature of romances. They may include much realism of detail in their depiction of aristocratic life: all the more so in Chaucer's time because by then there was a tendency for the nobility consciously to model their lives on romances—the traffic between romance and aristocratic reality moved in both directions. But the realistic detail is part of an idealizing celebration of the noble way of life, in its conspicuous consumption, its material luxury, its ostentatious splendour, its drive towards superlative grandeur and beauty. That celebratory quality is an especially marked feature of *The Knight's Tale*, and I shall have more to say later about its significance.

A third common feature of romances follows from their aristocratic subject matter. Because they are about aristocrats, they focus on what were seen as the two defining activities of aristocratic life, war and love. Aggression and sexual desire are in any case fundamental human instincts, but the medieval nobility began specifically as a warrior aristocracy, gaining power and imposing order in the chaos that followed the gradual decay of the Romans' European empire. The medieval nobleman originated as an armed and mounted warrior, and the huge expense of armour and warhorse (comparable, let us say, to possessing and maintaining one's own private tank) necessarily made him an exclusive figure, requiring the produce of much land and many peasants for his upkeep. By Chaucer's time, order had largely been restored, but what justified the privileged status of nobility and knighthood was still seen as being military prowess. Chaucer's Knight has devoted his life to the business of fighting, and he is characterized not only by the courage and specialized skill (*worthinesse* or prowess) necessary for this way of life but by a complex structure of virtues—'Trouthe [fidelity, just conduct] and honour, fredom [generosity, graciousness] and curteisie'. Cavalry has become chivalry, an ethic that in Chaucer's time was being consciously renewed by the formation of new chivalric orders all over Europe, King Edward III's Order of the Garter prominent among them. Both prowess and the system of chivalric virtues are central themes of medieval romances. So is love, the other activity that was seen as defining noble life. Aristocratic power and prosperity provided the possibility of leisure, both for ladies and for knights when not engaged in fighting; and that leisure was especially occupied with the cultivation of emotion around desire, at once masking and expressing the sexual instinct. In romances war and love tend to be closely linked: the knight performs deeds of prowess to win the lady's favour. In *The Knight's Tale*, as we shall see, the competitive aggression of Palamon and Arcite is the means by which it is to be settled which of them shall marry Emelye.

One other general characteristic of romances is that they are stories of adventure. Knights do not simply perform the duties required of them by their lords, but set out to encounter the unexpected—*aventure*, what happens by chance—so as to test themselves and the chivalric virtues they claim to live by, and perhaps to achieve a deeper understanding of their own nature and way of life. Appropriately, the settings of romances tend to be remote in time and/or place from everyday medieval life, settings in which the pattern of events cannot be confidently predicted, so that a knight will never know what test he may next have to face. The favourite setting of medieval romances is an imaginary Britain in what Chaucer's Wife of Bath calls 'th'olde dayes of the King Arthour'; and within such a general setting the characteristic location of knightly adventure is the forest, the mysterious area beyond human cultivation. (Much of medieval Europe was still heavily forested in reality.) In *The Knight's Tale*, adventure is not merely a feature of knightly activity, but becomes an explicit theme of the poem's thought: Fortune is repeatedly invoked as an explanatory concept, the 'lack of causal motivation' for events is insisted on, and 'The word *aventure* occurs in the *Tale* eleven times, while in the *Canterbury Tales* as a whole it appears only thirty times'[1]. Because of the philosophical dimension given to adventure in *The Knight's Tale*, I shall return to this topic later when considering the poem as a philosophical narrative.

War in The Knight's Tale[2]

For all its idealizing quality, the treatment of war in the Tale has many realistic features. The martial activities represented in the poem can frequently be paralleled from medieval chronicles, and must often be interpreted according to medieval conceptions of the laws of war, which were very different from our own. To many people in our time,

[1] Barbara Nolan, *Chaucer and the Tradition of the 'Roman Antique'* (Cambridge University Press, 1992).
[2] In this section I borrow without further acknowledgement from Stuart Robertson, 'Elements of Realism in the *Knight's Tale*', *Journal of English and Germanic Philology* 14 (1915); M. H. Keen, *The Law of War in the Later Middle Ages* (Routledge, 1965); Bruce Kent Cowgill, 'The *Knight's Tale* and the Hundred Years' War', *Philological Quarterly* 54 (1975); and G. A. Lester, 'Chaucer's Knight and the Medieval Tournament', *Neophilologus* 66 (1982).

war itself has come to seem unjustifiable in any circumstances, and belligerence 'has been shorn of its glamor (or
canalized into "business drive", sport, and so forth) to a
degree that would have been incomprehensible to most of
Chaucer's contemporaries'[1]. In Chaucer's time, warfare,
while inevitably brutal and destructive, had no means of
destroying the world or human civilization, and remained
largely a matter of face-to-face encounter; and male
honour, especially among the aristocracy, was generally felt
to depend on willingness and ability to use violence within
a certain code of conduct. The chronicler Froissart reports
on the contempt expressed by King Richard II's uncle, the
Duke of Gloucester, Constable of England, for the king's
unwillingness to pursue war against France, and his prefer-
ence for the arts of peace: 'this is no lyfe for men of werre
that wyll deserve to have honour by prowes of dedes of
arms!' Theseus's campaign against Creon, though
described by one modern critic as 'wanton violent destruction'[2], is clearly presented in the poem as a necessary,
though necessarily destructive, means of enforcing justice
against a tyrant and his followers. Theseus's own part in the
campaign is noble—'He faught, and slough him manly as a
knight / In pleyn bataille' (129–30)—and the whole procedure exactly follows approved medieval customs. Theseus
begins by 'displaying' his banner (108), the accepted sign
that open war had been declared. The battle takes place on a
plain outside the city, the defenders are beaten and retreat
within its walls, they are pursued, and the victors finally
destroy the city utterly. The action sounds barbarous, but

[1] Alcuin Blamires, 'Chaucer's Revaluation of Chivalric Honor', *Medi-
aevalia* 5 (1979).
[2] David Aers, *Chaucer* (Harvester, 1986).

the destruction of a city taken by assault was permitted by
the law of war, and was frequently carried out. Afterwards
the pillagers search the battlefield, and they recognize
Palamon and Arcite by their 'cote-armures' (158), the
medieval signs of identity among the noble. The two
knights are brought to Theseus, and he sends them to
prison for life. Chaucer three times mentions a detail not
found in his source, that Theseus would accept no ransom
for them. Here again an understanding in medieval terms is
necessary. To gain money by ransom was regarded as a
legitimate purpose of warfare, and it had been a major
source of income for English lords and knights in the
successful early stages of the Hundred Years War. Martial
honour and martial profit were not seen as necessarily
opposed for English soldiers in the fourteenth century, any
more than they were for English sailors at the time of the
Napoleonic Wars. It is true that captors were normally
expected to allow their prisoners to be ransomed on
reasonable terms; on the other hand, the Theban princes
are Theseus's deadly enemies, and if he releases them he
cannot be sure that they will not assemble their followers to
wage war on him, as indeed Palamon suggests that Arcite
will do once he has been freed at Perotheus's request
(427–32). The princes' perpetual imprisonment, set in
immediate contrast with Theseus's lifelong 'joye and . . .
honour' (170), is part of an aesthetic and philosophical
design that ultimately points to the notion of human life
itself as a prison from which the only escape is death; but
Chaucer has carefully set it in a realistic context, and one
that shows Theseus acting with prudence and with an
exceptional lack of concern for material gain.

When Palamon and Arcite meet for their secret duel,

Theseus is outraged that they should be fighting 'Withouten juge or oother officere' (854). This too is a medieval reaction, for a judicial duel between noble combatants, with death as a possible outcome, was still a recognized practice in Chaucer's time, one indeed for which the Duke of Gloucester had set down written rules; but it was regarded as legitimate only if conducted under the control of heralds to ensure that the rules were observed. The appeal of the onlooking ladies to Theseus to have mercy, and Theseus's consent, represent not merely a fantasy of ideal nobility but a possible medieval reality. In a famous case recorded by Froissart, Edward III's queen had interceded with the king to have mercy on six citizens of Calais whose lives were legitimately forfeit, and her appeal had been successful. The tournament by which the claim to Emelye's hand is to be settled, though doubtless made more magnificent by poetic licence, also reflects a genuine late-medieval love of spectacle and stylized violence. The specific combination ordained by Theseus of mêlée (or mock battle) with duel seems to have been unusual, but the procedure otherwise follows the pattern of actual tournaments as recorded by chroniclers. Religious observances (pagan ones, of course, in *The Knight's Tale*) regularly precede the fighting; Theseus as judge is entitled to modify the rules at the last moment, and his limitation of weapons to the spear and sword and of the outcome to capture rather than death was quite normal in medieval tournaments; the feasts held before and after were also common accompaniments to tournaments in Chaucer's time. All this must be understood if we are to recognize the nature of the Tale's appeal to its original audience and to avoid misinterpreting it.

At the same time, it must not be supposed that medieval attitudes towards fighting were simple and monolithic. Towards the close of the fourteenth century, when the war with France had already lasted, with brief intervals, for over fifty years, there seems to have been a growing sense of weariness and of horror that Christian nations should wage such destruction upon each other, rather than uniting in the sacred violence of a crusade to win back the Holy Land from the Saracens. The striking absence of Chaucer's Knight from the battles of the Hundred Years War may possibly indicate that Chaucer shared this feeling; we know that some of his friends at court did; and Richard II, who came to the throne as a boy in 1377, had very different tastes from his warlike grandfather and father, Edward III and the Black Prince. One notable late-fourteenth-century manifestation of the longing for European peace was the foundation of a new chivalric Order, that of the Passion of Jesus Christ, which included both English and French knights, and was explicitly dedicated to achieving an alliance between England and France and a new crusade to recapture Jerusalem, on the basis of a marriage between Richard and a French princess—not unlike the dynastic alliance between Athens and Thebes achieved at the end of *The Knight's Tale*. Along with its 'idealizing realism' in its treatment of fighting, the Tale includes a strong emphasis on the horrifying consequences of violence, whether the violence itself is legitimate or illegitimate—a city in ruins, a 'taas of bodies dede' (147) being ransacked by pillagers, human beings abandoning their humanity to act like wild beasts, and ultimately the gruesome and squalid death of Arcite, smothered in his own blood. Chaucer never suggests that there is any simple solution to this problem—would Theseus have done better to allow Creon's tyrannical rule to continue? or not to attempt to prevent Arcite and Palamon from fighting 'breme as it were bores two' (841)?—but his poem certainly evokes the misery as well as the grandeur of medieval warfare.

Love in The Knight's Tale

The other defining aristocratic activity is love, and this is no less important in *The Knight's Tale* than war. From the twelfth century on, a long tradition of European courtly writing, in lyrics, romances and allegorical visions, had refined and stylized a literary conception of love as idealization, suffering, and supreme value. One of the most influential expositions of the art of love (in French sometimes called *fin' amors*, rendered by Chaucer as 'the craft of fyn lovinge') was to be found in Guillaume de Lorris's thirteenth-century *Roman de la Rose*, which Chaucer had translated from French at an early stage of his poetic career. Here the process of falling in love is described allegorically in the form of a dream, in which Guillaume first finds his way into a rose-garden. This is the garden of love, and it is noticeable that certain unpleasant aspects of human life are explicitly excluded from it—poverty and old age, for example. In *The Knight's Tale*, similarly, the setting is exclusively aristocratic and untroubled by problems of money or time. Arcite, disguised as Philostrate, is given by Theseus 'gold to maintene his degree', and also goes on secretly receiving his 'rente' from 'his contree' (583–5), while despite the passage of many years in the course of the story, there is no indication that Palamon or Emelye has become any less attractive at the end of it. Inside the garden, Guillaume finds the God of Love himself, leading

Beauty by the hand and accompanied by a whole train of allegorical figures, including Idleness, the garden's gate-keeper. At the centre of the garden is a spring forming the pool by which Narcissus died of love for his own reflection—a perfect image of the unattainability of love's goal (as Emelye seems hopelessly unattainable to Palamon and Arcite when they first see her from their prison window). In *The Knight's Tale* Idleness, now gatekeeper to the garden of Venus, the Goddess of Love, is mentioned in the description of Venus's temple, and Narcissus also appears in the same description (1082–3). As Guillaume in the *Roman de la Rose* bends to admire a rosebud, the God of Love shoots an arrow which wounds his heart through his eye. The head of the arrow, which will not come out of the wound, is called Beauty, and the rosebud is a symbol of the object of his love. Exactly the same pattern of ideas recurs in *The Knight's Tale* when Palamon first sees Emelye wandering in her garden from his prison window. He falls in love at first sight, and the effect is of a sudden sickness or wound:

> He cast his eye upon Emelya,
> And therwithal he bleynte and cride, 'A!'
> As though he stongen were unto the herte.   (219–21)

Arcite then looks at Emelye too,

> Wher as this lady romed to and fro,
> And with that sighte hir beautee hurte him so,
> That, if that Palamon was wounded sore,
> Arcite is hurt as muche as he, or moore.
> And with a sigh he seyde pitously:
> 'The fresshe beautee sleeth me sodeynly
> Of hire that rometh in the yonder place.'   (255–61)

Emelye's beauty is killing him; and the same idea recurs with greater intensity when, disguised as Philostrate, he returns to Athens, and soliloquizes while Palamon secretly listens:

> And over al this, to sleen me outrely,
> Love hath his firy dart so brenningly
> Ystiked thurgh my trewe, careful herte,
> That shapen was my deeth erst than my sherte.
> Ye sleen me with youre eyen, Emelye;
> Ye been the cause wherfore that I die.   (705–10)

The wound given by Love's arrow is mortal. For most medieval people this was only a courtly metaphor, but for Arcite it is literally true: he is killed by his love for Emelye, and in the very act of looking at her (1821), after the tournament at the end of the poem.

The conception of love as an injury received through the eye, incurable and potentially mortal, is basic to the whole story of *The Knight's Tale*. Arcite and Palamon have no choice but to behave as they do; they *must* love Emelye, whatever extravagance or absurdity their love may lead them into, because they are suffering from a sickness. In this as in many other respects, what seems like poetic fancy in *The Knight's Tale* is closely linked to medieval science. The love-poetry of the Middle Ages and the Renaissance is full of disease imagery, with an attack of love producing many of the same symptoms as a bout of influenza. The reason for this is that love-sickness was regarded as a literal disease, known as *amor hereos*, and the best treatment for it was hotly disputed in medical treatises. When Arcite is banished from Athens and hence from Emelye, Chaucer gives a detailed account of the symptoms from which he suffers: he cannot eat, drink, or sleep, he is depressed, he cries easily, and he becomes so pale and thin as to be unrecognizable. This passage (503–21), one scholar has written, 'might almost be a paraphrase of a chapter on *hereos* from one of the medical treatises themselves'.[1] Another symptom of *amor hereos* is extreme moodiness, and this too is displayed by Arcite when, after singing a cheerful song, he falls suddenly 'Into a studie' (672), which results in his soliloquy just referred to. Chaucer indeed defines his sickness as 'the loveris maladye / Of Hereos' (515–16), and explains in physiological terms how it arises from an excess of the melancholic humour and can lead to mania. It was the young who were most liable to this disease; to those who had gained maturity, it might seem less like sickness than like folly, especially when the object of love was forbidden or otherwise unattainable—another man's wife, the kinswoman of an enemy, or a woman unaware of or indifferent to the passion she aroused. This is how Theseus sees Arcite and Palamon, when he finds them fighting over Emelye, who knows nothing of their love:

> Now looketh, is nat that an heigh folye?
> Who may been a fool, but if he love? (940–1)

But he too has suffered 'loves peyne' in his youth (957) and recognizes that, if *amor hereos* is foolishness, it is still unavoidable, for 'A man moot ben a fool, or yong or oold' (954).

Love, then, is a sickness, but it is also a literary code and a courtly game. Chaucer's readers might follow the development of the two lovers' cases in a spirit of connoisseurship,

---

[1] John Livingston Lowes, 'The Loveres Maladye of Hereos', *Modern Philology* 11 (1913–14); see also Edward C. Schweitzer, 'Fate and Freedom in *The Knight's Tale*', *Studies in the Age of Chaucer* 3 (1981), and Mary F. Wack, *Love-Sickness in the Middle Ages* (University of Pennsylvania Press, 1990).

watching the enactment of a game they perhaps played themselves somewhere between jest and earnest. Since the code of love was so exactly defined, a casuistry of love had been developed, and there could be lengthy discussion of such questions as whether one lover's situation was more or less happy than another's. Is the lover whose lady has died worse or better off than the lover whose lady has rejected his love? This is the question that underlies Chaucer's early poem, *The Book of the Duchess*; and just such a problem or *demande d'amour* is put directly to the audience of *The Knight's Tale* at the end of Part 1:

> Yow loveres axe I now this questioun:
> Who hath the worse, Arcite or Palamoun?
> That oon may seen his lady day by day,
> But in prison he moot dwelle alway;
> That oother wher him list may ride or go,
> But seen his lady shal he nevere mo.
> Now demeth as yow liste, ye that kan,
> For I wol telle forth as I bigan.   (489–96)

The audience envisaged here is manifestly not one of Canterbury pilgrims; whether or not this audience of courtier-lovers is also a fiction, Chaucer clearly had in mind readers who were willing to think of themselves as courtly experts on love.

The lady and the season

So much for the symptoms of love in the lover. What of the lady he loves? Medieval love is often a one-way affair: it is seen from the point of view of the man, whose feelings are of great interest and may be analysed at length, while the woman tends to exist only as an object arousing those feelings. The arrow is shot in one direction only. This is especially true in *The Knight's Tale*. The feelings of Emelye are never considered at all. In the *Roman de la Rose* we see everything through the eyes of the dreamer who falls in love, and the girl he loves is a rose-bud, part of the Maytime setting of the poem. Palamon and Arcite also fall in love in May, while Emelye is gathering flowers in a garden. And Emelye appears less as a person than as a personification of the Maytime garden; this is the effect of the imagery by which she is first described:

> Till it fil ones, in a morwe of May,
> That Emelye, that fairer was to sene
> Than is the lilie upon his stalke grene,
> And fressher than the May with floures newe—
> For with the rose colour stroof hire hewe,
> I noot which was the finer of hem two.   (176–81)

She is not quite an allegorical rose, but she looks very like one: an almost purely symbolic figure. A garden in May becomes the regular setting for love in medieval courtly poetry, and the events of *The Knight's Tale* seem to take place in a perpetual May. It is May when Palamon and Arcite fall in love, and Emelye has gone out 'To doon honour to May' (189)—to take part in the courtly seasonal ritual of going out early to sing and gather flowers and leaves. It is May again, seven years later, when Arcite, as Philostrate, has gone out

> To maken him a gerland of the greves
> Were it of wodebinde or hawethorn leves,
> And loude he song ayeyn the sonne shene:
> 'May, with alle thy floures and thy grene,
> Welcome be thou, faire, fresshe May,
> In hope that I som grene gete may'   (649–54)

and is overheard by Palamon. It is because Theseus loves hunting in May that he discovers the two fighting next day. And it is exactly one year later, and therefore still in May, that the lovers are brought together again and the lark is singing just as it did the year before. As Palamon rises to pray to Venus,

> Up roos the sonne, and up roos Emelye.   (1415)

She remains little more than a personification of the feelings associated with spring, the crystallization of an atmosphere. Later in the same day, the fatal tournament takes place, and we are told that

> Greet was the feeste in Atthenes that day,
> And eek the lusty seson of that May
> Made every wight to been in swich plesaunce
> That al that Monday justen they and daunce,
> And spenden it in Venus heigh servise.   (1625–9)

But by now the joy of May has come to seem deceptive.

The religion of love

Though Emelye is thus a figure of little interest as a person, she is given great power by the love her beauty arouses. Love, after all, is a god in the *Roman de la Rose*, and the code of love developed in courtly writing into a religion of love. This religion was a parody of Christianity, borrowing its conceptions and terminology, and it is constantly played against Christianity in Chaucer's poetry. If taken seriously, the courtly religion of love would have been a heretical rival to the true religion; but in reality it was never more than a game, an unsystematic collection of attitudes. Sometimes the object of the cult was the lady herself, and so when Palamon first sees Emelye he does not know whether she is human or divine. This is the traditional response of the lover to the first sight of the beloved, though Palamon, as a pagan, thinks she may be the goddess Venus. If the lady is thought of as her lover's goddess, then he can deserve no benefit at her hands, as if she were his equal. On this point a theology of love is developed, paralleling Christian theology. Just as man can be saved not by justice (for all human beings deserve damnation for the sin of Adam) but only by God's mercy or grace, so the lover must beg for a response to his love from his lady's mercy. Thus Arcite says, on first seeing Emelye:

> And but I have hir mercy and hir grace,
> That I may seen hire atte leeste weye,
> I nam but deed; ther nis namoore to seye.   (262–4)

And, at the very end of the poem, when Theseus is persuading Emelye to marry Palamon, he argues that Palamon has long served her and suffered for her, and 'gentil mercy oghte to passen right' (2231). Arcite has claimed no greater mercy of Emelye than to see her. In Christian theology the sight of God *is* heaven, or at least the chief reward of the blessed, and the deprivation of this sight is the chief punishment of the damned. This too has its parallel in the religion of love, and so later when Arcite has been freed from prison but banished from Athens, and hence from Emelye's presence, he argues that now he is in hell eternally, while in prison he would have been in heavenly bliss. As a result of this deprivation of the sight of his lady, he can expect to die in *wanhope*—despair, the ultimate sin in Christian terms, which makes salvation impossible.

The parody-theology mentioned so far has made the lady the god of the religion of love. But there is a different parody-theology that places the God of Love himself in this position, and this too comes into *The Knight's Tale*.

The medieval God of Love is Cupid, the son of Venus, but the medieval Cupid is usually very different from the pretty boy of Roman statuary or modern Valentines. He is a lord, a tyrant even (so he is accused of being in the Prologue to *The Legend of Good Women*), and terrifying in the power he possesses over his devotees. This view of Cupid is developed most fully in Theseus's long speech when he finds Palamon and Arcite fighting in the woods, the speech beginning

> The god of love, a, *benedicite!*
> How mighty and how greet a lord is he!
> Ayeyns his might ther gaineth none obstacles.
> He may be cleped a god for his miracles . . .   (927–30)
>
> Bihoold, for Goddes sake that sit above,
> Se how they blede!   (942–3)

The apparently incongruous 'for Goddes sake that sit above'—which might refer to the Christian God—is not an accidental anachronism, for Theseus goes on to emphasize that the service of Cupid really is folly, a folly exemplified in the way these two are striving to murder each other for the sake of a woman who doesn't even know of their existence. The contrast between the religion of Cupid and the true religion is a common one, made more piquant by the fact that Christianity is a religion of love and that the Christian God could also be called a God of Love. The contrast is wittily expressed in an earlier line, when Palamon and Arcite agree to fight: 'O Cupide, out of alle charitee!' (765). The line means literally 'O Cupid, lacking in all kindness', but it includes a play on the two kinds of love, *charitee* (Latin *caritas*) or Christian love, and *cupiditas*, the evil self-love of mere desire.

Love and friendship

But the relationship, fraught with paradoxes, between the two religions and the two loves is not much explored in *The Knight's Tale*: it is a more central theme of other courtly poems by Chaucer, and particularly of *Troilus and Criseyde*. A contrast which is more persistent, and more significant, in *The Knight's Tale* is that between love and friendship, *amor* and *amicitia*. Just as love was formalized and codified in medieval courtly society, so might friendship be; we are told something of the lifelong friendship between Theseus and Perotheus, which leads to Arcite's release from prison; and the carefully defined friendship between Palamon and Arcite is a more important theme in the poem than the modern reader may perhaps realize. The two are cousins by birth, but they are also 'sworn brothers'—that is, they have sworn to treat each other as brothers, as Palamon explains:

> That nevere, for to dyen in the peyne,
> Til that the deeth departe shal us tweyne,
> Neither of us in love to hindre oother,
> Ne in noon oother cas, my leeve brother;
> But that thou sholdest trewely forthren me
> In every cas, as I shal forthren thee.   (275–80)

But when they are both struck by the irresistible force of love for Emelye, there necessarily develops a conflict between their love and their brotherhood. Palamon claims that Arcite's oath of brotherhood binds him to assist him in his pursuit of Emelye, but Arcite answers by asserting a theory that love is above all laws, precisely because it cannot be resisted:

> I pose that thow lovedest hire biforn;
> Wostow nat wel the olde clerkes sawe,
> That 'who shal yeve a lovere any lawe?'

> Love is a gretter lawe, by my pan,
> Than may be yeve to any erthely man;
> And therfore positif lawe and swich decree
> Is broken al day for love in ech degree.
> A man moot nedes love, maugree his heed.
> He may nat fleen it thogh he sholde be deed.   (304–12)

They go through the same arguments at a later stage of the poem. When Palamon overhears Arcite soliloquizing on his love for Emelye, he breaks in angrily with:

> Arcite, false traitour wikke,
> Now artow hent, that lovest my lady so,
> For whom that I have al this peyne and wo,
> And art my blood, and to my conseil sworn,
> As I ful ofte have told thee heerbiforn.   (722–6)

And Arcite's answer is:

> For I defye the seurete and the bond
> Which that thou seist that I have maad to thee.
> What, verray fool, think wel that love is free,
> And I wol love hire maugree al thy might!   (746–9)

Amicitia remains powerful, however, and prevents Arcite from killing Palamon on the spot; instead they arrange a formal combat for the next day, and before it

> Everich of hem heelp for to armen oother
> As freendly as he were his owene brother.   (793–4)

And at the very end of the poem, there is a sense in which *amicitia* triumphs, for Arcite in his dying speech does not, as we might expect, curse Palamon, but recommends him to Emelye if she should ever marry. Friendship could scarcely go further, and we feel (and are perhaps meant to feel) that it is more noble than love. *Amor* is an all-powerful force operating on human beings from outside, but *amicitia* is a willed human response by which a person may achieve a spiritual triumph in the very moment of bodily defeat.

Gentillesse *and* pitee

The focus on nobility of birth and of conduct that characterizes romance is a prominent feature of *The Knight's Tale*. *Gentil* is the poem's highest term of praise, and, as explained above, it refers to a quality that is at once social and ethical. All the main characters of *The Knight's Tale*, without exception, are of the highest aristocracy, related to the royal or ducal houses of Thebes or Athens. This is true even of the Theban widows who accost Theseus at the beginning of the poem, and when the senior lady tells him that 'ther is noon of us alle / That she ne hath been a duchesse or a queene' (64–5), she is in effect asserting their suitability to the kind of story in which they find themselves. Their descent to misery is felt to be the more moving because of their high rank, and it is to Theseus's *gentillesse* (62) that they appeal for aid. When Arcite is disguised as Philostrate and is serving as page of Emelye's chamber, even in this comparatively humble situation,

> He was so gentil of condicioun
> That thurghout al the court was his renoun.   (573–4)

It is because Palamon and Arcite are 'gentil men . . . of greet estaat' (895) that Queen Ypolita, Emelye, and their ladies urge Theseus to reconsider his decision to condemn the two knights to death when he finds them fighting. With his dying breath, Arcite recommends Palamon to Emelye as *gentil*—'Foryet nat Palamon, the gentil man' (1939)— and it is indeed as 'gentil Palamon' (2219) that Theseus commends him to Emelye as husband.

Gentillesse is a general disposition embracing many different attributes, and some of these are listed in Arcite's dying speech, when he enumerates Palamon's qualities as a lover:

> trouthe, honour, knighthede,
> Wisdom, humblesse, estaat, and heigh kinrede,
> Fredom, and al that longeth to that art. (1931–3)

But a central element in *gentillesse* as Chaucer conceives it is *pitee*, pity or compassion, and this plays a key role in the poem. One of the great innovations of medieval Christianity, with its concentration on the human sufferings of Christ, was to make compassion one of the most highly prized virtues. To feel Christ's sufferings as if they were one's own, to share the sympathetic agony of Mary and John at the foot of the cross—these are the great goals of the mainstream of medieval religious devotion. And as the Middle Ages progressed, this concentration on suffering and pity for suffering extended into secular writing and became more and more intensified—sometimes, to modern tastes, excessive. Chaucer was a man of his age in the high value he gave to *pitee*, and some of his favourite scenes seem to be those of pathos, with spectators within the fiction dissolving into compassionate tears that the reader or listener is clearly intended to share. The final scenes of *The Clerk's Tale* (when Grisilde's supposedly dead children are restored to her) and of *The Prioress's Tale* (when the martyred Christian boy dies) may be mentioned as examples. But Chaucer was well aware of the dangers of *pitee* disproportionate to its object (what we would call sentimentality), as is shown by the satirical description of the Prioress in the *General Prologue*, who

> was so charitable and so *pitous*
> She wolde wepe, if that she saugh a mous
> Kaught in a trappe, if it were deed or bledde.

In *The Knight's Tale*, *pitee* plays a central part without ever running to the excess of tears indulged in for their own sake, to no practical purpose. *Pitee* was often thought of as a distinctively feminine quality, as when Theseus calls on Emelye to show her 'wommanly pitee' to Palamon (2225), but it is Theseus himself who is the Tale's chief embodiment of *pitee*, and in him it is a dynamic virtue, directed towards transformative action. When the widows appeal to his *gentillesse*, it is in *pitee* that they expect it to be displayed:

> Som drope of *pitee*, thurgh thy gentillesse,
> Upon us wrecched wommen lat thou falle.   (62–3)

They cry out to him *pitously* (91), and in turn

> This gentil duc doun from his courser sterte
> With herte *pitous*, whan he herde hem speke.   (94–5)

(In Boccaccio's version he had remained in his chariot.) As one scholar has noted, this 'dual meaning' of *pitous*, as both pitiable and pitying, 'manifests the dynamic quality of pity: cause instantaneously re-creates itself as effect'.[1] There is a similar scene later when Theseus discovers Palamon and Arcite fighting and impulsively sentences them both to death. Again he succumbs to a female appeal, for 'Greet pitee was it, as it thoughte hem alle' (893), and his softening is justified by a general statement once more associating *pitee* with *gentillesse*: 'For pitee renneth soone in gentil

---

[1] Jill Mann, *Geoffrey Chaucer* (Harvester Wheatsheaf, 1991). The religious associations of *pitous* mean that it can also often shade into the sense 'pious'.

herte' (903: for pity flows readily in the noble heart). That sentiment must have been near to Chaucer's heart, for the same line appears three times elsewhere in his writings.

THE AESTHETIC OF ROMANCE

My discussion of *The Knight's Tale* as a chivalric romance has been chiefly concerned with the values it expresses or assumes. It is time now to turn to the poem's artistry, which, like that of romances generally, differs radically from what may be more familiar to us in, say, the novel. There is no question here of an art that aims to conceal itself, so as to create the illusion of reality; rather, the art of romance is one of drastic stylization, more like that of opera than that of the classic novel or film, and the art of *The Knight's Tale* takes this tendency even further than in most romances. When Chaucer refers to the artistry displayed at Theseus's command in the creation of the amphitheatre and its temples, the emphasis is on extravagance, ostentation, brilliance of spectacle, manifold craftsmanship:

> For in the lond ther was no crafty man
> That geometrie or ars-metrike kan,
> Ne portreyour, ne kervere of images,
> That Theseus ne yaf him mete and wages,
> The theatre for to maken and devyse. (1039–43)

He emphasizes both the lavish use of valuable materials—'That coste largely of gold a fother' (1050) and 'With many a florin he the hewes boghte' (1230)—and the technical skill applied to them: the sculptor's 'noble kerving' (1057) and the painter's 'soutil pencel' (1191). The poem's verbal art is governed by the same aesthetic principles, and one way in which this can be seen is in its intensely ceremonial quality. Many of the events represented are ceremonies in themselves: Theseus's triumphant march home from his victory over the Amazons, the Maytime *observaunces* carried out by Emelye in Part I and by Arcite in Part II, and the prayers in the temples of the three gods. There are many ceremonies connected with the tournament: Theseus's feast before it, the processional appearance of the two chief champions, Lygurge and Emetreus (one following the other with such careful symmetry that each is described in exactly twenty-seven lines), and the tournament itself, with the precise equality of the two sides, its careful conduct by heralds and its definite rules of procedure. Finally there are the funeral of Arcite and the wedding of Palamon and Emelye. And even events that are not intrinsically ceremonial are turned into ceremonies. The company of Theban widows might seem a disorderly interruption of Theseus's triumphant return to Athens, but in fact they arrange themselves with perfect symmetry, 'tweye and tweye, / Ech after oother' (40–1), and only turn the triumph into a ceremony of a different kind, a ritual of pleading and assent. Again, when, amidst the confusion of the battlefield, the bodies of Palamon and Arcite are discovered by the pillagers, the two are symmetrically arranged, 'ligginge by and by, / Bothe in oon armes' (153–4). It hardly needs saying that such ceremonial stylization is not intended as a depiction of everyday experience.

More centrally, the rivalry between the two lovers which is the poem's main subject begins in private and is made more ceremonial by stages. It starts when Palamon overhears Arcite's soliloquy and Arcite draws his sword as if to kill him. But an impromptu scuffle will not do, for Palamon is unarmed, and so they arrange to meet more formally, though still unlawfully, next day for a duel in full armour. This meeting is interrupted by Theseus, and he substitutes for the furtive duel a full-scale public tournament, with a hundred supporters on each side, to be fought out with the greatest possible splendour. *The Knight's Tale* has rightly been described as pageant-like in its evocation of noble life.[1] As with actual medieval pageants, the ceremonies are intended not just to dazzle and impress but to convey meanings, and, as we shall see, the meanings are often sombre and disturbing; but in its pageantry the tale takes to an extreme the ceremonial tendencies that characterize romance as a medieval literary genre. The poem moves with cumbrous dignity under the weight of its formal magnificence; a little more ceremony and it almost seems that it might cease to move at all.

The aesthetic of stylization that I have been outlining operates in many different areas of *The Knight's Tale*, and one of these is the representation of the characters and their inner lives. The inner life of feeling is presented not with the fine discrimination that we expect of the novelist, separating one shade of feeling exactly from another, but through a consistent non-realistic convention. By this convention, all feelings are extreme, and are expressed by extreme outward signs. This is most noticeable in the case we have already touched on, of suffering and the pity it arouses. It can already be observed in the first incident of the poem, when Theseus is accosted by the widows. Their

---

[1] For a classic statement of this view, see the highly influential account by Charles Muscatine, *Chaucer and the French Tradition: A Study in Style and Meaning* (University of California Press, 1957).

grief is externalized in lamentation, rather than realized internally as experience, and the lamentation is of an extreme kind:

> swich a cry and swich a wo they make
> That in this world nis creature livinge
> That herde swich another waymentinge. (42–4)

Crying aloud is one sign of extreme grief; another is losing consciousness completely, and this too appears in the same scene, when Theseus asks the reason for their lamentation:

> The eldeste lady of hem alle spak,
> Whan she hadde swowned with a deedly cheere,
> That it was routhe for to seen and heere. (54–6)

Swoons tend to be presented in this matter-of-course way as interruptions of the poem's narrative line. The same thing happens in a later scene, when Arcite, disguised as Philostrate, is soliloquizing about his ignominious situation. He expresses his grief at great length,

> And with that word he fil doun in a traunce
> A longe time, and after he up sterte. (714–15)

An editor long ago wrote concerning these lines that Chaucer 'ought not to have seemed to stop the action in order to allow Arcite to faint'. The criticism seems reasonable, and indeed it would have a great deal of point if we were to consider this and similar passages as realistic accounts of human behaviour. It is true, certainly, that medieval people did allow themselves to express emotion in violent outward signs such as lamenting and perhaps even fainting more readily than people (at least in northern Europe) do nowadays. But, even when this is allowed for, it must be recognized that this way of presenting emotion belongs to an essentially non-realistic literary convention. By this convention, *all* emotions are heightened, so that the swoon becomes a kind of shorthand for expressing intense grief (as here) or, equally, intense joy (as when Grisilde in *The Clerk's Tale* is reunited with her children). A medieval reader, familiar with the convention, would never have considered how much time the swoon took up.

A further sign of intense grief is internal rather than external, in the sense that it takes the form of an intention rather than a deed, but it is none the less conventional. This is the threat to commit suicide. When Arcite is released from prison but banished from Athens, his reaction is described as follows:

> How greet a sorwe suffreth now Arcite!
> The deeth he feeleth thurgh his herte smite;
> He wepeth, waileth, crieth pitously;
> To sleen himself he waiteth prively. (361–4)

The first of these lines asserts the extreme quality of his feelings. The second emphasizes this extreme quality by relating it to death through the conventional image of a sword cutting (compare the arrow of love, which also deals a mortal wound). The third externalizes the emotion in the three outward forms of weeping, wailing and crying— a formulaic indication of grief which can be paralleled many times over in Chaucer's works. The fourth adds the intention to commit suicide in secret. But there is no indication, here or elsewhere, of any practical effect of this search for an opportunity to kill himself. Considered as a piece of realism, it is not in the least credible; but it is clearly not intended as a piece of realism. There is an even more striking example of the same convention in *The*

Franklin's Tale, when the heroine, having got herself into a situation where she cannot avoid being unfaithful to her husband, says several times that she would prefer death, gives a list of examples of women who have died rather than submit to dishonour, laments for 'a day or tweye,/ Purposinge evere that she wolde deye', but still does not in fact commit suicide, or show any sign of attempting to do so. Clearly in such cases we have to deal not with a lifelike account of actual human behaviour but with a convention which, like that of opera, presents emotion symbolically in a heightened form. This convention includes joy as well as sorrow, though joy is less common in *The Knight's Tale*. But when Theseus ordains that Palamon and Arcite shall fight in a tournament for Emelye in a year's time, the general reaction is one of joy, and it is described as follows:

> Who looketh lightly now but Palamoun?
> Who springeth up for joye but Arcite?
> Who kouthe telle, or who kouthe it endite,
> The joye that is maked in the place
> Whan Theseus hath doon so fair a grace?
> But doun on knees wente every maner wight,
> And thonked him with al hir herte and might,
> And namely the Thebans often sithe.   (1012–19)

Again the emotion is extreme, and again it is externalized, in cheerful looks, jumping up, kneeling, and multiple expressions of thanks.

THE CHARACTERS

Theseus

All the Tale's characters are presented as experiencing and expressing their emotions in these externalizing terms; as a result, there is little subtle distinction among them on the level of internal experience. There are four main characters: Theseus, Emelye, Palamon, and Arcite. Of these the most distinct as a personality is Theseus. The distinctness with which he is characterized is heightened by the contrast in the poem's opening stages between him and Creon, a contrast which personalizes the traditional opposition between the two cities over which they rule. Thebes is the city of Oedipus, a dark place of incest, fratricide, violence, and disaster; Athens is the city of philosophical enlightenment, presided over by Pallas Athene, the goddess of rational wisdom. Though Chaucer mentions neither Oedipus nor Pallas, it was in these terms that the cities were generally interpreted in the Middle Ages, and the two rulers are characterized correspondingly in *The Knight's Tale*. Creon is marked by *ire, iniquitee, despit, vileynye* (82–4), vices entirely typical of the tyrant as conceived in medieval thought,[1] and epitomized in Creon's contemptuous and sacrilegious treatment of his enemies' corpses. Theseus is lordly, courageous, and impulsive—witness his immediate response to the widows' appeal and his equally immediate death sentence on the two lovers when he finds them fighting. Yet, by contrast with 'the tiraunt Creon' (103), he is also open to the appeal of friendship (Perotheus), womanly *pitee*, or reason. His openness to reason is of special importance, and it is in this connection that we

---

[1] See J. D. Burnley, *Chaucer's Language and the Philosophers' Tradition* (D. S. Brewer, 1979). 'Tyrant' is a term with an exact meaning in medieval thought, and one that *The Knight's Tale* applies more than once to Creon but never to Theseus. When Palamon prays to Venus to have compassion on his and Arcite's lineage, 'That is so lowe ybroght by tirannye' (253), we are probably meant to understand that he sees Creon's injustice, not Theseus's, as the root cause of their downfall.

come closest to entering into an imaginable inner life. Finding the Theban princes illicitly fighting, he first trembles with anger, but then pauses to take other considerations into account:

> And although that his ire hir gilt accused,
> Yet in his resoun he hem bothe excused.   (907–8)

He ponders on the naturalness of the lovers' passion and their desire to escape from imprisonment, and on the appeal of the ladies' tears, and then 'his gentil herte' (914) leads him to draw a careful distinction between a ruler's appropriate responses to pride and to humility. Only now does the detailed account of what is going on in his mind lead into a formal speech; in it he gives an ironic but exact account of the lovers' situation, refers to his own past experience as a lover, and announces his forgiveness of Palamon and Arcite. The *pitee* he shows here and towards the widows is not arbitrary, nor is it unmanly weakness; as we have seen, it is associated with *gentillesse*, and it is also one aspect of the ideal ruler's justice, as this was understood in much medieval thought on moral and political issues. A scholar has aptly observed that in his response to the widows at the 'temple of the goddesse Clemence' (70), Theseus 'seems to be enacting Seneca's observation that the practitioner of true Stoic *clementia* [mercy] will "come to the aid of those who weep, but without weeping with them".'[1] Theseus is older and more mature than the other characters (though he can be comforted for Arcite's death by the wisdom and still longer experience of the still older

[1] Barbara Nolan, *Chaucer and the Tradition of the 'Roman Antique'*, quoting the *De clementia* of Seneca the Younger, a Roman philosopher (4 BC–AD 65) widely studied in the Middle Ages.

Egeus); he is reflective and wise. He is an admirable ruler precisely because he thinks philosophically, bringing general principles to bear on specific cases. Yet even when we have said all this, we are still very little aware of Theseus as a distinct personality. We have only to compare him with a character from a nineteenth- or twentieth-century historical novel, or even with one of Shakespeare's rulers—Duncan or Claudius—to recognize that our interest is not in him as an individual. It is rather, we may say provisionally, in him as part of a literary structure embodying a certain significance, a certain view of life.

Palamon and Arcite

The story focuses its main attention upon Palamon and Arcite, and in general the way in which they are presented is in line with the symmetry with which they are introduced. Approaching the Tale with the same expectations as in reading a novel, one might expect to find a carefully worked out and subtly depicted difference of character between the two knights. In this case, one would be disappointed. As characters, they are scarcely distinguishable. We first hear them speak in Theseus's prison. Palamon sees Emelye from the window, and immediately falls in love with her. Then Arcite sees her,

> And with that sighte hir beautee hurte him so,
> That, if that Palamon was wounded sore,
> Arcite is hurt as muche as he, or moore.   (256–8)

The whole point, clearly, is that their reactions are exactly the same. As a result, they quarrel, Palamon saying that he 'loved' her first, and accusing Arcite of breaking his oath of brotherhood by failing to aid him in this love. Arcite offers two lines of defence against this accusation. The first is that, though Palamon saw Emelye first, *he* loved her first 'paramour' (by way of human love). He points out that Palamon's first reaction was to wonder whether Emelye was a woman or a goddess, and so, he says,

> Thyn is affeccioun of hoolinesse,
> And myn is love, as to a creature.   (300–1)

Some modern scholars have seen a profound significance in this distinction between human and divine love; it has been argued that it reflects a difference of character between the two knights, one being a practical schemer, the other an idealistic dreamer. It has even been claimed that they represent allegorically the active and contemplative lives of medieval devotional writings. But in context it seems clear that Arcite's assertion is no more than an ingenious debating point, for he immediately abandons it and goes on to his second line of defence, saying, 'Suppose you did love her first; don't you know that love is a necessity above all laws?' This seems to be a more serious argument—Arcite develops it at greater length than the first—and also one whose truth is displayed in the working out of the story. For first we see love breaking the 'law' established between the two knights by their oath of brotherhood, and then we see it causing both of them to break a 'law' established between them and Theseus. Arcite, having been released, illicitly returns to Athens, and Palamon illicitly breaks out of prison. They then break a further law by engaging in a duel privately, without officers or witnesses, and it is only Theseus's generosity in allowing the dispute between them to be settled in a formal tournament that brings their quarrel within the bounds of law again. In all this it is clear that the focus of our interest is not in the characters as individuals, but in a general idea about human life: that love is an irresistible force and by being irresistible sets itself against all laws, and can only with great difficulty be brought within lawful ceremony.

There is no doubt intended to be a connexion between Palamon's initial feeling that Emelye may be the goddess Venus and the fact that before the tournament he prays to Venus for Emelye, while Arcite prays to Mars for victory. Venus and Mars are the planetary deities presiding over the two main aristocratic interests of love and war, and Palamon inclines towards one of these while Arcite inclines towards the other. Thus when Emelye prays to Diana that, if she must be given to one of the two knights, she should be given to the one who most desires her, her prayer is granted, and she is given to Palamon, who had set Venus above Mars. Similarly, Arcite gains the victory he desires, while Palamon gains the lady he desires, and so their prayers too are granted, though not as they expected. But none of this elaborate patterning throws much light on the characters of the two knights. We cannot see them even as human individuals embodying opposed moral abstractions, as Elinor Dashwood embodies sense and Marianne Dashwood sensibility in Jane Austen's novel. In the novel, it is through entering sympathetically and critically into the characters' minds that we come to understand what 'sense' and 'sensibility' are; and the characters themselves change bit by bit, so that we see Elinor acquiring more sensibility and Marianne much more sense. In *The Knight's Tale* there are no such processes of sympathetic understanding or moral change. Venus and Mars are forces so powerful as to reduce those through whom they operate to indistinguishability. It cannot be said, I think, that we care which of the knights, as a person, eventually wins Emelye.

Emelye

This is all the more true because Emelye herself, the last of the four central characters, is even less an individual than the other three. Like her sister Ypolita, she is an Amazon, and, if she has not inherited the warlike qualities of her tribe, she shows an Amazonian reluctance to accept the subordination to men that was the norm for medieval women and that is present in an exaggerated form in *The Knight's Tale*. Her wish is to remain chaste,

> And for to walken in the wodes wilde,
> And noght to ben a wyf and be with childe.　(1451–2)

Apart from this, we know little of her character except that, as is expected of all noble ladies, she readily feels *pitee*. I have said that she appears less as a person than as a personification of the May-morning convention. This gives her a certain power, but it is of a far less individual kind than that claimed and achieved by many of the women in Chaucer's poems, from Criseyde to the Wife of Bath, or from Alcestis in the Prologue to *The Legend of Good Women* to Alisoun in *The Miller's Tale*. The consciousnesses of many Chaucerian women are explored (that of Criseyde, especially, in the subtlest detail), while Emelye's remains almost totally opaque; and unlike the many dynamic, domineering and fascinating women imagined by Chaucer, Emelye is deprived of all initiative, all opportunity to shape the world in which she lives. Once she has served to arouse rivalrous love in the two knights, she recedes into the background, and she eventually obeys

Theseus's advice to marry Palamon without uttering a word. Indeed, her only words in the whole poem are her prayer to Diana, a prayer that the goddess is unable to grant.

From all this, it should be clear that the meaning of *The Knight's Tale* is not conveyed through individual characterization. That meaning is more general, more like a probing of the very nature of human life in the world, as will be explained later. For the moment it must be said that the lack of interest demanded by the poem for its characters as individuals, together with the generalized nature of its meaning, does not imply that it is a poem without human feeling. Feeling may be aroused for typical human situations as much as for individual persons, and there are many moments in the poem—the widows' statement of their plight, the brotherly arming of Palamon and Arcite before their savage duel, the solitariness and generosity of Arcite in his death—that move us deeply. At such moments we become aware not of the suffering of individuals in whom we are interested because they differ from others, but of the pathos of the general human situation, a situation in which we too are involved, regardless of our sex, social class, or religious belief, by the mere fact of our birth. Each of us is born of 'A womman travaillinge' (1225), and when we die we too shall be 'Allone, withouten any compaignye' (1921).

THE NARRATIVE PROCESS

Perhaps then our interest is to be aroused by the narrative itself, as in thrillers with perfunctory characterization, which we are driven to consume mainly by a simple wish to know what will happen next? We do not have to read very far into *The Knight's Tale* to recognize that this cannot be so. It has indeed a clear narrative line (quite unlike the interwoven complexities of the French romances that were fashionable in Chaucer's time), following a definite and simple pattern, and explicitly divided into four parts. The basic story could be told in a few paragraphs, even a few lines. Though *The Knight's Tale* is only a quarter the length of the *Teseida*, and Chaucer has omitted entire story-elements, such as Boccaccio's opening account of Theseus's war with the Amazons, what remains is narrated with lavish copiousness. *The Knight's Tale* is the second longest of the *Canterbury Tales*, shorter only than the Parson's concluding prose sermon. The pace of the narrative is slow, and it is frequently interrupted by passages that cannot be considered essential from the point of view of the action. At every opportunity, the characters make long and elaborate speeches, taking them far beyond exposition of their present feelings and intentions into considerations of a more general kind. Examples include Arcite's lament for his situation in Part I, which turns into a philosophical account of the human condition (365–416); the speech of Palamon immediately following this, in which he too turns philosopher and questions divine providence (423–75); Theseus's ironic discourse on the power of love in Part II (927–67); Saturn's statement of his powers (1595–1611); and Theseus's philosophical speech at the end of the whole poem, in which he returns to the questions raised by Arcite and Palamon in Part I (2129–2231). Even more noticeably, the action is interrupted again and again by elaborate descriptions: for example, of Emelye and the garden in which she is seen by the two knights (176–97); of Arcite's love-sickness (500–21); of the tournament (1741–77) and then of Arcite's agony (1885–1903) and funeral (1995–2106). The main concentration of descriptive passages comes in Part III, which indeed consists almost entirely of description—of the lists and the three temples erected by Theseus, with all their allegorical decoration, and of Lygurge and Emetreus, the champions of the two sides in the tournament. This predominance of description over action is of course connected with the ceremonial quality already noted; it is precisely through description that the effect of ceremony is given. In these ways too *The Knight's Tale* takes to an extreme tendencies already present in medieval chivalric romance, doing so in accordance with the learned *ars poetica* (art of poetry), which was taught in medieval schools as part of the grammatical and rhetorical study of Latin literature, and was subsequently extended to vernacular writing as this became more learned and ambitious.

The art of poetry

Numerous medieval Latin treatises on the art of poetry survive; in *The Nun's Priest's Tale*, Chaucer refers to the author of one of them, Geoffrey of Vinsauf, as though the name would be familiar to his audience, and in *Troilus and Criseyde* he translates without acknowledgement a few lines from Geoffrey's *Poetria nova*. Treatises of this kind are often of special interest for the basic assumptions they state or take for granted about literary composition, and one of these assumptions was implied at the beginning of the present Introduction: a writer will not invent his own story, like a modern novelist, but will begin from a narrative that already exists in some authoritative form—from the field of

'olde stories'. This narrative source will then be rehandled
to convey the meaning the new writer finds in it, and the
basic processes involved will be amplification and abbreviation, to give heightened emphasis to some parts of the
material and lessened emphasis to others. This is the case
with *The Knight's Tale*: the poem as a whole is much
shorter than the *Teseida*, but certain parts of it, particularly the philosophical speeches and the descriptions of the
temples in Part III, are amplifications of Boccaccio's
material. The treatises on *ars poetica* list and exemplify
various means by which abbreviation and amplification
may be carried out. One of these, much used in *The
Knight's Tale*, is called *occupatio* or *praeteritio*—mentioning something only to state that one is not going to
mention it further. Thus at the very beginning of the Tale,
Chaucer compresses more than a whole book of the
Teseida into a few lines by simply mentioning its main
events and saying that he has not time to tell us about
them:

> And certes, if it nere to long to heere,
> I wolde have toold yow fully the manere
> How wonnen was the regne of Femenye
> By Theseus and by his chivalrye;
> And of the grete bataille for the nones
> Bitwixen Atthenes and Amazones;
> And how asseged was Ypolita,
> The faire, hardy queene of Scithia;
> And of the feste that was at hir weddinge,
> And of the tempest at hir hoom-cominge;
> But al that thing I moot as now forbere.   (17–27)

Here the *occupatio* is genuine and functional; but it may
also be used in a more sophisticated way to describe even
while seeming to pass over. It is used in this way in the

description of the feast given by Theseus before the tour-nament:

> The minstralcye, the service at the feeste,
> The grete yiftes to the meeste and leeste,
> The riche array of Theseus paleys,
> Ne who sat first ne last upon the deys,
> What ladies fairest been or best daunsinge,
> Or which of hem kan dauncen best and singe,
> Ne who moost felingly speketh of love;
> What haukes sitten on the perche above,
> What houndes liggen on the floor adoun—
> Of al this make I now no mencioun.   (1339–48)

Still more strikingly, it is used in the description of Arcite's funeral in such a way that forty-six lines are spent in mentioning what is *not* going to be described. The decep-tion is transparent, and, whatever other purpose Chaucer may have had, we are clearly intended to admire the virtuosity with which the device is spun out. Such virtuoso effects are the natural consequence of a conception of 'art' as technique, proficiency in which may be enjoyed for its own sake. 'The fascination of what's difficult' was strongly operative on medieval poets and their audiences, and their art of poetry tended to display rather than conceal itself. Similarly, in performances of ballet or opera today, the artists may be applauded for feats of physical or vocal athleticism, even though these are not strictly necessary at the point at which they occur.

The main part of the *artes poeticae* is concerned with amplifying rather than abbreviating one's material. Chaucer uses many of the amplifying devices they recom-mend. Among these may be mentioned first the *exclamatio* or *apostrophatio*, in which the story is held up while a speech is addressed to some person or thing just mentioned

48

or suggested by what has just been mentioned. (Characteristically it begins with an 'O!') Under this heading comes the narrator's comment at the point where Palamon and Arcite have arranged to meet next day to have a duel:

> O Cupide, out of alle charitee!
> O regne, that wolt no felawe have with thee!
> Ful sooth is seyd that love ne lordshipe
> Wol noght, his thankes, have no felaweshipe.
> Wel finden that Arcite and Palamoun. (765–9)

In this example, the two *exclamationes* are followed by another common amplifying device, called *sententia*. This is a generalization about life, often based on a proverb, suggested by the particular event narrated in the story. *Sententiae* thus tend to begin with some such form of words as 'Ful sooth is seyd that . . .'. We might compare this with an earlier example, when Chaucer comments that Palamon, hiding in the woods, would not have expected to find Arcite there:

> God woot he wolde have trowed it ful lite.
> But sooth is seyd, go sithen many yeres,
> That 'feeld hath eyen and the wode hath eres.'
> It is ful fair a man to bere him evene,
> For al day meeteth men at unset stevene. (662–6)

Here two *sententiae* are juxtaposed. Another amplifying device is the *exemplum*, which may be seen as the opposite of the *sententia*. Where *sententia* supports a specific detail in the narrative by a generalization, *exemplum* supports a generalization with a particular instance. Thus Theseus, having digressed from the spectacle of Palamon and Arcite fighting to the death for a lady who does not know of their existence to say how powerful the God of Love is, reverts to their particular case as an *exemplum* illustrating Cupid's power:

> Lo heere this Arcite and this Palamoun ...   (933)

Again, the portraiture on the walls of the temple of Venus is conceived as a series of *exempla* illustrating Venus's power. Chaucer lists various people who were depicted there, draws the general moral, and then remarks that he has only given a few of the thousand *ensamples* (i.e. *exempla*) that prove its truth:

> Thus may ye seen that wisdom ne richesse,
> Beautee ne sleighte, strengthe ne hardinesse,
> Ne may with Venus holde champartie,
> For as hir list the world than may she gye.
> Lo, alle thise folk so caught were in hir las,
> Til they for wo ful ofte seyde 'allas!'
> Suffiseth heere ensamples oon or two,
> And though I koude rekene a thousand mo.   (1089–96)

A further means of amplification is the *comparatio* or comparison. This is easily recognized:

> Ther nas no tigre in the vale of Galgopheye,
> Whan that hir whelp is stole whan it is lite,
> So crueel on the hunte as is Arcite
> For jelous herte upon this Palamon.   (1768–71)

Another, equally easy to recognize, is the *circumlocutio* or periphrasis. When Emelye goes to pray to Diana, she does not begin 'O Diana', but with a series of periphrases meaning the same thing but implying a scholarly knowledge of classical mythology:

> O chaste goddesse of the wodes grene,
> To whom bothe hevene and erthe and see is sene,
> Queene of the regne of Pluto derk and lowe,
> Goddesse of maidens ...   (1439–42)

Descriptions

Finally we may mention the commonest device of all in *The Knight's Tale*, *descriptio* or description, of which I have already mentioned some prominent examples. Some of the *artes poeticae* are devoted almost entirely to description, and indeed much medieval poetry does consist of description, aiming to offer a verbal equivalent for the visual arts of painting and tapestry. It is significant that in *The Knight's Tale* the descriptions of the three temples are accounts of what was displayed on the walls in pictorial form. And this verbal description tends to follow the method of pictorial art in the Middle Ages, enumerating detail in an almost encyclopaedic way, rather than selecting a few salient details which will suggest the total impression. In pictorial art this mass of detail may be organized spatially so as to combine to form a single total effect; in verbal art, however, the detail can only be enumerated, and the result of this may be confusion and monotony. But in *The Knight's Tale* this danger is usually avoided, by making the descriptions convey not merely pictorial effects but certain ideas, which themselves act as organizing elements of the pictorial field. It cannot be said that this technique was learned by Chaucer from the *artes poeticae*, because they have little to say about the *use* of descriptions. Geoffrey of Vinsauf writes simply: 'Descriptions spread out one's material. For when one has to make the brief statement that "Such a woman is beautiful", if a description of her beauty is given, then the brevity will be expanded.' Clearly he thinks of amplification as an end to be pursued for its own sake. The technique of using descriptions to convey ideas comes not from the *artes poeticae* but from what Chaucer makes of their doctrine through his own genius.

What his technique involves in *The Knight's Tale* can best be seen by examining a particular example in detail: the scene in which Emelye goes out to gather flowers in the garden in Maytime (175–221). This will involve some recapitulation of remarks made earlier. Descriptions of spring and descriptions of beautiful women are prescribed in the *artes poeticae* and are lavishly supplied in the poetry based on them. In both cases, every detail of the description tends to be laid down by tradition. In descriptions of spring we find bright sunshine, blue skies, flowers of various colours and kinds, birds singing, and so on, while the woman always has fair hair, grey eyes, a high forehead, graceful movements, and so on. What Chaucer has done is not simply to go through these conventional hoops, but to abbreviate both descriptions and run them together, so that the woman and the season become different aspects of a single complex idea. This idea cannot be simply stated, for it is uniquely created by this very passage, but it includes renewal, youth, vigour, and grace. The woman is compared with and vies with the spring flowers; her clothing is 'fressh', like the morning and the flowers; she rises as the sun rises; she gathers flowers with which to adorn her own head; she sings as the birds usually sing in the conventional spring-description. The woman becomes a personification of the season and the place; the season and the place become extensions of herself. Thus the description is unified and organized with a unique life. But this is not all. Having established the unity of woman and season, Chaucer goes on to juxtapose a description of a quite different kind:

> The grete tour, that was so thikke and stroong,
> Which of the castel was the chief dongeoun

> (Ther as the knightes weren in prisoun
> Of which I tolde yow and tellen shal)
> Was evene joinant to the gardyn wal
> Ther as this Emelye hadde hir pleyinge.   (198–203)

The tower and the garden are next to each other, indeed enclosed by the same wall.

In medieval romances, place tends to be symbolic rather than realistic, and in *The Knight's Tale* Chaucer shows so little interest in realism of place that he admits certain contradictions: thus, although Theseus in capturing Thebes 'rente adoun bothe wall and sparre and rafter' (132), later Palamon and Arcite can still ride home 'To Thebes, with his olde walles wide' (1022); and, although Theseus constructs his amphitheatre in the grove where he finds Palamon and Arcite fighting (1004), the same grove still exists to be cut down to make Arcite's funeral pyre (1999 ff.). In medieval culture generally, enclosed spaces (walled cities, castles, gardens) represent civilization; unenclosed spaces (forests, oceans, deserts) represent wilderness. So, for example, it is in the grove beyond the walls of Theseus's palace, 'Out of the court, were it a mile or tweye' (646), that Palamon and Arcite meet to fight like wild beasts. In the Maytime scene I have been discussing, though, two opposed aspects of civilization—prison and garden, brutal constraint and protected freedom—are tellingly brought together, as if to convey that you cannot have one without the other. The prison is the price paid for the garden; or, as Freud puts it, civilization is based on repression. The very sequence of the description intertwines them, for next we see the woman and the garden again, through the eyes of Palamon in the tower,

> In which he al the noble citee seigh,
> And eek the gardyn, ful of braunches grene,
> Ther as this fresshe Emelye the shene
> Was in hire walk, and romed up and doun.   (208–11)

Then we return to the tower itself, its harsh massiveness powerfully evoked in the very sound of consonant-clusters through which the tongue must force its way with difficulty:

> That thurgh a window, thikke of many a barre
> Of iren greet and square as any sparre,
> He cast his eye upon Emelya.
>   (217–19)

Here the paradox of the union of garden and tower is particularly striking, since the massiveness of the tower is felt most fully in the description of the window through which Palamon sees Emelye in the garden. The garden and the tower are both symbolic features of the courtly life, and the total effect of this interlocking description is to suggest that in this life (and in the general human life of which it is a specialized and idealized version), opposite extremes of experience are violently yoked together. In this the description is a small-scale representation of the effect of the whole Tale.

A similar technique is used throughout *The Knight's Tale*, but it is particularly noticeable in Part III, which consists almost entirely of descriptions. If we were expecting the action to bear the chief burden of the poem's meaning, we should no doubt expect this book to be the least relevant, the most extraneous and merely decorative. But the opposite is the case. *The Knight's Tale* is a poem in which the description gives meaning to the action, and so Part III becomes the core of the work's meaning. We shall be examining the nature of this meaning in a later part of this Introduction.

Descriptions of action

This, however, will be a convenient place to say something of descriptions of a rather different kind—those of action. Most of the poem's descriptions are of people or places; hence they are lacking in physical movement, and the development that occurs in them is a development of ideas. But the poem also includes a number of descriptions of violent physical action, particularly in connexion with the tournament in Part IV, and these are strikingly successful in a quite different way from the static descriptions. They employ the same basic technique of the accumulation of details, but their success depends not on the unifying of details by a single dominant idea, but on manipulation of the way we perceive the action itself. The descriptive technique used here is similar in some ways to that of the film. The poet's eye moves like the camera, giving the sense of bustling activity by switching rapidly from one shot to another, and pausing every so often to give a close-up of some especially significant or characteristic detail. In the description of the busy scene before the tournament (1633–64), an atmosphere of breathless haste is evoked by the running on of the sense from one line to another and from one couplet to another:

> Knightes of retenue, and eek squieres
> Nailinge the speres . . .   (1644–5)

> The fomy steedes on the golden bridel
> Gnawinge . . .   (1648–9)

At the same time, between two distant shots of people on horseback, a *ther maystow seen* in line 1638 draws us in for a close-up of richly decorated armour and equipment; and then the camera's eye, which has been ranging over the whole city, focuses on the random and busily talking groups in the palace, and we move among them, hearing snatches of their gossip. In the description of the tournament itself (1743–77), alliteration is used very heavily, to communicate directly the noise and impetus of battle. Chaucer here is not following exactly the structure of the alliterative verse which was being written in the north and west of England in his own time, but he did know of this verse (he makes the Parson refer to it, saying 'I kan nat geeste "rum, ram, ruf" by lettre') and no doubt recognized its special gift for conveying martial noise and movement. Again the effect is cinematic, mingling general views of the field (catching for instance the flash of silver as the swords are drawn), with rapidly successive shots of particular incidents, and finally coming to rest in formal descriptions of the two champions.

The foregrounding of narration

A noticeable effect of many of the devices I have been discussing under the heading of 'The narrative process' is to call attention to that process itself. As I have stressed earlier, the art of this poem, far from concealing itself, conspicuously displays itself; it has rightly been observed that '*The Knight's Tale* is the most insistently "artificial" of all Chaucer's major poems, constantly calling attention to itself as a thing "made".'[1] At the simplest level, by contrast with the seamless editing aimed at in the classic Hollywood film as a means of sustaining the illusion of a reality

[1] V. A. Kolve, *Chaucer and the Imagery of Narrative: The First Five Canterbury Tales* (Edward Arnold, 1984).

unmediated by any storyteller, no attempt is made to mask the joints between one narrative segment and another; on the contrary, a device that the *artes poeticae* sometimes call *transitio* is used to call attention to these joints. After Arcite has been banished from Athens, Chaucer tells us more about Palamon and then returns to his cousin in Thebes:

> Now wol I stynte of Palamon a lite,
> And lete him in his prisoun stille dwelle,
> And of Arcita forth I wol yow telle.   (476–8)

Later, he wishes to leave Palamon and Arcite fighting their duel to explain that Theseus was hunting in the same wood, and he makes this transition equally explicit:

> And in this wise I lete hem fighting dwelle,
> And forth I wole of Theseus yow telle.   (803–4)

Open transitions of this kind may also be used to bracket a digression which interrupts the narrative line only briefly. At the very beginning of the Tale, we are told of Theseus's triumphant homecoming. Chaucer then inserts the *occupatio* mentioned earlier, in which he remarks that he has no time to tell us of Theseus's victory and wedding feast, and afterwards returns to his homecoming. Although this *occupatio* is a means of abbreviation, it is so positioned as to be a digression interrupting the narrative, and so it is prefaced with one transition:

> And thus with victorie and with melodye
> Lete I this noble duc to Atthenes ride,
> And al his hoost in armes him biside   (14–16)

and concluded by another:

> And ther I lefte, I wol ayeyn biginne.
> This duc of whom I make mencioun . . .   (34–5)

The process of storytelling is equally if less explicitly foregrounded in many others of the devices used. When ignorance is professed as to some narrative detail, trivial or of major importance—

> For with the rose colour stroof hire hewe,
> I noot which was the finer of hem two   (180–1)
>
> I noot which hath the wofuller mester   (482)
>
> His spirit chaunged hous and wente ther,
> As I cam nevere, I kan nat tellen wher.
> Therfore I stynte, I nam no divinistre   (1951–3)

—we are kept aware that the story does not tell itself: all this information is coming (or failing to come) from some human source. When we are reminded of what has been said previously or alerted to what will be said in due course—

> (Ther as the knightes weren in prisoun
> Of which I tolde yow and tellen shal)   (200–1)
>
> Cleer was the day, as I have toold er this   (825)
>
> Thanne seyde he thus, as ye shal after heere   (1906)

—the situation in which a story is being told to us as readers or listeners is kept in our minds. When a rhetorical question is asked or a *sententia* is introduced to justify some statement that has been made, as in the following passage where both devices occur in succession—

> What helpeth it to tarien forth the day
> To tellen how she weep bothe eve and morwe?
> For in swich cas wommen have swich sorwe,
> Whan that hir housbondes ben from hem ago,
> That for the moore part they sorwen so . . .   (1962–6)

—we cannot help recalling the difficulties involved in storytelling and the need to appeal to some ground of experience shared by teller and public if understanding is to be achieved. 'What need is there to waste time in telling you how Emelye wept incessantly when Arcite died? That's how women always behave when their husbands pass away'—and we are left either to accept this as an undeniable truth about life or, if we choose, to suspect ironic exaggeration. *Exclamatio*, to take one more instance, manifestly expresses a response to the story being told, at once implying the teller's emotional participation and reminding us that he must stand outside his story in order for such response to become explicit. But the most striking of all these devices that foreground the activity of storytelling is the *occupatio* used to describe Arcite's funeral. Beginning at line 2060, where Chaucer tells us that he is not going to tell us the names of the trees used to make the pyre (but in doing so mentions the names of twenty-one trees!), and continuing down to lines 2105–6, where he tells us that he will not tell us how people returned to Athens after the funeral games, it is an extraordinary display of rhetorical skill, demanding admiration simultaneously for the ceremonies described and the ingenuity with which the poet finds ways of refusing to describe them.

To continue with this analysis is unnecessary: any reader of *The Knight's Tale* must notice how rarely more than a few lines pass without some such foregrounding of the storytelling process itself. But why should this be? Two apparently obvious answers to this question are, first, that Chaucer was writing with a listening audience in mind, and such an audience would need careful guidance as to the sequence of the plot and the appropriate way to respond to it, and, second, that he wished to keep our attention fixed on a fictional narrator distinct from himself (in this case presumably the Knight). I used to think both these answers contained some truth, and in the version of this Introduction originally published I explained the foregrounding of narratorial process along these lines. I have now come to believe that what seem the obvious explanations are mistaken. The first is perhaps not completely mistaken; it was certainly normal, so far as we can tell, for medieval poetry to be read aloud to listeners, as in a scene in *Troilus and Criseyde* in which a 'romaunce . . . of Thebes' is read aloud to Criseyde and her ladies by a maiden; and the general technique of storytelling in vernacular verse retained many recollections of an earlier medieval past in which poetry had been not just been orally delivered but also orally composed. But *The Canterbury Tales* does not merely reflect this situation but fictionalizes it: oral storytelling is part of the fiction, and what we have is clearly a consciously written imitation of spoken narrative, in which the audience addressed as 'yow' or 'yow loveres' (for example line 489) is as much a fiction as the notion that the Knight is reciting over two thousand lines of rhyming couplets to a miscellaneous collection of pilgrims. The second explanation is still taken as correct by many scholars, but, as I indicated earlier, I now believe it to be totally erroneous. The 'I' of the narratorial elements in *The Knight's Tale* is no more than a grammatical space; 'the narrator' is not characterized in any noticeable way that evokes a consistent and distinct person or that differentiates him from the 'I' of a great many of Chaucer's other poems, including most of the *Canterbury Tales*. The most we could deduce about this 'I', supposing that we knew nothing of the fictional frame attributing the tale to the Knight, is that he is a heterosexual male adult who is writing a poem. He is, in effect, the sum of the forms in which Chaucer chooses to represent himself in writing while recounting 'the love of Palamon and Arcite'; and we all know, if only from the experience of composing thank-you letters, that the 'I' of writing need not be, and often cannot be, self-consistent, and that the written 'I' is a phenomenon of a totally different kind from the living 'I'.

Why then is the storytelling process so markedly foregrounded in *The Knight's Tale*? I suggest that the reason is that this is devised to be, as it was put by the scholar I quoted earlier, 'the most insistently "artificial" of all Chaucer's major poems, constantly calling attention to itself as a thing "made"'. The process of 'making'—a word that Chaucer and other medieval English writers employed to refer specifically to poetic composition—is to be seen as laborious, difficult, demanding, a never-ending and never totally successful struggle to shape recalcitrant material into art and to give it meaning as well as beauty. In *The Knight's Tale*, 'making' is itself thematized; and I shall return later to consider how this relates to the poem's other, more explicit philosophical themes.

CHAUCER'S RESHAPING OF ROMANCE

So far I have been treating *The Knight's Tale* as a medieval chivalric romance; but it is not an entirely typical example of this kind of composition. Chaucer undoubtedly knew many romances in both English and French, and his poetic style and storytelling methods must owe much to his reading and listening in this field; but there is also much to suggest that 'Chaucer, who seems so much at home in the fabliau, the miracle of the Virgin, and the saint's life, felt less easy with the very genre which we regard as most characteristic of his period, the romance'.[1] One of the two *Canterbury Tales* that he attributes to himself, *Sir Thopas*, is a scathing and hilarious parody of the literary and social ineptitude of popular Middle English romances; another of the *Tales*, *The Squire's Tale*, seems to be in part a genial but still penetrating burlesque of fashionable French romances with their excessively complicated plots and impossible magic devices; and a third, *The Wife of Bath's Tale*, begins with some amusing satirical commentary on 'th'olde dayes of the King Arthour', emphasizing their remoteness from the realities of Chaucer's own time. We can also find in *The Canterbury Tales* passing remarks that indicate a contemptuous scepticism about the Arthurian legends, as when the Nun's Priest assures us that his tale of talking animals

> is also trewe, I undertake,
> As is the book of Launcelot de Lake,
> That wommen holde in ful greet reverence.

Good enough for women, perhaps, but not for rational adults!

In general it would seem that Chaucer found three chief causes for dissatisfaction with the chivalric romances he knew: they lacked classical simplicity in their plotting, they were remote from reality in their subject-matter, and, following from these two faults, they lacked seriousness— not solemnity, which had little appeal for him, but significant relation to the most important human experiences. Chaucer was not content merely to criticize and parody,

---

[1] J. A. Burrow, in *The Cambridge Chaucer Companion*, ed. Piero Boitani and Jill Mann (Cambridge University Press, 1986).

though; he also undertook large-scale attempts to reconstruct romance as a more adult literary form. His three major attempts are *Troilus and Criseyde*, *The Franklin's Tale*, and *The Knight's Tale*. His chief guide in this enterprise was Boccaccio, and all three poems have Boccaccian sources—*Troilus* is translated from the *Filostrato*, *The Franklin's Tale* is loosely based on a story in the *Filocolo*, and *The Knight's Tale*, as we have seen, is adapted from the *Teseida*. From Boccaccio Chaucer learned not only the possibility of literary composition in a vernacular language that would match Latin in dignity and scope; he also learned to write romances that would have relatively simple plots set in the real history of the classical past, rather than in an Arthurian never-never-land. All three of the poems mentioned are attempts to imagine that classical past in its own right, as an autonomous culture distant and different from the medieval present, and that meant imagining it as pagan, not as Christian. And this in turn made it possible for Chaucer to use chivalric romance as a means of exploring serious philosophical issues—more serious than those taken up by Boccaccio—that arose from the paganism of the worlds he imagined in his three 'philosophical romances'. The rest of this Introduction will be chiefly concerned with the topics indicated in the present paragraph.

ROMANCE AS PAGAN HISTORY

Medieval conceptions of history were very different from ours, and in particular the sense of the difference of the past—the sense that, as L. P. Hartley put it, 'The past is a foreign country: they do things differently there'—was largely lacking in the Middle Ages. We can see this vividly revealed in medieval paintings or manuscript illuminations representing scenes from pagan or Old Testament times: the characters are generally shown wearing medieval costume, armed with medieval weapons, surrounded by medieval buildings, and so on. It was in fourteenth-century Italy, where more than anywhere else people lived amid the remains of ancient Roman buildings, that they seem first to have begun to think of the past, and especially of classical antiquity, as essentially different from the present. The great poet and scholar Petrarch recorded the powerful impact made on him in the 1330s by his first sight of the ruins of ancient Rome, and shortly after this he began writing a Latin poem, called *Africa*, which was the first medieval attempt at a total re-creation of classical epic poetry, reproducing classical subject-matter in the authentic style of Virgil's *Aeneid*. It is this growth of a sense of historical difference, and of the possibility of overcoming it by scholarship and imaginative identification, that marks the beginning of what we now call the Renaissance. Boccaccio's *Teseida* represented an early stage in the same movement; and Chaucer was alone among fourteenth-century English writers in encountering it, by visiting Italy, and in seeing the possibility of following in the footsteps of Petrarch and Boccaccio. Chaucer needed Boccaccio as a model for his own attempts to re-enter imaginatively the classical past, but he was careful to conceal his debt; as we have seen, he gave the impression that in *The Knight's Tale* he was working only with authentic classical sources, such as Statius's *Thebaid*, and indeed that the story of Palamon and Arcite was itself historical, a continuation found in 'olde stories' of the history of Thebes as Statius had told it. (Chaucer may actually have believed that this story was history rather than fiction; in his time those two fields were not distinguished in the same way as they are in ours, and he must certainly have felt that what could be read about Creon, Theseus, Hippolyta, and those associated with them was at least *truer* than 'the book of Launcelot de Lake'.)

Before discussing in more detail in what ways *The Knight's Tale* offers itself to be read as 'pagan history', I need to venture some preliminary generalizations about fourteenth-century attempts to re-create classical antiquity in modern writing. First, these attempts were based on a different conception of historical knowledge from our own. Petrarch and Boccaccio were men of impressive classical learning; Boccaccio, for example, composed in his later years an enormous Latin encyclopaedia of classical mythology, called *De genealogia deorum gentilium* (On the genealogy of the pagan gods). Chaucer was probably somewhat less learned, but he had a good acquaintance with Latin poets such as Virgil and Ovid and with other sources of information about Roman thought. (He knew no Greek, and seems to have seen the classical world as a single homogeneous culture, not distinguishing Athens from Rome.) He lived, too, in a country where a number of exceptionally well-informed friars had been carefully compiling information about the classical past, and he knew something of their work. In *The Knight's Tale* he shows some concern to establish and display his classical knowledge, as when, describing the decoration of Diana's temple, he carefully distinguishes between two mythological figures whose names were similar in Middle English,

and at the same time shows that he knows Daphne's
ancestry:

> Ther saugh I Dane, yturned til a tree—
> I mene nat the goddesse Diane,
> But Penneus doghter, which that highte Dane.   (1204–6)

But Chaucer had little means of distinguishing historical
fact from literary fiction, and much of what he took to be
fact would now be regarded as legend. Hence his picture of
classical antiquity in *The Knight's Tale* is strongly and
unconsciously medievalized. To take a single example, we
have seen that he imagines knighthood in medieval terms;
this is almost certainly not because, like earlier poets, he
gave no thought to possible differences between the past
and the present, but because he followed medieval scholars
in believing that the chivalry of their time really did have
classical origins. Medieval Latin terms for 'knight', such as
miles and *eques*, were assumed to have had the same sense
in antiquity, rather than meaning simply 'soldier' and
'horseman'. Thus a chronicler praised King Henry V
because 'he maintained the discipline of chivalry well, as
did the Romans formerly'; and even Romulus, the founder
of Rome, 'because he raised a band of a thousand mounted
warriors, was taken to be the founder of chivalry'.[1] There
would be many other respects too in which the very
language of the medieval vernaculars would carry associations belonging to their own time rather than to the
classical past. (Remember that this must equally be true of
our language; scholars in the future will be able to see how
our views of the past are pervaded with associations that

---

[1] J. Huizinga, *The Waning of the Middle Ages* (Penguin, 1955).

evoke our own present.) Some at least of what has traditionally been read as naively unconscious medievalization in Chaucer's conception of Athens and Thebes was probably intended as historical learning.

Second, what most fascinated the early Renaissance about classical antiquity was its paganism. Ancient Rome, it was acknowledged, possessed a civilization superior in almost every respect to that of fourteenth-century Europe: its architecture, its civil engineering, its sculpture, its poetry, its philosophy—all these achievements and others were the standards against which the best-informed of Chaucer's contemporaries would have measured the enterprises of their own time, and their best hope would be not to fall too far short of what the ancients had already done. But there was one respect in which the situation was reversed. Ancient Rome had been pagan; medieval Europe was Christian, and saw itself as having the immeasurable blessing of a divine revelation that was unknown to its great predecessor. (We may need to remind ourselves that Catholic Christianity was the universal religion of western Europe in Chaucer's time: there were a few unorthodox believers regarded as heretics, such as John Wyclif's followers the Lollards, but few medieval people would ever have met an agnostic, an atheist, a pagan, a Jew, a Muslim, or, of course, a Protestant.) The incomparable poetry of Virgil and Ovid, Statius and Horace, was permeated by a false mythology; great thinkers such as Cicero and Seneca, for all their power of understanding and their skill in reasoning, knew nothing of such vital truths as the sin of Adam, the Incarnation of God as man, the Crucifixion and Redemption. This deep paradox was of intense interest; some medieval thinkers argued that the great pagan poets and philosophers must have had veiled glimpses of Christian truth concealed within their false mythology, others that God might find some means to save virtuous pagans even though they were ignorant of the one true faith. The latter possibility was of particular concern in the fourteenth century, when the question of the means to salvation was a topic of heated discussion. One view among theologians was that God had bound himself to grant salvation to all who did the best they could according to the understanding granted to them; an opposing view was that God remained entirely free to grant or refuse salvation in accordance with his own inscrutable will. The case of the virtuous pagan would clearly be a test: if a virtuous pagan could earn salvation, the same would surely be true of any Christian who did his best to follow his conscience and the Church's teachings. In *The Knight's Tale* Arcite dies virtuously. Faced with the unexpected death that medieval Christians most feared, lacking the presence of a priest and the religious comfort and hope available to them, he nevertheless commits his soul to the protection of the highest god he knows (Jupiter), and selflessly begs Emelye to grant Palamon her love. The question of the fate of his soul in the next world is then explicitly raised:

> His spirit chaunged hous and wente ther,
> As I cam nevere, I kan nat tellen wher.
> Therfore I stynte, I nam no divinistre;
> Of soules finde I nat in this registre,
> Ne me ne list thilke opinions to telle
> Of hem, though that they writen wher they dwelle.
> Arcite is coold, ther Mars his soule gye!   (1951–7)

In the *Teseida*, Boccaccio in fact states that Arcite's soul goes to heaven; but since the *Teseida* was unknown in England, Chaucer was free to state misleadingly that he found nothing in his source about souls, and to add that in any case he preferred not to repeat the opinions of theologians (*divinistres*) on this controversial topic. But he has raised the question, and there can be little doubt that one kind of interest aroused by his re-creation of pagan life would have been precisely that of the means to salvation—a dangerous issue, possibly leading to heresy, and therefore best discussed in the context of the distant past and without proposing any definite solution. We shall see that in *The Knight's Tale* it is the paganism of the poem's characters that interests Chaucer beyond all other aspects of historical difference.

A third generalization is that the Renaissance sense of history, while it focuses on the difference of the past, and especially of pagan antiquity, sees that difference as enriching rather than denying the existence of a single universal human nature. There is a real gap between the ancients and ourselves, so Boccaccio or Chaucer might have thought, but it can be bridged by the exercise of imagination and imitation. That may have been what especially fascinated the inner circle of Chaucer's readers about poems such as *Troilus and Criseyde* and *The Knight's Tale*: they re-created a pagan past in all its splendour and hopelessness, but in doing so they introduced us to men and women like ourselves and to situations like our own.

THE KNIGHT'S TALE AS PAGAN HISTORY

The story of *The Knight's Tale* emerges at the point of intersection of two great bodies of ancient Greek legend— that concerning the hero Theseus, and that concerning the city of Thebes. After Theseus had killed the Minotaur in Crete, he became king of Athens. He then led an expedition against the Amazons, a tribe of warlike women, defeated them, and returned to Athens with their queen as his bride. Meanwhile the series of events known as 'the seven against Thebes' had been taking place. The twin brothers Polyneices and Eteocles had been made joint kings of Thebes, but Eteocles had banished Polyneices. Polyneices then gathered seven champions to support him (including the 'Cappaneus' mentioned in *The Knight's Tale*, 74), and they led an expedition against Thebes. After the twins had killed each other, the expedition was defeated by Creon, their uncle, with great loss of life. Creon then became ruler of Thebes, and refused to allow the bodies of his dead enemies to be buried, but left them to be eaten by dogs. This is the legendary background to the story of *The Knight's Tale*, which actually begins with Theseus on his triumphant return to Athens being accosted by a party of the widows of those killed in the attack on Thebes. Thus the story of Arcite and Palamon, though not itself of classical origin, is carefully related to the legendary classical past, and Theseus, a leading figure in ancient Greek legend, remains one of its central characters.

The world imagined by Chaucer as that in which this story takes place differs in several important ways from his own. It is the world of history as conceived by ancient epic poetry—a patriarchal world in which public issues predominate almost totally over private ones. In Chaucer's own society, the public sphere was largely male, and the place of women was largely confined to private life, but in *The Knight's Tale* he seems deliberately to have exaggerated this opposition. War, politics and philosophy are the ultimate concerns in his imagined Athens and Thebes, cities structured by male bonding and male rivalry: women's roles are emotionally as well as politically subordinate, and women's chief function is to be the objects of rivalry and exchange among men. In *Troilus and Criseyde* Chaucer describes a rich private sphere of domestic spaces in which men and women interact, in conversation, tale-telling, play, flirtation, love-making; in *The Knight's Tale* there is no such sphere. There the only private spaces we see are the exclusively male prison and the exclusively female garden; Theseus's *chambre* (the room which in many medieval romances is the setting for the warmth and passion of relations between the sexes) is mentioned only as the place where he holds himself back from the public eye (1667) in anticipation of his self-display at a window to preside over the preparations for the tournament. Ypolita, with whom he presumably shares the ducal *chambre*, goes unmentioned. Chaucer's omission of Boccaccio's full account of the Amazons and their resistance to Theseus is in keeping with his creation of a male-dominated public world in *The Knight's Tale*. One effect of this repression both of the female and of interaction between the sexes, except at the distance of gazes, is paradoxical: whether or not intentionally, the female becomes the feminine, and thus gains a secret and subversive power. Seen, as it is throughout the Tale, by men, femininity is an alien and forbidden sphere of existence, disturbing precisely because unknown, and the narrative's controlled surface is troubled on occasion by fear or nervous laughter at what is being repressed.[1] Only

[1] For a fuller study of this aspect of *The Knight's Tale*, see A. C. Spearing, *The Medieval Poet as Voyeur: Looking and Listening in Medieval Love-Narratives* (Cambridge University Press, 1993), ch.8.

in the heavens, strangely enough, in Venus's squabble with Mars and the childish tears by which she gains Saturn's indulgence, do we seem to glimpse a realm that corresponds to more conventional medieval conceptions of relations between women and men.

Of the many ceremonies represented in *The Knight's Tale*, some, such as the Maying engaged in by Emelye (176–97) and Arcite (633–54), belong to Chaucer's own time; others, such as the chivalric ceremonies associated with the tournament, can be recognized as medieval by us but might well have been thought classical by Chaucer. (When he says of the armour worn by Palamon's party, 'Ther is no newe gyse that it nas old' [1267], we may get a glimpse of his feeling the need to make some excuse for his lack of detailed knowledge of ancient customs.) On the other hand, the religious ceremonies that play so important a part in the narrative are clearly not medieval and Catholic but classical and pagan. Creon will not allow his enemies' corpses to be 'yburied nor ybrent' (88); burial was a Catholic practice, but cremation was pagan, and 'the brenninge / Of the bodies' (138–9) is eventually carried out 'as was tho the gyse' (135). The temples that Theseus has constructed as part of his amphitheatre are dedicated to the pagan gods, Mars, Venus and Diana, and their altars, statues and other decorations evoke in many ways the world of pagan antiquity. (When Chaucer notes that the deaths of Julius Caesar, Nero and Antony were depicted in Mars's temple, he is careful to retain accurate chronology by explaining that this was possible only by prophecy, because at the time the Tale is set these Romans had not yet been born.) The ceremonies in the temples are performed, as we are told of Arcite's sacrifice to Mars, 'With alle the rites of his payen wise' (1512), and the details given, especially of Emelye's sacrifice to Diana (discussed more fully below), are exotic in the extreme—burning fires, washing in well-water, crowning with evergreen oak, and so on. Still more exotic are Arcite's funeral ceremonies, with the vessels 'Al ful of hony, milk, and blood, and wyn' (2050), the gigantic funeral pyre into which the mourners cast treasures 'And coppes fulle of wyn, and milk, and blood' (2091), and the funeral games in which warriors wrestle 'naked with oille enoint' (2103). The paganism is heightened by Chaucer's comment that when the grove was cut down to make the pyre,

> the goddes ronnen up and doun,
> Disherited of hire habitacioun,
> In which they woneden in reste and pees,
> Nymphes, fawnes and amadrides . . .   (2067–70)

No earlier English poetry, with the possible exception of Chaucer's own *Troilus and Criseyde*, had so vividly and learnedly evoked the world of classical paganism. Reference by the characters to the revealed doctrines peculiar to Christianity is systematically excluded from the poem, while they see themselves, and are seen by Chaucer, as living in a world governed by the gods of the pagan past. The first of these to be mentioned is the one who is eventually responsible for Arcite's death, Saturn. He is mentioned as an alternative to or explanation of a reference to Fortune. When Arcite tells Palamon not to cry out in anguish at their imprisonment 'for it may noon oother be', he goes on:

> Fortune hath yeven us this adversitee.
> Som wikke aspect or disposicioun
> Of Saturne, by som constellacioun,
> Hath yeven us this, although we hadde it sworn;
> So stood the hevene whan that we were born.   (228–32)

Next we hear of a goddess, when Palamon wonders whether Emelye is Venus, and prays to her (243–53). Palamon at the end of Part I laments that he is in prison because of Saturn, and also because of another goddess, Juno, who is offended with the Thebans, while on the other hand he is tormented with jealousy caused by Venus (470–5). It is from another god, Mercury, whom he sees in a dream, that Arcite gets the idea of returning to Athens (527–34). It is Venus who changes Arcite's joy into melancholy, in the same way as she causes changes in the weather of her day, Friday (676–81). He apostrophizes Mars and Venus as causers of his family's fall from prosperity. We are told of Theseus when he goes hunting that 'after Mars he serveth now Diane' (824). But it is in Part III that the gods really take control, both of the action and of the poetry. First we have the long descriptions of the three temples of Venus, Mars, and Diana; then the prayers in each of them, and the responses received; then, for the first time, we are taken among the gods themselves. We see the quarrel between Mars and Venus and its settlement by Saturn, who defines his own nature in a long speech. After this, we are returned from the heavens to see Saturn's decision worked out on earth, in the intervention of the 'furie' which kills Arcite after he has gained the victory, and thus allows both Mars and Venus to keep their promises to their devotees. The great and increasing importance of the gods as motivating forces in the story is obvious. We must now ask who or what these gods are.

The functions of the gods

Their names are those of the Roman gods. The story of the poem is set in ancient Greece, but these gods are still appropriate, for there was a close correspondence between

Greek and Roman mythology, and in the Middle Ages, when Greek was little known in Western Europe, the Greek gods were usually called by their Roman names. It may be useful to insert here a brief account of who the gods mentioned in the poem were, information which can easily be skipped by those to whom it is already familiar.

Jupiter was the king of the gods. His father was *Saturn*, whom he had deposed, but who remains a potent force in mythology, and especially in this poem. Jupiter's wife was *Juno*. Among the other chief deities are *Mercury*, the messenger of the gods, with whom oracles were associated, and who was also the god of sleep and dreams; *Mars*, the god of war; *Venus*, the goddess of love, whose husband was *Vulcan*, the smith of the gods, and whose son was *Cupid*, the god of love in medieval courtly poetry; *Pluto*, the god of the underworld; and *Diana*, the goddess of the moon, of hunting, of chastity, and of childbirth. Various fables concerning the relations of these gods with each other and with certain mortals are alluded to here and there in *The Knight's Tale*, and are explained at the appropriate points in the Notes. Chaucer would have learned about the special powers of the gods, and the emblems associated with them, not only from classical Latin literature but also from medieval encyclopaedias of mythology, among them probably Boccaccio's *De genealogia deorum gentilium*.

The temples of the gods

In the *Teseida* Chaucer found a story where the gods already played a considerable part, and in translating it he brought them into even more striking prominence, and made them more completely responsible for the poem's action. To take a small example, it was Chaucer who introduced the vision of Mercury by which Arcite is persuaded to return to Athens; to take a larger example, the entire part played by Saturn is Chaucer's addition. But his intensification of the gods' importance and significance is most apparent in Part III, and we must now turn to examine this in more detail.

The descriptions of the three temples of Venus, Mars, and Diana are used by Chaucer to convey thought about the meaning of the gods. For him this meaning is both more important and more sombre than it was for Boccaccio. In the description of the temple of Venus (1060–1108), the opening lines, with their generalizing list of the sufferings 'That loves servantz in this lyf enduren', are a Chaucerian addition. Then comes a list of personifications connected with love, where good and bad qualities are mingled in utter disorder, for Venus has nothing to do with morality. Next there is a description of Venus's dwelling, which gradually merges into the garden of love as depicted in the *Roman de la Rose*, and this in turn merges into a list of well-known legendary figures who suffered through love. Here particularly, if we are to make any sense at all of the description, it is necessary to interpret its meaning intellectually rather than rely on an instinctive response to its decorative quality. Narcissus died through falling in love with his own reflexion in a pool; Solomon was led into idolatry by his wives and concubines; Hercules was killed by a poisoned shirt sent to him by his wife out of jealousy (jealousy has been among the list of personifications); Medea murdered her own children; Circe turned men into animals; Turnus was killed fighting for the love of Lavinia. What is illustrated by this list is not simply the universal power of Venus, but the fact that this power is destructive and brings human beings to miserable ends. And this point is made more explicitly at the end, in some lines that were also added by Chaucer:

> Lo, alle thise folk so caught were in hir las,
> Til they for wo ful ofte seyde 'allas!'   (1093–4)

Finally comes the statue of Venus herself, full of appeal to the senses and surrounded by the traditional emblems listed by medieval writers on mythology; but here too there is a suggestion of the destructive, for she is accompanied by her son Cupid armed with 'arwes brighte and kene'. Thus the force in human life that Venus represents—sexual love—is very fully defined in this description: alluring, all-powerful, morally neutral, and destructive.

The description of the temple of Mars (1109–92) similarly functions as a statement of the nature of the force Mars represents. What this force is, is best conveyed by the memorable poetry of the description itself, rather than by any abstract definition, but it may be roughly summed up as violence. The description begins less abstractly than that of the temple of Venus, by evoking the atmosphere of 'the grete temple of Mars in Trace', which is painted on the wall. The dead forest rocked by the wind, the effect of which is conveyed through the alliterative harshness and difficulty of the actual sound—

> With knotty, knarry, bareyne trees olde,
> Of stubbes sharpe and hidouse to biholde,
> In which ther ran a rumbel in a swough,
> As though a storm sholde bresten every bough   (1119–22)

—the glitter of steel, the frightening noises, the cold dim light, the brutal strength of the iron reinforcing the doors and the pillars: all this offers an unforgettable *poetic* definition of heartless violence. There follows a survey of the operations of Mars in the actual world, in which personified abstractions are jumbled together with typical persons and scenes, so that Fear and a pickpocket jostle in the same line. Many of the items in this list are horribly memorable in themselves: the vignette of the suicide bathed in his own blood—

> The sleere of himself yet saugh I ther—
> His herte-blood hath bathed al his heer   (1147–8)

—or the justly famous line in which the essentials of treachery are collected with the utmost economy:

> The smilere with the knyf under the cloke.   (1141)

The total effect of the list, mixing allegory with genre-painting, and putting the abstract Conquest in place of the individual Damocles—

> And al above, depeynted in a tour,
> Saugh I Conquest sittinge in greet honour,
> With the sharpe swerd over his heed
> Hanginge by a soutil twines threed   (1169–72)

—is to make us feel the abstractions at work in everyday life, not merely in their own special world. The influence of Mars is felt in all nations and all classes—Julius Caesar rubs shoulders with the cook and the pickpocket—and his power shows itself as much in the squalid accidents of everyday life as in world-historical events. (In this way Chaucer goes beyond the normal social limits of chivalric romance: the characters of his Tale may all be of high birth, but in the temples we see that the same forces operate on the common people.) Finally comes the statue of Mars himself, surrounded like that of Venus by his traditional emblems, here the chariot and the man-eating wolf (the last detail being a Chaucerian addition). When we revisit the temple of Mars with Arcite, though the response to his prayer is apparently favourable and is accompanied by a sweet smell rising from the ground, there are also further suggestions of the sinister—the doors 'clatereden ful faste' (1565), the mail-coat worn by the god's statue rings aloud, and even the promise of victory emerges from 'a murmuringe/ Ful lowe and dim' (1574–5).

The third temple description, that of Diana (1193–1230) was entirely added by Chaucer, but its method is the same as the others, a definition by extension of the force in human life that the pagan goddess represents. The nature of this force is considerably harder to define than in the case of Mars or Venus. Sex and violence are everyday phenomena, and the presence of the temples of these gods over the amphitheatre's *gateways* may indicate that they are the familiar means of entering 'the arena of passionate experience';[1] the less conspicuous location of Diana's temple 'in a touret on the wal' (1051) may suggest that she has a different kind of meaning. Certainly the complex of ideas and feelings represented by Diana is not easily perceived as a unity, and there is no single word to express it. Her multiple roles as goddess not only of hunting in the wilderness outside human civilization, but also of both chastity and childbirth, of the underworld and of the changeable moon, seem to associate her with the feminine itself—woman as a dangerous mystery, defined as such by man, the elusive other who always escapes male categorizations. As one critic more

[1] Kolve, *Chaucer and the Imagery of Narrative*.

bluntly puts it, 'Diana's power is fuelled by male guilt and fear: guilt at what the masculine world does to women, and fear of how they may feel about it'.[1] That her suppliant should be the Amazon Emelye, member of a female tribe representing a parallel complex of repression and fear, might seem to support this interpretation. Whether or not this is so, in the temple description Diana too, like Venus and Mars, is seen as a force whose power is directed towards destruction. Chaucer gives a list of her victims compiled from Ovid's *Metamorphoses*: Callisto transformed into a bear, Daphne into a laurel tree, Actaeon (as punishment for seeing the goddess naked) into a stag which was killed by his own hunting-hounds, and so on. There follows the usual description of the goddess's statue, containing emblematic allusions to her connexions with the fickle moon, with the sinister underworld, and with the pain of childbirth. The return visit to the temple redoubles the sense of bewildering mystery, with its details of pagan ritual and above all of Emelye's purification ceremony, which Chaucer seems to find fascinatingly improper:

> This Emelye, with herte debonaire,
> Hir body wessh with water of a welle.
> But hou she dide hir rite I dar nat telle,
> But it be any thing in general;
> And yet it were a game to heeren al.
> To him that meneth wel it were no charge;
> But it is good a man been at his large.   (1424–30)

The vagueness of these lines makes them hard to translate accurately (see Notes), but their obscurity is not accidental. The implied speaker, whether imagined as Chaucer or the Knight, is specifically male (1429–30: 'him . . . a man'), and

---

[1] Leicester, *The Disenchanted Self*.

the lines convey a certain embarrassed excitement aroused by his imagined presence at pagan rites open only to females and involving nude washing. (Even 'Hir body' in line 1425 evokes what it fails to describe: Chaucer could easily have written 'Hirselven wessh' if he had wanted to avoid calling up a fleeting bodily image.) The lines convey feelings more exactly than facts: something like, 'I dare not tell—it would be fun to hear—there's no harm in imagining it'. Chaucer here puts his reader in the position of Actaeon, a male spying on Diana's naked female followers, uneasily defensive about his position, and fearing perhaps the possibility of Actaeon's punishment, referred to in the earlier description of the temple.

This is one of the points at which female power, doubly repressed in Theseus's defeat of the Amazons and in Chaucer's refusal to include any account of them in his version of the story, returns surreptitiously to disturb the surface of the tightly controlled narrative. As the Amazons were defeated and Emelye is subordinate to her brother-in-law Theseus, so Diana is powerless among her fellow-deities; yet the sense of fascinating danger remains associated with the feminine mystery this goddess represents. One, more conventional, version of femininity in the Tale is represented by Venus, whom we see getting her own way with the supreme patriarch Saturn by the traditional woman's weapon of tears (1620, 1806–8). This is a femininity that accepts its subordination to male rule, and is correspondingly accepted as the object of indulgent male patronage. Diana represents a different and, as it were, underground version of the feminine, defeated and yet unwilling to compromise, hence still the source of instability and male unease. Ypolita seems to have passed from

Diana to Venus, and the story's end implies that Emelye
will do the same.

The conflict of the gods and Saturn's solution

These then are the forces by which the world of *The
Knight's Tale* is immediately governed, and they are
defined by the descriptions in Part III as universally
powerful and universally destructive. But the course of the
story now brings these forces into conflict among themselves. Palamon prays to Venus for possession of Emelye,
and Arcite prays to Mars for victory in the tournament
which is to determine possession of her, and both their
prayers are granted. The result, naturally, is strife in heaven
between Venus and Mars, since they appear to have made
incompatible promises. In the *Teseida* this strife is settled
by an ingenious device, the origin of which is not specified.
But Chaucer, with greater consistency, continues the celestial motivation. First of all Jupiter attempts to put an end
to the quarrel, but he has no success. Saturn, the father of
Jupiter, and oldest of the gods, takes his place, and

> Foond in his olde experience an art
> That he ful soone hath plesed every part. (1587–8)

In doing so, he makes a speech which is in effect a
definition of his own nature, and thus provides a parallel to
the three earlier temple descriptions. It works in the same
way as these descriptions, and particularly that of Mars, in
asserting the universality of the god's power by juxtaposing
a variety of examples of its effect. Saturn is the force that
produces disasters, and he lists them in his speech—
drowning, imprisonment, strangling, rebellion, the collapse
of buildings, plague. The speech is magnificently sombre,

organized by a rhetoric that constantly returns to an assertion of personal power:

> *Myn* is the drenching in the see so wan;
> *Myn* is the prison in the derke cote;
> *Myn* is the strangling and hanging by the throte,
> The murmure and the cherles rebelling ...   (1598–1601)

Moreover, its different details are unified by having applied to them adjectives that express the nature of Saturn himself, as the planet conceived by medieval astrology. He is responsible for 'the drenching in the see so *wan*', for 'the prison in the *derke* cote', for 'the maladies *colde*', for 'The *derke* tresons, and the castes *olde*'. All these adjectives stand for attributes of the planet-god himself. Chaucer has made the ponderous symmetries of Part III point towards the oldest and most inimical of the seven planetary gods—*Infortuna major*, as he was called by the astrologers. This is the arbitrating force in the poem's universe, a force that crushes mankind beneath inexplicable disasters. And the solution he finds to the conflict between Mars and Venus is in keeping with his nature as defined in this speech.

He first allows Arcite to be victorious in the tournament, so that Mars may carry out his promise. Venus thinks she is shamed—

> What seith she now? What dooth this queene of love,
> But wepeth so, for wantinge of hir wille,
> Til that hir teeres in the listes fille?   (1806–8)

—but Saturn replies, 'Doghter, hoold thy pees', and then sends the 'furie infernal' which startles Arcite's horse and causes him to be fatally injured. Thus Palamon may eventually possess Emelye, and Venus's promise too can be carried out. But this solution is of course utterly callous of human suffering, and we are not allowed to disregard the suffering it involves. The death agony of Arcite is described in the fullest possible medical detail, including the 'clothered blood', the swelling of 'The pipes of his longes', and the accumulation of 'venym and corrupcioun' in his chest. Significantly, most of this detail, which is completely accurate in terms of medieval medicine, was added by Chaucer, and there can be no doubt, I think, that his purpose was to fix our attention on the horror of Arcite's death, rather than to allow it to rest complacently on the ingenious solution chosen by Saturn. The contrast between human suffering and divine callousness is striking, and a similar contrast seems to arise a little later, in Arcite's dying speech, between human generosity and divine pettiness. Arcite has been made to die in agony at the moment of his apparent triumph in order to settle a quarrel between gods who are presented as bickering like children. But he can rise above the squalid circumstances of his death to a final display of *gentillesse*, in recommending his rival to Emelye. Arcite is less powerful but more noble than the gods who have killed him, and thus the aristocratic value-system centring in *gentillesse* comes to have metaphysical implications. In order to discuss these, we shall have finally to consider the poem's explicit philosophizing; but before that I need to say more about the identity of the pagan gods with the planets.

The pagan gods as planets

So far I have been discussing the gods as elements of the pagan world Chaucer imagines in *The Knight's Tale*, but I have just noted that Saturn is also a planet. The same is true of all the deities who play significant parts in the Tale, and this fact makes an important contribution to the universalization of its meaning. As I suggested was generally true of the Renaissance fascination with pagan antiquity, beyond historical difference lies a universal human nature. In one sense, classical paganism was dead in Chaucer's England—nobody would ever have met a worshipper of Mars, Venus or Diana as living gods—but in another sense the gods themselves were still living, because their names were assigned to the seven planets then known (the sun and moon being included among them)—Mercury, Venus, Mars, Jupiter, Saturn, Diana (or Luna, the moon), and Phoebus Apollo (or Sol, the sun). In the Middle Ages there was widespread belief in astrology, according to which the heavenly bodies, and especially the planets, had a direct effect on human life. Whereas now, at least in the West, astrology survives only as superstition or entertainment, in Chaucer's time it was seen as a genuine and serious science, not yet distinguished from astronomy. Chaucer himself took a keen interest in it; he wrote at least one substantial prose work on the practice of astrology/astronomy (*A Treatise on the Astrolabe*), and may have written another of which the authorship is uncertain (*The Equatorie of the Planetis*). In the *Treatise* he denied any belief in the possibility of using horoscopes to foretell an individual's unavoidable future, associating this practice with 'rytes of payens' (pagan rites); in *The Man of Law's Tale*, on the other hand, he describes the heavens as a book in which people's deaths can be read:

> For in the sterres, clerer than is glas,
> Is writen, God woot, whoso koude it rede,
> The deeth of every man, withouten drede.

(For, God knows, in the stars is written clearer than glass, for anyone able to read it, the death of every man, without doubt.) Chaucer may have changed his mind one way or the other, but in his time both the characters and the fates of individuals were widely held to be influenced by the state of the heavens at their birth; this is what Arcite is referring to when he tells Palamon, 'So stood the hevene whan that we were born' (232). Moreover, certain planets were dominant in certain periods and at certain times of day, and were then able to influence human life in general. ('Influence' here must be understood not in its abstract modern sense, but as a medieval scientific term, implying a kind of radiation or invisible rain emanating from celestial bodies and affecting human beings.) It was thus perfectly possible for Chaucer and his contemporaries to go on believing in the power of the pagan gods, about whom they read so much in the Latin literature on which medieval education was based—the gods as planets, and thus in a form that was not incompatible with Christianity. The medieval Church did not deny that the planets influenced human life. Its beliefs were by no means finally settled and monolithic, and in the theological controversies of the fourteenth century there were those who laid greater stress on human freewill and those, including Wyclif and his followers, who laid greater stress on divine predestination. The latter need have no difficulty in seeing predestination as exercised *through* the planets; the former could accept the reality of planetary influence, while denying that its effect was totally determinative. The precise extent to which and means by which the planets governed human lives were probably matters that most non-theologians did not bother to define: they could believe simultaneously in God and in the planetary 'gods'.

What effect does this have on our understanding of *The Knight's Tale*? The characters' fates are influenced by 'the hevene', but one way in which that influence works is through their own temperaments. To take a small example, when Arcite falls into love-sickness, he dreams that the god Mercury appears to him and tells him:

> To Atthenes shaltou wende,
> Ther is thee shapen of thy wo an ende.   (533–4)

Mercury's traditional role is as the messenger of the gods; but as a planet Mercury was also thought to be specially responsible for producing dreams, which were in any case likely to come to those dominated by 'humour malencolik' (517). Intervention by a pagan god, influence from a planet, and the operation of human physiology and psychology— all three are different ways of explaining the same event, and while only a pagan would literally believe that one of his gods would appear to him in his sleep, the other two explanations would be thought universally valid. To take a larger example, in Part III Arcite visits Mars's temple in an hour dedicated to Mars (1509) and prays there to Mars because he is himself 'martial', dominated by the aggressive impulses for which Mars stands—he is the kind of man who *would* pray to Mars, and would beg, 'Yif me victorie, I aske thee namoore' (1562). In the same way Palamon prays to Venus because he is the kind of man who would pray to Venus, and would beg, 'Yif me my love' (1402). When, as gods, Mars and Venus make apparently incompatible promises, that is another way of saying that the state of the heavens seems to foretell incompatible futures. Again, when Venus weeps at Arcite's victory in the tournament, 'Til that hir teeres in the listes fille' (1808), that is another way of saying that there is a shower of rain (for the planetary gods control the weather), and we can understand, if we choose, that this is further explanation for the fall of Arcite's horse: a 'furie infernal' (1826) caused it to shy, but perhaps too the ground was slippery. One last instance: the gruesome clinical details of Arcite's injury and death are given in accordance with medieval medical knowledge, but many of them at the same time mark the influence of Saturn, the ultimate cause of the melancholia of which Arcite's love-sickness is one variety, and now the causer of his death. Saturn's influence is reflected in the blackness of complexion produced by the rush of blood to Arcite's face (1834–5); and Saturn, too, 'reigns over the retentive "virtue", or force, in man's body, and it is the domination of the retentive virtue over the expulsive which finally prevents any relief of the "venym and corrupcioun" gathered in Arcite's shattered breast'.[1]

Chaucer and his contemporaries would have expected pagans to be fatalists, believing themselves unable to resist their preordained fates, which are also the consequence of their inborn temperaments. Arcite believes from the beginning that 'Som wikke aspect or disposicioun / Of Saturne' (229–30) has ordained the fates of himself and Palamon, so that 'We moste endure it; this is the short and plain' (233). Having fallen in love with Emelye, he laments the power of 'felle Mars' (701) and announces that 'shapen was my deeth erst than my sherte' (708); and it is perhaps because he believes so firmly that his death has been preordained from the moment of his birth that it comes to be so. Only after

[1] Salter, *Fourteenth-Century English Poetry*, referring to lines 1890–1900. For a fuller account, see W. C. Curry, *Chaucer and the Mediaeval Sciences*, revised edition (Allen and Unwin, 1960), ch. 6.

he has received his final wound does he achieve the moral insight that enables him to renounce the 'strif and rancour' (1926) that have governed him in the past, to wish that Jupiter should protect his soul, and to urge Emelye to accept his rival as her husband. Moreover, medieval Christians would have expected the pagan gods to deceive their worshippers by communicating with them in deliberate ambiguities—what Chaucer in *Troilus and Criseyde* refers to as 'double wordes slye, / Swiche as men clepen a word with two visages' (sly, double words, of the kind that people refer to as words with two faces)—and this is what happens all through *The Knight's Tale*. When Mercury promises Arcite that in Athens an end is predestined to his woes, it turns out to be so, but the end is his own death. When Mars promises him 'Victorie!' (1575), that is what he achieves in the tournament, but only to be killed before he can enjoy what he has hoped to gain by victory, marriage to Emelye. And when Venus makes a sign from which Palamon understands that his prayer for his love has been granted, that also turns out to come true, even though he is the loser in the tournament arranged to decide who shall win Emelye.

What happens in *The Knight's Tale* is the combined outcome of planetary influences working both through and on the characters. Some modern readers argue that to explain the Tale's events in terms of the working of the planetary gods is to obscure the operation of human agency—to pretend that human beings are not responsible for the terrible things that happen in the Tale, from the destruction of Thebes to the death of Arcite. 'If the gods are thought of as the causes of what happens in human life,' writes one scholar, 'they distract attention from the real forces, especially those within human beings themselves, that they fail to control.' He goes on to argue that 'the prayers of Palamon, Arcite, and Emelye, taken together, complete what might be called the undoing or deconstruction of the gods, whereby they are replaced, in a special and complex sense, by the characters.'[1] I think such views mistaken, because they disregard the reality of the gods' existence as planets, and thus as forces that shape both nature and human nature. It was certainly possible for a medieval poet to deconstruct the poetic figures employed to mystify human agency: a century or so after Chaucer, Stephen Hawes in his *Pastime of Pleasure* has a character addressing Fortune and pointing out that she is no more than a personified idea:

> The man is fortune in the propre dede,
> And not thou that causeth hym to spede.

(It is not you who make man succeed; he is fortune by his own actions.) But the speaker in this case is Mars, who ascribes Fortune's unreality to the fact that she is 'In heven or erthe without a dwellynge place'. Fortune is a personification, but the same is not true of Mars or the other planetary gods, as they were understood in the culture that Chaucer and Hawes shared: they are real heavenly bodies, which really cause things to happen, but they do so as much by being forces 'within human beings themselves' as by acting on human beings from the outside.

[1] Leicester, *The Disenchanted Self.*

Introduction

THE KNIGHT'S TALE AS PHILOSOPHICAL ROMANCE

The planetary gods, then, are one means by which Chaucer turns the story he found in Boccaccio's *Teseida* into a philosophical romance, one with a larger and more explicit meaning than any earlier romance in English. Romances are about war and love, the two activities seen by the medieval aristocracy as defining their existence, but here war and love are focused as the planetary gods Mars and Venus, forces that operate throughout the whole world; and alongside these forces are the others represented by Diana, Saturn, Mercury and Jupiter. The overall effect of this framework for the story is to give an extremely pessimistic picture of life. Human beings, according to the poem's 'scientific' mythology, are enslaved both by their own passions and by the nature of the world they inhabit, and by both equally they are driven towards misery and death.

This picture of life is not confined to the poem's mythological superstructure. It also pervades *The Knight's Tale* in other forms, and most noticeably in its most characteristic imagery. Two trains of imagery run throughout the Tale and serve to reinforce its mythology. These are beast-images and prison-images, and their effect is to suggest that human beings are animals, both in their uncontrollable passions and in their subjection to external forces beyond their understanding, and that life itself is a prison. These images will be worth examining in some detail.

Animal imagery and the role of Theseus

Animal images indicating ferocity are applied most strikingly to the two knights. Love, according to Arcite's speech on the subject after he and Palamon have both seen Emelye for the first time, is a force that overrides all laws and reduces humanity to a Hobbesian state of nature: 'Ech man for himself, ther is noon oother' (324). In the same speech he imagines himself and Palamon as two dogs fighting for a bone. And love does indeed release an animal-like ferocity in the two. When they meet unexpectedly in Athens, they are immediately at each other's throats, and Arcite 'As fiers as leon pulled out his swerd' (740). They agree to meet next day on equal terms, but the *gentillesse* of their conduct in helping to arm each other only makes more striking the contrast between the civilized surface and the animal passions beneath it. First we are told that they are like hunters of the lion or bear waiting for their prey to rush at them. Then three animal similes follow in quick succession:

> Thou mightest wene that this Palamon
> In his fighting were a wood leon,
> And as a crueel tigre was Arcite;
> As wilde bores gonne they to smite,
> That frothen whit as foom for ire wood.   (797–801)

When they are interrupted by Theseus, the last image is repeated:

> He was war of Arcite and Palamon,
> That foughten breme as it were bores two.   (840–1)

Theseus is out hunting when he comes upon them, and here hunting seems to carry suggestions of the restraint or ordering of the animal qualities. Theseus stands as an opposite to all that the animal imagery implies about humanity, and at one point he specifically repudiates the idea that a ruler should be lion-like (915–17). He can control his own passions, and his aim is always to moderate, to impose order on disorder: he turns the illegal private duel into a ceremonial public act. But there is perhaps a certain ambivalence in the idea of Theseus as a hunter, in the light of the previous hunting image, in which the hunter, engaged in a desperate battle for survival, seemed as savage as his prey, and as reduced from rational status. The savage aspect of hunting is emphasized in the conception of Diana as a huntress. A persistent irony follows Theseus, by which his attempts to impose a civilized order on human life lead only to greater destruction, clothed though this may be in chivalric pageantry. This has been seen on a small scale in the poem's first episode, where his generous response to the widows' plea for mercy led to the total destruction of the city of Thebes. He marched against Thebes with two emblems: a banner showing an image of Mars (and we have seen what Mars stands for), and his private pennon

> Of gold ful riche, in which ther was ybete
> The Minotaur, which that he slough in Crete. (121–2)

The Minotaur was a monster, half man and half bull, and thus a perfect image of the bestial element in man. Theseus had killed it, but now he carries it as his emblem, and it is difficult to resist seeing in this a telling irony: Theseus is himself an exponent of the very force he is proud of having destroyed. The pattern is repeated in the main part of the poem. Theseus first converts the private duel into a public tournament, and then ordains that in the tournament no one shall be killed; but the result of all this is that Arcite dies a horrible death. And the magnificent pageantry of the tournament itself, which from one point of view is the supreme expression of the civilized chivalric order, in fact expresses, rather than conceals, the disorder and savagery which the order is intended to govern.

The lists constructed by Theseus are in the form of an amphitheatre, and their circular shape is itself the traditional symbol of order and perfection. Theseus, when he constructs the amphitheatre, is like God creating the world by reducing chaos to order; and, just as God when the world was made saw that it was good, so we are told of Theseus that 'Whan it was doon, him liked wonder weel' (1234). The chief decorative features of the amphitheatre are the temples of Venus, Mars, and Diana, but these keystones of the amphitheatre's ceremonial order themselves symbolize the very opposite: disruptive violence. The temple descriptions include much animal imagery. The power of Venus is exemplified by Circe, who transformed men into beasts. Mars has at his feet a wolf devouring a man. Diana is represented by a number of metamorphoses, including those of the transformation of Callisto into a bear and of Actaeon into a stag. But the animal imagery culminates in another part of the pageantry, the processional appearance of the two champions, Lygurge and Emetreus. Both are terrifyingly like wild animals in appearance and trappings. Lygurge stares like a griffin, with eyes that 'gloweden bitwixen yelow and reed'. He wears a black bear-skin, complete with claws, and his hair shines 'As any ravenes fethere'. He rides in a chariot drawn by bulls and followed by dogs 'To hunten at the leoun or the deer.' Emetreus is compared first to Mars and then to a lion. He has an animal's yellowish-green eyes, carries an eagle on his wrist, and is followed by lions and leopards. Emetreus particularly is totally metamorphosed into a wild beast, or rather into a composite symbol of savagery, and the two together make up a magnificent and terrifying image of the animal in man. When the tournament itself is reached, the beast images applied to the duel are repeated in a formalized and expanded form as epic similes:

> Ther nas no tigre in the vale of Galgopheye,
> Whan that hir whelp is stole whan it is lite,
> So crueel on the hunte as is Arcite
> For jelous herte upon this Palamon.
> Ne in Belmarye ther nis so fel leon,
> That hunted is, or for his hunger wood,
> Ne of his praye desireth so the blood,
> As Palamon to sleen his foo Arcite.   (1768–75)

Again hunting and savagery are connected.

Animal imagery of a different kind is also used to express the indignity or even absurdity of the human condition. At the end of Part 1, Palamon has a philosophical speech in which he asks indignantly what meaning there is in the universe, and the backbone of the speech is a comparison between human beings and animals. He begins by asking the 'crueel goddes':

> What is mankinde moore unto you holde
> Than is the sheep that rouketh in the folde?
> For slain is man right as another beest . . .   (449–51)

He goes on to point out that the animals can satisfy their desires in life and suffer no pain after death, whereas human beings must deprive themselves in life and are then punished when they die. Our position is worse than that of animals. Before this, Arcite has said that, in our ignorance of what is good for us, we go through life 'as he that dronke is as a mous' (403), and there too the animal image, though applied only obliquely, is degrading. Somewhat similarly, though with amusement rather than Palamon's indignation or Arcite's despair, Theseus points out that the two lovers are about to slaughter each other in their duel for Emelye, while

> She woot namoore of al this hoote fare,
> By God, than woot a cokkow or an hare!   (951–2)

Sheep, mouse, cuckoo, hare: such images debase the human condition by seeing it as absurd.

Prison imagery

Prison imagery is used less often in *The Knight's Tale* than animal imagery, but because it is narrative rather than merely verbal, it has perhaps no less force. We have seen how powerfully the actual prison in which Palamon and Arcite are put for life is realized in the poem as a matter of walls and bars 'greet and square as any sparre'. Naturally their thoughts revert to it again and again, until imprisonment comes to seem an image of the human condition itself:

> For wel thou woost thyselven, verraily,
> That thou and I be dampned to prisoun
> Perpetuelly; us gaineth no raunsoun.   (316–18)

Medieval Christian thought saw Christ's redemption (literally, 'buying back') of humanity as a form of ransom paid to release the souls that were kept in the devil's prison; but Palamon and Arcite are pagans, and they can know of no hope of ransom, even in the next world. Later Palamon addresses the planetary gods in terms that evoke the physical conditions of imprisonment:

> O crueel goddes that governe
> This world with binding of youre word eterne,
> And writen in the table of atthamaunt
> Youre parlement and youre eterne graunt . . .   (445–8)

The binding chains of the gods' word and the stony tablet on which their decisions are written imply that their role is as gaolers to human beings. The idea of earthly life as a prison from which we can escape only by death is traditional to Christianity and also to Platonism, by which the thought of early Christianity was strongly influenced. It is also a fundamental notion in a philosophical work by a Christian Platonist that more specifically underlies the thought of *The Knight's Tale*. This is the *De consolatione philosophiae* (On the consolation of philosophy) of the Roman philosopher and statesman Boethius. The *Consolation*, Boethius's most famous work, was written shortly before his execution for treason in AD 524, and it was an attempt to see how far the philosophical truths available to human intelligence, without the benefit of any religious revelation, can console someone who has been unjustly toppled from high distinction to absolute ruin—Boethius's own situation. It forms a dialogue, in which Boethius himself voices objections to the way the world is run that would naturally occur to someone who has been unfairly accused and persecuted, and Lady Philosophy shows him how unreasonable his complaints are. Boethius was a Christian, but in this work he wrote as if he were a philosophically minded pagan, presumably because he wanted to provide arguments that would offer comfort to present and future readers whatever their beliefs. The *Consolation*, widely read in the Middle Ages, meant much to Chaucer, who translated it from Latin into English around or just before the time at which he was translating the *Teseida*. Its ostensibly pagan framework, as a consolation not of theology but of philosophy, made it especially useful to him as a source of thought that could be attributed to pagan characters struggling to make sense of the world, and *The Knight's Tale* is deeply influenced by it. What matters here is that the *Consolation* was generally understood to have been written during Boethius's final imprisonment, and it was the stimulus for a whole series of medieval prison-writings, in which the state of being a lover, or simply a human being, was identified with imprisonment. In *The Knight's Tale*, this idea occurs in the long speech derived from Boethian philosophy in which Theseus attempts to expound the significance and moral of the poem's events, when he argues

> That goode Arcite, of chivalrie the flour,
> Departed is with duetee and honour
> Out of this foule prisoun of this lyf.   (2201–3)

In the same speech, Theseus refers to the 'faire cheyne of love' by which the elements are kept within 'certeyn boundes, that they may nat flee' (2133–5), and here the imagery of chains and binding seems to turn the universe itself into a prison, even though one benevolently designed.

EXPLICIT PHILOSOPHY

In the 1380s, Chaucer's friend Thomas Usk, in a Boethian prison-writing called *The Testament of Love* composed shortly before he too was executed for treason, referred to Chaucer as 'the noble philosophical poet in English'. *The Knight's Tale* is a noble philosophical poem, and it is so not just by implication but explicitly. Its characters do not simply lament or rejoice at the personal situations they find themselves in, but seek for some general explanation for the world they live in and the way it treats them. Life as they experience it is a matter of violent contrasts and changes: between Theseus's lifelong happiness and Palamon and Arcite's lifelong imprisonment; between the prison and the garden; between Arcite's liberation and rise in Theseus's service and Palamon's continuing imprisonment; between Arcite's happiness as he sings a roundel and the fit of melancholy that suddenly comes upon him; between his former princely state and his new, more lowly position as squire; between the two knights' friendship in arming each other and their savagery in the duel; between Arcite's victory in the tournament and his sudden downfall. Pervasively the Tale conveys a sense of human life as full of contrast, veering violently and unpredictably from one extreme to another. It is a vision of life summed up with piercing economy by Arcite in his dying speech, in the contrast between the warm companionship of love and the cold solitude of the grave:

> What is this world? what asketh men to have?
> Now with his love, now in his colde grave
> Allone, withouten any compaignye.   (1919–21)

It is towards this kind of insight into the nature of the general human condition that the Tale drives, and this is why, as we saw earlier, Chaucer makes little attempt to interest us in the characters as individuals. They are human beings, and human beings, according to the view of life embodied in the Tale, are forced by their common destiny into a unity more important than the accidental differences of character.

Introduction

Fortune

The vision of life as a matter of violent contrasts and changes is conceptualized, particularly in the earlier stages of *The Knight's Tale*, under the name of Fortune. In the opening incident of the widows, which seems in many ways to function as a paradigm for the whole poem, the eldest widow first addresses Theseus as

> Lord, to whom *Fortune* hath yiven
> Victorie, and as a conqueror to liven,   (57–8)

and then, having said that all the ladies were once royal or noble, adds:

> Now be we caytyves, as it is wel seene,
> Thanked be *Fortune* and hire false wheel,
> That noon estaat assureth to be weel.   (66–8)

Arcite, thinking that Palamon's cry is one of anguish at their imprisonment, tells him to be patient because

> *Fortune* hath yeven us this adversitee.   (228)

When Arcite has been freed, he envies Palamon's lot, saying:

> Wel hath *Fortune* yturned thee the dys.   (380)

And when Theseus arranges the tournament, he is aware of placing the choice of Emelye's husband in Fortune's hands:

> Thanne shal I yeve Emelya to wyve
> To whom that *Fortune* yeveth so fair a grace.   (1002–3)

In the Middle Ages, the idea of Fortune had a powerful hold on people's imaginations. Medieval people were probably more conscious than most of us are nowadays of the insecurity of human life and the dramatic changes that can come upon anyone unawares. They tended to think of Fortune as a personal force, female because patriarchal thought traditionally sees women as fickle, imagining her as incessantly turning a great wheel, on which all human beings moved up and down. This is what the widow means by 'Fortune and hir false wheel, / That noon estaat assureth to be weel'. Every condition of life is unstable; no one, however high his or her position, can be sure that it will last, and indeed, as the wheel image suggests, the higher the position, the more likely is a sudden descent. An important source of this idea of Fortune is Boethius's *De consolatione philosophiae*. Book II of the *Consolation* is concerned chiefly with Fortune. Philosophy presents the whole world as governed by Fortune, but denies that what happens to people in their subjection to her is to be interpreted as reward or punishment. In herself, Fortune is a non-moral force, and she does not bring people to prosperity for their virtues or to disgrace (like Boethius's) for their sins; that is simply what the world is like. Fortune, in fact, is a personification of the way we perceive what is ordained for us by higher forces (a mere illusion, as Stephen Hawes noted, in a way the planetary gods are not). In *The Knight's Tale* Chaucer presents a world similar to that described by Philosophy in Book II of the *Consolation*, a world in which the only certainty is that things will change, for (to quote from Chaucer's translation), 'It is certeyn and establissched by lawe perdurable that nothing that is engendred nis stedfast ne stable' (It is certain, and fixed by unchanging law, that nothing that comes into being is steadfast or stable). Fortune, then, is the goddess who personifies that unstable *aventure* that is the unchanging law of chivalric romance.

If the truth were really so obvious to all intelligent human beings, would it need to be so heavily underlined? What this part of the speech (the first thirty lines, which come entirely from Boethius, not Boccaccio) seems to express is, above all, the *difficulty* philosophy has in ordering the universe. It conveys a sense of strain, a wrenching and grinding of gears, as Theseus struggles to find metaphysical order underlying the disorder of human experience.

After this comes a series of examples of mutability: the long-lived oak, the hard stone, the broad river, the great cities; all these come to an end in time, and so must human lives, by whatever means. This argument is more convincing in itself, but what it proves is not that Arcite's death is just or rational, but, less ambitiously, that it is what happens to everyone. Here Theseus reverts to the philosophical concept of the First Cause, asking:

> What maketh this but Juppiter, the king,
> That is prince and cause of alle thing,
> Convertinge al unto his propre welle
> From which it is dirrived, sooth to telle?   (2177–80)

But the naming of the First Cause as Jupiter raises questions. We, unlike Theseus himself, have been allowed to see the heavenly pattern behind the poem's earthly events, and it was one in which Jupiter was powerless to settle a dispute between Venus and Mars, and Saturn imposed his will instead. Theseus had no temple to Saturn erected as part of his amphitheatre, and he never mentions his name; it is as if he were unaware of Saturn's very existence. Moreover, Theseus seems to identify the First Mover with the First Cause or 'cause of alle thing', and, in terms of the cosmology generally accepted in Chaucer's time, the term 'First

Mover' could properly be applied not to any of the spheres on which the planets were thought to revolve around the earth, but to the outermost crystalline sphere by which God himself applied motion to the whole system. Perhaps Theseus, as a pagan, is supposed not to know of this sphere's existence; but he must still be mistaken to think of Jupiter as the First Mover, because Jupiter's sphere is enclosed by Saturn's, 'that hath so wide for to turne' (1596), Saturn being the outermost of the planets known in the Middle Ages. Theseus believes the world of the poem to be ruled by the benevolent Jupiter; we know that it is ruled by the malevolent Saturn. Within this imagined pagan realm, Saturn's claim to have 'moore power than woot any man' (1597) seems to be literally true.

At this point a further shift of direction occurs in Theseus's speech:

> And heer-agains no creature on live,
> Of no degree, availleth for to strive.
> Thanne is it wisdom, as it thinketh me,
> To maken vertu of necessitee,
> And take it weel that we may nat eschue. (2181–5)

From an assertion of order Theseus has passed to one of inevitability; and now he leaves metaphysics behind entirely, and goes on to offer practical advice about the best way to behave in a world where change and death are part of the very nature of things. We must make a virtue of necessity—rejoice that Arcite's death occurred when his glory was at its height (an attitude that Chaucer might have regarded as characteristically pagan, since it sees no higher good than earthly fame), and that now he has at last escaped from 'this foule prisoun of this lyf'. And finally, with a certain self-consciousness about the length and complication of his argument, Theseus adds:

> What may I conclude of this longe serye,
> But after wo I rede us to be merye,
> And thanken Juppiter of al his grace? (2209–11)

The reference to Jupiter's 'grace' raises still more questions, for what grace of his has been displayed in the story we have been following? But Theseus concludes his speech with a more definite and practical proposal: let Emelye accept Palamon as her husband, and turn the sorrow of funeral into the joy of marriage. Like a medieval English monarch, Theseus claims to be acting 'With al th'avis heere of my parlement' (2218); Emelye and Palamon silently acquiesce in this dynastic arrangement, with its obvious political advantages—

> To have with certein contrees alliaunce,
> And have fully of Thebans obeisaunce (2115–16)

—and the poem ends as it began, with a wedding. Thus the pessimism that has so far reigned is mitigated at the last moment, not by being refuted, but by being allowed to fade from our attention in a 'happy ever after' conclusion. Theseus has moved from unconvincing philosophical speculation to sensible practical advice; he has not shown that all is for the best in the world of the poem, but he has shown how to go on living in a world ruled by Saturn.

The question of what to make of Theseus's final speech is not easy to settle, once we set aside the notion that it is meant to be, and is, a convincing justification of the ways of the gods to man. Some recent critics have suggested that Theseus's philosophizing is mere mystification of a hard-headed search for political advantage, in which 'thoroughly limited class and nationalistic self-interests' are made to masquerade as transcendental values.[1] In view of Chaucer's repeated praise of Theseus's conduct, this seems to me unlikely, appealing though it may be to the cynicism of readers six centuries later. Another solution is to distinguish between the Jupiter of the narrative, a 'good-natured but rather ineffectual planetary influence', and the Jupiter of Theseus's speech, 'the figurative representative, in the classical pantheon, of the Prime Mover' of medieval Christian thought.[2] It is true that learned medieval poets sometimes used classical mythology figuratively to refer to Christian truth (Dante even addresses God as 'supreme Jupiter, who wast crucified on earth for us'), but Chaucer never draws any such distinction between a planetary and a figurative Jupiter, and, since it was he who created Saturn's entire role in the story, we must surely suppose that he intended us to notice the gap between the reality of Saturn's control and the power and 'grace' that Theseus attributes to Jupiter. A better way to interpret the speech, in my view, is to see it in the light of Theseus's role in the whole poem. We have seen on Theseus's part a series of nobly intended but partly frustrated attempts to impose order on chaos: his just avenging of the Theban widows leads to the destruction of Thebes, his conversion of the Theban princes' illicit struggle into a formal tournament puts two hundred knights instead of two at risk, and his command that there shall be 'no destruccion of blood' at the tournament (1706) is rendered invalid by Saturn's interference. His final speech too is wisely and nobly intended, and on the practical level it is successful (so far as we learn) in

[1] Aers, *Chaucer.*
[2] Derek Pearsall, *The Canterbury Tales* (Allen and Unwin, 1985).

producing an alliance between Athens and Thebes and happiness for Palamon and Emelye; but on the philosophical level it fails, because Theseus, as a pagan, is bound to lack the doctrinal resources necessary to achieve a convincingly optimistic interpretation of the world he lives in. He senses that, beyond the chaos that culminates in Arcite's death, there must lie some benevolent order, and, just as Arcite in his dying speech committed his soul to Jupiter, so Theseus identifies the source of this order with the most beneficent of the planetary gods known to him. He is wrong, but in a sense he is right to be wrong: he is a virtuous pagan on the brink of a Christian understanding that can only disrupt the one cosmology he knows.

Theseus cannot be anything but a pagan; Chaucer was a Christian, but he could try to imagine what it would be like to be a pagan. In *The Knight's Tale* he enters into questions and doubts about the cosmic order that belong to the pagan world but that could also be part of Christian experience, though in medieval England they must usually have been foreclosed by the unquestionable truths of Christian doctrine. Chaucer needed to imagine pagan worlds in order to gain the impetus and the courage to interrogate his own God. The possibility of imagining what it would be like to live in a world ruled by Saturn was something new; it demanded a daring and freedom of the imagination that no earlier English poet had possessed, and that would not be matched in England before the great Elizabethans. (The pagan world of *The Knight's Tale* has aptly been compared with that of *King Lear*, as a means by which the most fundamental questions about the world can be pressed home, without being cut short by religious dogma.) To give expression to this imaginative vision also demanded extraordinary artistic skill. The shaping power that Theseus struggles to apply to his world, as artistic patron and as ruler, is matched by Chaucer's own working of the painful material of his story into the most nobly symmetrical of all his poems. Neither Theseus nor Chaucer can be a creator in the fullest sense, like God making the world out of nothing; both begin with recalcitrant stuff—a world governed by cruel gods, a story derived from 'bookes olde'—and for both the outcome is not easy mastery and total success but unremitting effort. In Chaucer's case, we sense that effort throughout the Tale, in the sudden shifts and uncertainties of tone, in the uncovenanted returns of repressed material, in the unconcealed rhetoric of narration that acts out the struggle to keep the story within the bounds of art. *The Knight's Tale* is not a perfect achievement, but its very imperfection makes it all the more gripping and admirable.

NOTE ON THE TEXT

The text which follows is based upon that of F. N. Robinson (*The Complete Works of Geoffrey Chaucer*, 2nd ed., 1957). The punctuation has been revised, with special reference to the exclamation marks. Spelling has been partly rationalized, by substituting *i* for *y* wherever the change aids the modern reader and does not affect the semantic value of the word. Thus *smylyng* becomes 'smiling', and *nyghtyngale* 'nightingale', but *wyn* (wine), *lyk* (like), and *fyr* (fire) are allowed to stand.

No accentuation has been provided in this text, for two reasons. First, because it produces a page displeasing to the eye; secondly, because it no longer seems necessary or entirely reliable in the light of modern scholarship. It is not now thought that the later works of Chaucer were written in a ten-syllable line from which no variation was permissible. The correct reading of a line of Chaucer is now seen to be more closely related to the correct reading of a comparable line of prose with phrasing suited to the rhythms of speech. This allows the reader to be more flexible in his interpretation of the line, and makes it unreasonably pedantic to provide a rigid system of accentuation.

NOTE ON PRONUNCIATION

These equivalences are intended to offer only a rough guide.

SHORT VOWELS

ă represents the sound now written *u*, as in 'cut'
ĕ as in modern 'set'
ĭ as in modern 'is'
ŏ as in modern 'top'
ŭ as in modern 'put' (not as in 'cut')
final -*e* represents the neutral vowel sound in '*a*bout' or 'atten*tio*n'. It is silent when the next word in the line begins with a vowel or an *h*.

Note on the Text

LONG VOWELS

ā as in modern 'car' (not as in 'name')

ē (open—i.e. where the equivalent modern word is spelt with *ea*) as in modern 'there'

ē (close—i.e. where the equivalent modern word is spelt with *ee* or *e*) represents the sound now written *a* as in 'take'

ī as in modern 'machine' (not as in 'like')

ō (open—i.e. where the equivalent modern vowel is pronounced as in 'br*o*ther', 'm*oo*d', or '*goo*d') represents the sound now written *aw* as in 'fawn'

ō (close—i.e. where the equivalent modern vowel is pronounced as in 'road') as in modern 'note'

ū as in French *tu* or German *Tür*.

DIPHTHONGS

ai and *ei* both roughly represent the sound now written *i* or *y* as in 'die' or 'dye'

au and *aw* both represent the sound now written *ow* or *ou* as in 'now' or 'pounce'

ou and *ow* have two pronunciations: as in *through* where the equivalent modern vowel is pronounced as in 'through' or 'mouse'; and as in *pounce* where the equivalent modern vowel is pronounced as in 'know' or 'thought'.

WRITING OF VOWELS AND DIPHTHONGS

A long vowel is often indicated by doubling, as in *roote* or *eek*. The *ŭ* sound is sometimes represented by an *o* as in *yong*. The *au* sound is sometimes represented by an *a*, especially before *m* or *n*, as in *cha(u)mbre* or *cha(u)nce*.

CONSONANTS

Largely as in modern English, except that many consonants now silent were still pronounced. *Gh* was pronounced as in Scottish 'lo*ch*', and both consonants should be pronounced in such groups as the following: '*gn*acchen', '*kn*ave', 'wor*d*', 'fol*k*', '*w*rong'.

THE PORTRAIT OF THE KNIGHT

From *The General Prologue*, lines 43–78

A KNIGHT ther was, and that a worthy man,
That fro the time that he first bigan
To riden out, he loved chivalrie,
Trouthe and honour, fredom and curteisie.
Ful worthy was he in his lordes werre,
And therto hadde he riden, no man ferre,
As wel in cristendom as in hethenesse,
And evere honoured for his worthiness.
At Alisaundre he was whan it was wonne.
Ful ofte time he hadde the bord bigonne
Aboven alle nacions in Pruce;
In Lettow hadde he reysed and in Ruce,
No Cristen man so ofte of his degree.
In Gernade at the seege eek hadde he be
Of Algezir, and riden in Belmarye.
At Lyeys was he and at Satalye,
Whan they were wonne; and in the Grete See
At many a noble armee hadde he be.
At mortal batailles hadde he been fiftene,
And foughten for oure feith at Tramissene
In listes thries, and ay slain his foo.
This ilke worthy knight hadde been also
Sometime with the lord of Palatye
Again another hethen in Turkye.
And everemoore he hadde a sovereyn prys;
And though that he were worthy, he was wys,

And of his port as meeke as is a maide.
He nevere yet no vileinye ne saide
In al his lif unto no maner wight.
He was a verray, parfit gentil knight.
But, for to tellen yow of his array,
His hors were goode, but he was nat gay.
Of fustian he wered a gipon
Al bismotered with his habergeon,
For he was late ycome from his viage,
And wente for to doon his pilgrimage.

THE KNIGHT'S TALE

PART I

Whilom, as olde stories tellen us,
Ther was a duc that highte Theseus;
Of Atthenes he was lord and governour,
And in his time swich a conquerour
That gretter was ther noon under the sonne.
Ful many a riche contree hadde he wonne;
What with his wisdom and his chivalrie,
He conquered al the regne of Femenye,
That whilom was ycleped Scithia,
And weddede the queene Ypolita,   10
And broghte hire hoom with him in his contree
With muchel glorie and greet solempnitee,
And eek hir yonge suster Emelye.
And thus with victorie and with melodye
Lete I this noble duc to Atthenes ride,
And al his hoost in armes him biside.

And certes, if it nere to long to heere,
I wolde have toold yow fully the manere
How wonnen was the regne of Femenye
By Theseus and by his chivalrye;   20
And of the grete bataille for the nones
Bitwixen Atthenes and Amazones;
And how asseged was Ypolita,
The faire, hardy queene of Scithia;
And of the feste that was at hir weddinge,
And of the tempest at hir hoom-cominge;
But al that thing I moot as now forbere.
I have, God woot, a large feeld to ere,

30
And wayke been the oxen in my plough.
The remenant of the tale is long ynough.
I wol nat letten eek noon of this route;
Lat every felawe telle his tale aboute,
And lat se now who shal the soper winne;
And ther I lefte, I wol ayeyn biginne.

This duc of whom I make mencioun,
Whan he was come almoost unto the toun,
In al his wele and in his mooste pride,
He was war, as he caste his eye aside,
Where that ther kneled in the heighe weye
40
A compaignye of ladies, tweye and tweye,
Ech after oother, clad in clothes blake;
But swich a cry and swich a wo they make
That in this world nis creature livinge
That herde swich another waymentinge;
And of this cry they nolde nevere stenten
Til they the reines of his bridel henten.

'What folk been ye, that at myn hom-cominge
Perturben so my feste with cryinge?'
Quod Theseus. 'Have ye so greet envye
50
Of myn honour, that thus compleyne and crye?
Or who hath yow misboden or offended?
And telleth me if it may been amended,
And why that ye been clothed thus in blak.'

The eldeste lady of hem alle spak,
Whan she hadde swowned with a deedly cheere,
That it was routhe for to seen and heere.
She seyde: 'Lord, to whom Fortune hath yiven
Victorie, and as a conqueror to liven,
Nat greveth us youre glorie and youre honour,
60
But we biseken mercy and socour.

Have mercy on oure wo and oure distresse.
Som drope of pitee, thurgh thy gentillesse,
Upon us wrecched wommen lat thou falle.
For certes, lord, ther is noon of us alle
That she ne hath been a duchesse or a queene.
Now be we caytyves, as it is wel seene,
Thanked be Fortune and hire false wheel,
That noon estaat assureth to be weel.
And certes, lord, to abiden youre presence,
Heere in this temple of the goddesse Clemence   70
We han ben waitinge al this fourtenight.
Now help us, lord, sith it is in thy might.

    I, wrecche, which that wepe and waile thus,
Was whilom wyf to king Cappaneus,
That starf at Thebes—cursed be that day!—
And alle we that been in this array
And maken al this lamentacioun,
We losten alle oure housbondes at that toun
Whil that the seege theraboute lay.
And yet now the olde Creon, weylaway!   80
That lord is now of Thebes the citee,
Fulfild of ire and of iniquitee,
He, for despit and for his tirannye,
To do the dede bodies vileynye
Of alle oure lordes whiche that been yslawe,
Hath alle the bodies on an heep ydrawe,
And wol nat suffren hem, by noon assent,
Neither to been yburied nor ybrent,
But maketh houndes ete hem in despit.'

    And with that word, withouten moore respit,   90
They fillen gruf and criden pitously,
'Have on us wrecched wommen som mercy,

119

And lat oure sorwe sinken in thyn herte.'
This gentil duc doun from his courser sterte
With herte pitous, whan he herde hem speke.
Him thoughte that his herte wolde breke,
Whan he saugh hem so pitous and so maat,
That whilom weren of so greet estaat;
And in his armes he hem alle up hente,
100   And hem conforteth in ful good entente,
And swoor his ooth, as he was trewe knight,
He wolde doon so ferforthly his might
Upon the tiraunt Creon hem to wreke,
That al the peple of Grece sholde speke
How Creon was of Theseus yserved
As he that hadde his deeth ful wel deserved.
And right anoon, withouten moore abood,
His baner he desplayeth, and forth rood
To Thebes-ward, and al his hoost biside.
110   No neer Atthenes wolde he go ne ride,
Ne take his ese fully half a day,
But onward on his wey that night he lay,
And sente anon Ypolita the queene
And Emelye, hir yonge suster sheene,
Unto the toun of Atthenes to dwelle,
And forth he rit; ther is namoore to telle.
The rede statue of Mars, with spere and targe,
So shineth in his white baner large
That alle the feeldes gliteren up and doun;
120   And by his baner born is his penoun
Of gold ful riche, in which ther was ybete
The Minotaur, which that he slough in Crete.
Thus rit this duc, thus rit this conquerour,
And in his hoost of chivalrie the flour,

Til that he cam to Thebes and alighte
Faire in a feeld, ther as he thoughte to fighte.
But shortly for to speken of this thing,
With Creon, which that was of Thebes king,
He faught, and slough him manly as a knight
In pleyn bataille, and putte the folk to flight;   130
And by assaut he wan the citee after,
And rente adoun bothe wall and sparre and rafter;
And to the ladies he restored again
The bones of hir housbondes that were slain,
To doon obsequies, as was tho the gyse.
But it were al to longe for to devyse
The grete clamour and the waymentinge
That the ladies made at the brenninge
Of the bodies, and the grete honour
That Theseus, the noble conquerour,   140
Dooth to the ladies whan they from him wente;
But shortly for to telle is myn entente.

Whan that this worthy duc, this Theseus,
Hath Creon slain, and wonne Thebes thus,
Stille in that feeld he took al night his reste,
And dide with al the contree as him leste.

To ransake in the taas of bodies dede,
Hem for to strepe of harneys and of wede,
The pilours diden bisynesse and cure
After the bataille and disconfiture.   150
And so bifel that in the taas they founde,
Thurgh-girt with many a grevous blody wounde,
Two yonge knightes ligginge by and by,
Bothe in oon armes, wroght ful richely,
Of whiche two Arcita highte that oon,
And that oother knight highte Palamon.

Nat fully quyke, ne fully dede they were,
But by hir cote-armures and by hir gere
The heraudes knewe hem best in special
As they that weren of the blood roial
Of Thebes, and of sustren two yborn.
Out of the taas the pilours han hem torn,
And han hem caried softe unto the tente
Of Theseus; and he ful soone hem sente
To Atthenes, to dwellen in prisoun
Perpetuelly—he nolde no raunsoun.
And whan this worthy duc hath thus ydon,
He took his hoost, and hoom he rit anon
With laurer crowned as a conquerour;
And ther he liveth in joye and in honour
Terme of his lyf; what nedeth wordes mo?
And in a tour, in angwissh and in wo,
This Palamon and his felawe Arcite
For everemoore; ther may no gold hem quite.

    This passeth yeer by yeer and day by day,
Till it fil ones, in a morwe of May,
That Emelye, that fairer was to sene
Than is the lilie upon his stalke grene,
And fressher than the May with floures newe—
For with the rose colour stroof hire hewe,
I noot which was the finer of hem two—
Er it were day, as was hir wone to do,
She was arisen and al redy dight;
For May wole have no slogardie a-night.
The sesoun priketh every gentil herte,
And maketh him out of his slep to sterte,
And seith 'Arys and do thyn observaunce.'
This maked Emelye have remembraunce

To doon honour to May, and for to rise.
Yclothed was she fressh, for to devyse: 190
Hir yelow heer was broided in a tresse
Bihinde hir bak, a yerde long, I gesse.
And in the gardyn, at the sonne upriste,
She walketh up and doun, and as hire liste
She gadereth floures, party white and rede,
To make a subtil gerland for hire hede;
And as an aungel hevenisshly she soong.
The grete tour, that was so thikke and stroong,
Which of the castel was the chief dongeoun
(Ther as the knightes weren in prisoun 200
Of which I tolde yow and tellen shal)
Was evene joinant to the gardyn wal
Ther as this Emelye hadde hir pleyinge.
Bright was the sonne and cleer that morweninge,
And Palamoun, this woful prisoner,
As was his wone, by leve of his gayler
Was risen and romed in a chambre an heigh,
In which he al the noble citee seigh,
And eek the gardyn, ful of braunches grene,
Ther as this fresshe Emelye the shene 210
Was in hire walk, and romed up and doun.
This sorweful prisoner, this Palamoun,
Goth in the chambre rominge to and fro,
And to himself compleyninge of his wo.
That he was born, ful ofte he seyde, 'allas!'
And so bifel, by aventure or cas,
That thurgh a window, thikke of many a barre
Of iren greet and square as any sparre,
He cast his eye upon Emelya,
And therwithal he bleynte and cride, 'A!' 220

123

As though he stongen were unto the herte.
And with that cry Arcite anon up sterte,
And seyde, 'Cosin myn, what eyleth thee,
That art so pale and deedly on to see?
Why cridestow? Who hath thee doon offence?
For Goddes love, taak al in pacience
Oure prisoun, for it may noon oother be.
Fortune hath yeven us this adversitee.
Som wikke aspect or disposicioun

230 Of Saturne, by som constellacioun,
Hath yeven us this, although we hadde it sworn;
So stood the hevene whan that we were born.
We moste endure it; this is the short and plain.'

    This Palamon answerde and seyde again:
'Cosin, for sothe, of this opinioun
Thow hast a veyn imaginacioun.
This prison caused me nat for to crye,
But I was hurt right now thurghout myn ye
Into myn herte, that wol my bane be.

240 The fairnesse of that lady that I see
Yond in the gardyn romen to and fro
Is cause of al my crying and my wo.
I noot wher she be womman or goddesse,
But Venus is it soothly, as I gesse.'
And therwithal on knees doun he fil,
And seyde: 'Venus, if it be thy wil
Yow in this gardyn thus to transfigure
Bifore me, sorweful, wrecched creature,
Out of this prisoun help that we may scapen.

250 And if so be my destinee be shapen
By eterne word to dyen in prisoun,
Of oure linage have som compassioun,

That is so lowe ybroght by tirannye.'
And with that word Arcite gan espye
Wher as this lady romed to and fro,
And with that sighte hir beautee hurte him so,
That, if that Palamon was wounded sore,
Arcite is hurt as muche as he, or moore.
And with a sigh he seyde pitously:
'The fresshe beautee sleeth me sodeynly   260
Of hire that rometh in the yonder place,
And but I have hir mercy and hir grace,
That I may seen hire atte leeste weye,
I nam but deed; ther nis namoore to seye.'

    This Palamon, whan he tho wordes herde,
Dispitously he looked and answerde,
'Wheither seistow this in ernest or in pley?'

    'Nay,' quod Arcite, 'in ernest, by my fey!
God helpe me so, me list ful yvele pleye.'

    This Palamon gan knitte his browes tweye.   270
'It nere,' quod he, 'to thee no greet honour
For to be fals ne for to be traitour
To me, that am thy cosin and thy brother
Ysworn ful depe, and ech of us til oother,
That nevere, for to dyen in the peyne,
Til that the deeth departe shal us tweyne,
Neither of us in love to hindre oother,
Ne in noon oother cas, my leeve brother;
But that thou sholdest trewely forthren me
In every cas, as I shal forthren thee—   280
This was thyn ooth, and myn also, certeyn;
I woot right wel, thou darst it nat withseyn.
Thus artow of my conseil, out of doute,
And now thow woldest falsly been aboute

To love my lady, whom I love and serve,
And evere shal til that myn herte sterve.
Nay, certes, false Arcite, thow shalt nat so.
I loved hire first, and tolde thee my wo
As to my conseil and my brother sworn
290   To forthre me, as I have toold biforn.
For which thou art ybounden as a knight
To helpen me, if it lay in thy might,
Or elles artow fals, I dar wel seyn.'
   This Arcite ful proudly spak ageyn:
'Thow shalt,' quod he, 'be rather fals than I;
And thou art fals, I telle thee outrely,
For paramour I loved hire first er thow.
What wiltow seyen? Thou woost nat yet now
Wheither she be a womman or goddesse!
300   Thyn is affeccioun of hoolinesse,
And myn is love, as to a creature;
For which I tolde thee myn aventure
As to my cosin and my brother sworn.
I pose that thow lovedest hire biforn;
Wostow nat wel the olde clerkes sawe,
That "who shal yeve a lovere any lawe?"
Love is a gretter lawe, by my pan,
Than may be yeve to any erthely man;
And therfore positif lawe and swich decree
310   Is broken al day for love in ech degree.
A man moot nedes love, maugree his heed.
He may nat fleen it thogh he sholde be deed,
Al be she maide, or widwe, or elles wyf.
And eek it is nat likly al thy lyf
To stonden in hir grace; namoore shal I;
For wel thou woost thyselven, verraily,

That thou and I be dampned to prisoun
Perpetuelly; us gaineth no raunsoun.
We strive as dide the houndes for the boon;
They foughte al day, and yet hir part was noon.   320
Ther cam a kite, whil that they were so wrothe,
And baar awey the boon bitwixe hem bothe.
And therfore, at the kinges court, my brother,
Ech man for himself, ther is noon oother.
Love, if thee list, for I love and ay shal;
And soothly, leeve brother, this is al.
Heere in this prisoun moote we endure,
And everich of us take his aventure.'
  Greet was the strif and long bitwix hem tweye,
If that I hadde leyser for to seye,   330
But to th'effect. It happed on a day,
To telle it yow as shortly as I may,
A worthy duc that highte Perotheus,
That felawe was unto duc Theseus
Sin thilke day that they were children lite,
Was come to Atthenes his felawe to visite,
And for to pleye as he was wont to do;
For in this world he loved no man so,
And he loved him als tendrely again.
So wel they lovede, as olde bookes sayn,   340
That whan that oon was deed, soothly to telle,
His felawe wente and soughte him doun in helle;
But of that storie list me nat to write.
Duc Perotheus loved wel Arcite,
And hadde him knowe at Thebes yeer by yere,
And finally at requeste and preyere
Of Perotheus, withouten any raunsoun,
Duc Theseus him leet out of prisoun

Frely to goon wher that him liste over al,
In swich a gyse as I you tellen shal.
    This was the forward, pleynly for t'endite,
Bitwixen Theseus and him Arcite
That if so were that Arcite were yfounde
Evere in his lif, by day or night, oo stounde
In any contree of this Theseus,
And he were caught, it was acorded thus,
That with a swerd he sholde lese his heed.
Ther nas noon oother remedie ne reed;
But taketh his leve, and homward he him spedde.
Lat him be war! his nekke lith to wedde.
    How greet a sorwe suffreth now Arcite!
The deeth he feeleth thurgh his herte smite;
He wepeth, waileth, crieth pitously;
To sleen himself he waiteth prively.
He seyde, 'Allas that day that I was born!
Now is my prisoun worse than biforn;
Now is me shape eternally to dwelle
Noght in purgatorie, but in helle.
Allas, that evere knew I Perotheus!
For elles hadde I dwelled with Theseus,
Yfetered in his prisoun everemo.
Thanne hadde I been in blisse and nat in wo.
Oonly the sighte of hire whom that I serve,
Though that I nevere hir grace may deserve,
Wolde han suffised right ynough for me.
O deere cosin Palamon,' quod he,
'Thyn is the victorie of this aventure.
Ful blisfully in prison maistow dure—
In prison? certes nay, but in paradys.
Wel hath Fortune yturned thee the dys,

That hast the sighte of hire, and I th'absence.
For possible is, sin thou hast hire presence,
And art a knight, a worthy and an able,
That by som cas, sin Fortune is chaungeable,
Thow maist to thy desir somtime atteyne.
But I, that am exiled and bareyne
Of alle grace, and in so greet dispeir,
That ther nis erthe, water, fir, ne eir,
Ne creature that of hem maked is,
That may me helpe or doon confort in this,   390
Wel oughte I sterve in wanhope and distresse.
Farwel my lif, my lust, and my gladnesse!
   Allas, why pleynen folk so in commune
On purveiaunce of God, or of Fortune,
That yeveth hem ful ofte in many a gyse
Wel bettre than they kan hemself devyse?
Som man desireth for to han richesse,
That cause is of his mordre or greet siknesse;
And som man wolde out of his prisoun fain,
That in his hous is of his meynee slain.   400
Infinite harmes been in this mateere.
We witen nat what thing we preyen heere:
We faren as he that dronke is as a mous.
A dronke man woot wel he hath an hous,
But he noot which the righte wey is thider,
And to a dronke man the wey is slider.
And certes, in this world so faren we;
We seken faste after felicitee,
But we goon wrong ful often, trewely.
Thus may we seyen alle, and namely I,   410
That wende and hadde a greet opinioun
That if I mighte escapen from prisoun

Thanne hadde I been in joye and perfit heele,
Ther now I am exiled fro my wele.
Sin that I may nat seen you, Emelye,
I nam but deed; ther nis no remedye.'
   Upon that oother side Palamon,
Whan that he wiste Arcite was agon,
Swich sorwe he maketh that the grete tour
420   Resouneth of his youling and clamour.
The pure fettres on his shynes grete
Weren of his bittre, salte teeres wete.
'Allas,' quod he, 'Arcita, cosin myn,
Of al oure strif, God woot, the fruit is thyn.
Thow walkest now in Thebes at thy large,
And of my wo thow yevest litel charge.
Thou mayst, sin thou hast wisdom and manhede,
Assemblen alle the folk of oure kinrede,
And make a werre so sharp on this citee,
430   That by som aventure or some tretee
Thow mayst have hire to lady and to wyf
For whom that I moste nedes lese my lyf.
For, as by wey of possibilitee,
Sith thou art at thy large, of prisoun free,
And art a lord, greet is thyn avauntage
Moore than is myn, that sterve here in a cage.
For I moot wepe and waile, whil I live,
With al the wo that prison may me yive,
And eek with peyne that love me yeveth also,
440   That doubleth al my torment and my wo.'
Therwith the fyr of jalousie up sterte
Withinne his brest, and hente him by the herte
So woodly that he lyk was to biholde
The boxtree or the asshen dede and colde.

Thanne seyde he, 'O crueel goddes that governe
This world with binding of youre word eterne,
And writen in the table of atthamaunt
Youre parlement and youre eterne graunt,
What is mankinde moore unto you holde
Than is the sheep that rouketh in the folde?   450
For slain is man right as another beest,
And dwelleth eek in prison and arreest,
And hath siknesse and greet adversitee,
And ofte times giltelees, pardee.

What governance is in this prescience,
That giltelees tormenteth innocence?
And yet encresseth this al my penaunce,
That man is bounden to his observaunce,
For Goddes sake, to letten of his wille,
Ther as a beest may al his lust fulfille.   460
And whan a beest is deed he hath no peyne;
But man after his deeth moot wepe and pleyne,
Though in this world he have care and wo.
Withouten doute it may stonden so.
The answere of this lete I to divinis,
But wel I woot that in this world greet pyne is.
Allas, I se a serpent or a theef,
That many a trewe man hath doon mescheef,
Goon at his large, and where him list may turne.
But I moot been in prisoun thurgh Saturne,   470
And eek thurgh Juno, jalous and eek wood,
That hath destroyed wel ny al the blood
Of Thebes with his waste walles wide;
And Venus sleeth me on that oother side
For jalousie and fere of him Arcite.'
Now wol I stynte of Palamon a lite,

131

For al day meeteth men at unset stevene.
Ful litel woot Arcite of his felawe,
That was so ny to herknen al his sawe,
For in the bussh he sitteth now ful stille.

670   Whan that Arcite hadde romed al his fille,
And songen al the roundel lustily,
Into a studie he fil sodeynly,
As doon thise loveres in hir queynte geres,
Now in the crope, now doun in the breres,
Now up, now doun, as boket in a welle.
Right as the Friday, soothly for to telle,
Now it shineth, now it reyneth faste,
Right so kan geery Venus overcaste
The hertes of hir folk; right as hir day
680   Is gereful, right so chaungeth she array.
Selde is the Friday al the wowke ylike.

Whan that Arcite had songe, he gan to sike,
And sette him doun withouten any moore.
'Allas,' quod he, 'that day that I was bore!
How longe, Juno, thurgh thy crueltee,
Woltow werreyen Thebes the citee?
Allas, ybroght is to confusioun
The blood roial of Cadme and Amphioun—
Of Cadmus, which that was the firste man
690   That Thebes bulte, or first the toun bigan,
And of the citee first was crouned king.
Of his linage am I and his ofspring
By verray ligne, as of the stok roial,
And now I am so caytyf and so thral
That he that is my mortal enemy,
I serve him as his squier povrely.
And yet dooth Juno me wel moore shame,

138

For I dar noght biknowe myn owene name;
But ther as I was wont to highte Arcite,
Now highte I Philostrate, noght worth a mite.   700
Allas, thou felle Mars, allas, Juno!
Thus hath youre ire oure linage al fordo,
Save oonly me and wrecched Palamoun,
That Theseus martireth in prisoun.
And over al this, to sleen me outrely,
Love hath his firy dart so brenningly
Ystiked thurgh my trewe, careful herte,
That shapen was my deeth erst than my sherte.
Ye sleen me with youre eyen, Emelye;
Ye been the cause wherfore that I die.   710
Of al the remenant of myn oother care
Ne sette I nat the montance of a tare,
So that I koude doon aught to youre plesaunce.'
And with that word he fil doun in a traunce
A longe time, and after he up sterte.

This Palamoun, that thoughte that thurgh his herte
He felte a coold swerd sodeynliche glide,
For ire he quook, no lenger wolde he bide.
And whan that he had herd Arcites tale,
As he were wood, with face deed and pale,   720
He stirte him up out of the buskes thikke,
And seide: 'Arcite, false traitour wikke,
Now artow hent, that lovest my lady so,
For whom that I have al this peyne and wo,
And art my blood, and to my conseil sworn,
As I ful ofte have told thee heerbiforn,
And hast byjaped heere duc Theseus,
And falsly chaunged hast thy name thus!
I wol be deed, or elles thou shalt die.

730 Thou shalt nat love my lady Emelye,
But I wol love hire oonly and namo;
For I am Palamon, thy mortal foo.
And though that I no wepene have in this place,
But out of prison am astert by grace,
I drede noght that outher thow shalt die,
Or thow ne shalt nat loven Emelye.
Chees which thou wolt, for thou shalt nat asterte.'

   This Arcite, with ful despitous herte,
Whan he him knew, and hadde his tale herd,
740 As fiers as leon pulled out his swerd,
And seyde thus: 'By God that sit above,
Nere it that thou art sik and wood for love,
And eek that thow no wepne hast in this place,
Thou sholdest nevere out of this grove pace
That thou ne sholdest dyen of myn hond.
For I defye the seurete and the bond
Which that thou seist that I have maad to thee.
What, verray fool, think wel that love is free,
And I wol love hire maugree al thy might!
750 But for as muche thou art a worthy knight,
And wilnest to darreyne hire by bataille,
Have heer my trouthe, tomorwe I wol nat faille,
Withoute witing of any oother wight,
That heere I wol be founden as a knight,
And bringen harneys right ynough for thee;
And ches the beste, and leef the worste for me.
And mete and drinke this night wol I bringe
Ynough for thee, and clothes for thy beddinge.
And if so be that thou my lady winne,
760 And sle me in this wode ther I am inne,
Thow mayst wel have thy lady as for me.'

This Palamon answerde, 'I graunte it thee.'
And thus they been departed til amorwe,
Whan ech of hem had leyd his feith to borwe.

O Cupide, out of alle charitee!
O regne, that wolt no felawe have with thee!
Ful sooth is seyd that love ne lordshipe
Wol noght, his thankes, have no felaweshipe.
Wel finden that Arcite and Palamoun.
Arcite is riden anon unto the toun,   770
And on the morwe, er it were dayes light,
Ful prively two harneys hath he dight,
Bothe suffisaunt and mete to darreyne
The bataille in the feeld bitwix hem tweyne;
And on his hors, allone as he was born,
He carieth al the harneys him biforn.
And in the grove, at time and place yset,
This Arcite and this Palamon ben met.
Tho chaungen gan the colour in hir face,
Right as the hunters in the regne of Trace,   780
That stondeth at the gappe with a spere,
Whan hunted is the leon or the bere,
And hereth him come russhing in the greves,
And breketh bothe bowes and the leves,
And thinketh, 'Heere cometh my mortal enemy!
Withoute faille, he moot be deed, or I;
For outher I moot sleen him at the gappe,
Or he moot sleen me, if that me mishappe,'—
So ferden they in chaunging of hir hewe,
As fer as everich of hem oother knewe.   790

Ther nas no good day, ne no saluing,
But streight, withouten word or rehersing,
Everich of hem heelp for to armen oother

As freendly as he were his owene brother;
And after that, with sharpe speres stronge
They foynen ech at oother wonder longe.
Thou mightest wene that this Palamon
In his fighting were a wood leon,
And as a crueel tigre was Arcite;
800 As wilde bores gonne they to smite,
That frothen whit as foom for ire wood.
Up to the ancle foghte they in hir blood.
And in this wise I lete hem fighting dwelle,
And forth I wole of Theseus yow telle.

The destinee, ministre general,
That executeth in the world over al
The purveiaunce that God hath seyn biforn,
So strong it is that, though the world had sworn
The contrarie of a thing by ye or nay,
810 Yet sometime it shal fallen on a day
That falleth nat eft withinne a thousand yeer.
For certeinly oure appetites heer,
Be it of werre or pees, or hate or love,
Al is this reuled by the sighte above.

This mene I now by mighty Theseus,
That for to hunten is so desirus,
And namely at the grete hert in May,
That in his bed ther daweth him no day
That he nis clad and redy for to ride
820 With hunte and horn and houndes him biside.
For in his hunting hath he swich delit
That it is al his joye and appetit
To been himself the grete hertes bane,
For after Mars he serveth now Diane.

Cleer was the day, as I have toold er this,

And Theseus with alle joye and blis,
With his Ypolita, the faire queene,
And Emelye, clothed al in grene,
On hunting be they riden roially.
And to the grove that stood ful faste by,   830
In which ther was an hert, as men him tolde,
Duc Theseus the streighte wey hath holde.
And to the launde he rideth him ful right,
For thider was the hert wont have his flight,
And over a brook, and so forth on his weye.
This duc wol han a cours at him or tweye
With houndes swiche as that him list comaunde.
    And whan this duc was come unto the launde,
Under the sonne he looketh, and anon
He was war of Arcite and Palamon,   840
That foughten breme as it were bores two.
The brighte swerdes wenten to and fro
So hidously that with the leeste strook
It semed as it wolde felle an ook.
But what they were no thing he ne woot.
This duc his courser with his spores smoot,
And at a stert he was bitwix hem two,
And pulled out a swerd, and cride, 'Hoo!
Namoore, up peyne of lesinge of youre heed!
By mighty Mars, he shal anon be deed   850
That smiteth any strook that I may seen.
But telleth me what myster men ye been,
That been so hardy for to fighten heere
Withouten juge or oother officere,
As it were in a listes roially.'
    This Palamon answerde hastily,
And seyde, 'Sire, what nedeth wordes mo?

We have the deeth disserved bothe two.
Two woful wrecches been we, two caytyves,
860   That been encombred of oure owene lives;
And as thou art a rightful lord and juge,
Ne yif us neither mercy ne refuge,
But sle me first, for seinte charitee!
But sle my felawe eek as wel as me;
Or sle him first, for though thow knowest it lite,
This is thy mortal foo, this is Arcite,
That fro thy lond is banisshed on his heed,
For which he hath deserved to be deed.
For this is he that cam unto thy gate
870   And seyde that he highte Philostrate.
Thus hath he japed thee ful many a yer,
And thou hast maked him thy chief squier;
And this is he that loveth Emelye.
For sith the day is come that I shal die,
I make pleynly my confessioun
That I am thilke woful Palamoun
That hath thy prisoun broken wikkedly.
I am thy mortal foo, and it am I
That loveth so hoote Emelye the brighte
880   That I wol die present in hir sighte.
Wherfore I axe deeth and my juwise;
But sle my felawe in the same wise,
For bothe han we deserved to be slain.'
    This worthy duc answerde anon again
And seyde, 'This is a short conclusioun.
Youre owene mouth, by youre confessioun,
Hath dampned yow, and I wol it recorde;
It nedeth noght to pine yow with the corde.
Ye shal be deed, by mighty Mars the rede!'

The queene anon for verray wommanhede   890
Gan for to wepe, and so dide Emelye
And alle the ladies in the compaignye.
Greet pitee was it, as it thoughte hem alle,
That evere swich a chaunce sholde falle;
For gentil men they were of greet estaat,
And no thing but for love was this debaat;
And saugh hir blody woundes wide and soore,
And alle crieden, bothe lasse and moore,
'Have mercy, Lord, upon us wommen alle!'
And on hir bare knees adoun they falle,   900
And wolde have kist his feet ther as he stood;
Til at the laste aslaked was his mood,
For pitee renneth soone in gentil herte.
And though he first for ire quook and sterte,
He hath considered shortly, in a clause,
The trespas of hem bothe, and eek the cause,
And although that his ire hir gilt accused,
Yet in his resoun he hem bothe excused,
As thus: he thoghte wel that every man
Wol helpe himself in love, if that he kan,   910
And eek delivere himself out of prisoun.
And eek his herte hadde compassioun
Of wommen, for they wepen evere in oon;
And in his gentil herte he thoughte anon,
And softe unto himself he seyde, 'Fy
Upon a lord that wol have no mercy,
But been a leon, bothe in word and dede,
To hem that been in repentaunce and drede,
As wel as to a proud despitous man
That wol maintene that he first bigan.   920
That lord hath litel of discrecioun

That in swich cas kan no divisioun,
But weyeth pride and humblesse after oon.'
And shortly, whan his ire is thus agoon,
He gan to looken up with eyen lighte,
And spak thise same wordes al on highte:
  'The god of love, a, *benedicite!*
How mighty and how greet a lord is he!
Ayeyns his might ther gaineth none obstacles.

930   He may be cleped a god for his miracles;
For he kan maken, at his owene gyse,
Of everich herte as that him list divyse.
Lo heere this Arcite and this Palamoun,
That quitly weren out of my prisoun,
And mighte han lived in Thebes roially,
And witen I am hir mortal enemy,
And that hir deth lith in my might also;
And yet hath love, maugree hir eyen two,
Broght hem hider bothe for to die.

940   Now looketh, is nat that an heigh folye?
Who may been a fool, but if he love?
Bihoold, for Goddes sake that sit above,
Se how they blede! be they noght wel arrayed?
Thus hath hir lord, the god of love, ypayed
Hir wages and hir fees for hir servise!
And yet they wenen for to been ful wise
That serven love, for aught that may bifalle.
But this is yet the beste game of alle,
That she for whom they han this jolitee

950   Kan hem therfore as muche thank as me.
She woot namoore of al this hoote fare,
By God, than woot a cokkow or an hare!
But all moot ben assayed, hoot and coold;

146

A man moot ben a fool, or yong or oold—
I woot it by myself ful yore agon,
For in my time a servant was I oon.
And therfore, sin I knowe of loves peyne,
And woot hou soore it kan a man distreyne,
As he that hath ben caught ofte in his laas,
I yow foryeve al hoolly this trespaas,   960
At requeste of the queene, that kneleth heere,
And eek of Emelye, my suster deere.
And ye shul bothe anon unto me swere
That nevere mo ye shal my contree dere,
Ne make werre upon me night ne day,
But been my freendes in all that ye may.
I yow foryeve this trespas every deel.'
And they him sworen his axing faire and weel,
And him of lordshipe and of mercy preyde,
And he hem graunteth grace, and thus he seyde: 970
   'To speke of roial linage and richesse,
Though that she were a queene or a princesse,
Ech of you bothe is worthy, doutelees,
To wedden whan time is, but nathelees
I speke as for my suster Emelye,
For whom ye have this strif and jalousye.
Ye woot yourself she may nat wedden two
Atones, though ye fighten everemo.
That oon of you, al be him looth or lief,
He moot go pipen in an ivy leef;   980
This is to seyn, she may nat now han bothe,
Al be ye never so jalouse ne so wrothe.
And forthy I yow putte in this degree,
That ech of yow shal have his destinee
As him is shape, and herkneth in what wise;

Lo heere youre ende of that I shal devyse.
  My wil is this, for plat conclusioun,
Withouten any repplicacioun—
If that you liketh, take it for the beste:
That everich of you shal goon where him leste
Frely, withouten raunson or daunger;
And this day fifty wykes, fer ne ner,
Everich of you shal bringe an hundred knightes
Armed for listes up at alle rightes,
Al redy to darreyne hire by bataille.
And this bihote I yow withouten faille,
Upon my trouthe, and as I am a knight,
That wheither of yow bothe that hath might—
This is to seyn, that wheither he or thow
May with his hundred, as I spak of now,
Sleen his contrarie or out of listes drive—
Thanne shal I yeve Emelya to wyve
To whom that Fortune yeveth so fair a grace.
The listes shal I maken in this place,
And God so wisly on my soule rewe,
As I shal evene juge been and trewe.
Ye shul noon oother ende with me maken,
That oon of yow ne shal be deed or taken.
And if yow thinketh this is weel ysaid,
Seyeth youre avis, and holdeth you apayd.
This is youre ende and youre conclusioun.'
  Who looketh lightly now but Palamoun?
Who springeth up for joye but Arcite?
Who kouthe telle, or who kouthe it endite,
The joye that is maked in the place
Whan Theseus hath doon so fair a grace?
But doun on knees wente every maner wight,

990

1000

1010

And thonked him with al hir herte and might,
And namely the Thebans often sithe.
And thus with good hope and with herte blithe   1020
They taken hir leve, and homward gonne they ride
To Thebes, with his olde walles wide.

PART III

I trowe men wolde deme it necligence
If I foryete to tellen the dispence
Of Theseus, that gooth so bisily
To maken up the listes roially,
That swich a noble theatre as it was
I dar wel seyen in this world ther nas.
The circuit a mile was aboute,
Walled of stoon, and diched al withoute.   1030
Round was the shap, in manere of compas,
Ful of degrees, the heighte of sixty pas,
That whan a man was set on o degree
He letted nat his felawe for to see.

Estward ther stood a gate of marbul whit,
Westward right swich another in the opposit.
And shortly to concluden, swich a place
Was noon in erthe, as in so litel space;
For in the lond ther was no crafty man
That geometrie or ars-metrike kan,   1040
Ne portreyour, ne kervere of images,
That Theseus ne yaf him mete and wages,
The theatre for to maken and devyse.
And for to doon his rite and sacrifise,
He estward hath, upon the gate above,
In worshipe of Venus, goddesse of love,

Doon make an auter and an oratorie;
And on the gate westward, in memorie
Of Mars, he maked hath right swich another,
1050 That coste largely of gold a fother.
And northward, in a touret on the wal,
Of alabastre whit and reed coral,
An oratorie, riche for to see,
In worshipe of Diane of chastitee,
Hath Theseus doon wroght in noble wise.

 But yet hadde I foryeten to devyse
The noble kerving and the portreitures,
The shap, the contenaunce, and the figures,
That weren in thise oratories thre.

1060 First in the temple of Venus maystow se
Wroght on the wal, ful pitous to biholde,
The broken slepes and the sikes colde,
The sacred teeris and the waymentinge,
The firy strokes of the desiringe
That loves servantz in this lyf enduren;
The othes that hir covenantz assuren;
Plesaunce and Hope, Desir, Foolhardinesse,
Beautee and Youthe, Bauderie, Richesse,
Charmes and Force, Lesinges, Flaterye,
1070 Despense, Bisynesse; and Jalousye,
That wered of yelewe gooldes a gerland,
And a cokkow sittinge on hir hand;
Festes, instrumentz, caroles, daunces,
Lust and array, and alle the circumstaunces
Of love which that I rekned and rekne shal,
By ordre weren peynted on the wal,
And mo than I kan make of mencioun.
For soothly al the mount of Citheroun,

Ther Venus hath hir principal dwellinge,
Was shewed on the wal in portreyinge,　　　　1080
With al the gardyn and the lustinesse.
Nat was foryeten the porter, Idelnesse,
Ne Narcisus the faire of yore agon,
Ne yet the folye of king Salomon,
Ne yet the grete strengthe of Ercules,
Th'enchauntementz of Medea and Circes,
Ne of Turnus with the hardy fiers corage,
The riche Cresus, kaytyf in servage.
Thus may ye seen that wisdom ne richesse,
Beautee ne sleighte, strengthe ne hardinesse,　　1090
Ne may with Venus holde champartie,
For as hir list the world than may she gye.
Lo, alle thise folk so caught were in hir las,
Til they for wo ful ofte seyde 'allas!'
Suffiseth heere ensamples oon or two,
And though I koude rekene a thousand mo.

　The statue of Venus, glorious for to se,
Was naked, fletinge in the large see,
And fro the navele doun al covered was
With wawes grene, and brighte as any glas.　　1100
A citole in hir right hand hadde she,
And on hir heed, ful semely for to se,
A rose gerland, fressh and wel smellinge;
Above hir heed hir dowves flikeringe.
Biforn hire stood hir sone Cupido;
Upon his shuldres winges hadde he two,
And blind he was, as it is often seene;
A bowe he bar and arwes brighte and kene.

　Why sholde I noght as wel eek telle yow al
The portreiture that was upon the wal　　　　1110

Withinne the temple of mighty Mars the rede?
Al peynted was the wal, in lengthe and brede,
Lyk to the estres of the grisly place
That highte the grete temple of Mars in Trace,
In thilke colde, frosty regioun
Ther as Mars hath his soverein mansioun.

First on the wal was peynted a forest,
In which ther dwelleth neither man ne best,
With knotty, knarry, bareyne trees olde,
Of stubbes sharpe and hidouse to biholde,
In which ther ran a rumbel in a swough,
As though a storm sholde bresten every bough.
And dounward from an hille, under a bente,
Ther stood the temple of Mars armipotente,
Wroght al of burned steel, of which the entree
Was long and streit, and gastly for to see.
And therout came a rage and swich a veze
That it made al the gate for to rese.
The northren light in at the dores shoon,
For windowe on the wal ne was ther noon
Thurgh which men mighten any light discerne.
The dore was al of adamant eterne,
Yclenched overthwart and endelong
With iren tough; and for to make it strong,
Every piler, the temple to sustene,
Was tonne-greet, of iren bright and shene.

Ther saugh I first the derke imagining
Of Felonye, and al the compassing;
The crueel Ire, reed as any gleede;
The pykepurs, and eek the pale Drede;
The smilere with the knyf under the cloke;
The shepne brenninge with the blake smoke;

1120
1130
1140

The tresoun of the mordringe in the bedde;
The open werre, with woundes al bibledde;
Contek, with blody knyf and sharp manace.
Al ful of chirking was that sory place.
The sleere of himself yet saugh I ther—
His herte-blood hath bathed al his heer;
The nail ydriven in the shode a-night;
The colde deeth, with mouth gaping upright.   1150
Amiddes of the temple sat Meschaunce,
With disconfort and sory contenaunce.
Yet saugh I Woodnesse, laughinge in his rage,
Armed Compleint, Outhees, and fiers Outrage;
The careyne in the busk, with throte ycorve;
A thousand slain, and nat of qualm ystorve;
The tiraunt, with the pray by force yraft;
The toun destroyed, ther was no thing laft.
Yet saugh I brent the shippes hoppesteres;
The hunte strangled with the wilde beres;   1160
The sowe freten the child right in the cradel;
The cook yscalded, for al his longe ladel.
Noght was foryeten by the infortune of Marte
The cartere overriden with his carte:
Under the wheel ful lowe he lay adoun.
Ther were also, of Martes divisioun,
The barbour, and the bocher, and the smith,
That forgeth sharpe swerdes on his stith.
And al above, depeynted in a tour,
Saugh I Conquest sittinge in greet honour,   1170
With the sharpe swerd over his heed
Hanginge by a soutil twines threed.
Depeynted was the slaughtre of Julius,
Of grete Nero, and of Antonius;

Al be that thilke time they were unborn,
Yet was hir deth depeynted ther-biforn
By manasinge of Mars, right by figure.
So was it shewed in that portreiture,
As is depeynted in the sterres above
1180 Who shal be slain or elles deed for love.
Suffiseth oon ensample in stories olde;
I may nat rekene hem alle though I wolde.

The statue of Mars upon a carte stood
Armed, and looked grim as he were wood;
And over his heed ther shinen two figures
Of sterres, that been cleped in scriptures
That oon Puella, that oother Rubeus—
This god of armes was arrayed thus.
A wolf ther stood biforn him at his feet
1190 With eyen rede, and of a man he eet;
With soutil pencel depeynted was this storie
In redoutinge of Mars and of his glorie.

Now to the temple of Diane the chaste,
As shortly as I kan, I wol me haste,
To telle yow al the descripsioun.
Depeynted been the walles up and doun
Of hunting and of shamefast chastitee.
Ther saugh I how woful Calistopee,
Whan that Diane agreved was with here,
1200 Was turned from a womman til a bere,
And after was she maad the loode-sterre;
Thus was it peynted, I kan sey yow no ferre.
Hir sone is eek a sterre, as men may see.
Ther saugh I Dane, yturned til a tree—
I mene nat the goddesse Diane,
But Penneus doghter, which that highte Dane.

Ther saugh I Attheon an hert ymaked,
For vengeaunce that he saugh Diane al naked;
I saugh how that his houndes have him caught
And freeten him, for that they knewe him naught. 1210
Yet peynted was a litel forther moor
How Atthalante hunted the wilde boor,
And Meleagre, and many another mo,
For which Diane wroghte him care and wo.
Ther saugh I many another wonder storie,
The which me list nat drawen to memorie.

This goddesse on an hert ful hye seet,
With smale houndes al aboute hir feet;
And undernethe hir feet she hadde a moone—
Wexinge it was and sholde wanye soone.   1220
In gaude grene hir statue clothed was,
With bowe in honde, and arwes in a cas.
Hir eyen caste she ful lowe adoun
Ther Pluto hath his derke regioun.
A womman travaillinge was hire biforn;
But for hir child so longe was unborn,
Ful pitously Lucina gan she calle,
And seyde, 'Help, for thou mayst best of alle!'
Wel koude he peynten lifly that it wroghte;
With many a florin he the hewes boghte.   1230

Now been thise listes maad, and Theseus,
That at his grete cost arrayed thus
The temples and the theatre every deel,
Whan it was doon, him liked wonder weel.
But stynte I wole of Theseus a lite,
And speke of Palamon and of Arcite.

The day approcheth of hir retourninge,
That everich sholde an hundred knightes bringe

The bataille to darreyne, as I yow tolde.
1240 And til Atthenes, hir covenant for to holde,
Hath everich of hem broght an hundred knightes,
Wel armed for the werre at alle rightes.
And sikerly ther trowed many a man
That nevere, sithen that the world bigan,
As for to speke of knighthod of hir hond,
As fer as God hath maked see or lond,
Nas of so fewe so noble a compaignye.
For every wight that lovede chivalrye,
And wolde his thankes han a passant name,
1250 Hath preyed that he mighte been of that game;
And wel was him that therto chosen was.
For if ther fille tomorwe swich a cas,
Ye knowen wel that every lusty knight
That loveth paramours and hath his might,
Were it in Engelond or elleswhere,
They wolde, hir thankes, wilnen to be there—
To fighte for a lady, *benedicitee*,
It were a lusty sighte for to see.
    And right so ferden they with Palamon.
1260 With him ther wenten knightes many on;
Som wol ben armed in an haubergeoun,
And in a brestplate and a light gypoun;
And som wol have a paire plates large;
And som wol have a Pruce sheeld or a targe;
Som wol ben armed on his legges weel,
And have an ax, and som a mace of steel—
Ther is no newe gyse that it nas old.
Armed were they, as I have yow told,
Everich after his opinioun.
1270   Ther maistow seen cominge with Palamoun

Lygurge himself, the grete king of Trace.
Blak was his berd and manly was his face;
The cercles of his eyen in his heed,
They gloweden bitwixen yelow and reed,
And lik a grifphon looked he aboute,
With kempe heeris on his browes stoute;
His lymes grete, his brawnes harde and stronge,
His shuldres brode, his armes rounde and longe;
And as the gyse was in his contree,
Ful hye upon a chaar of gold stood he,   1280
With foure white boles in the trais.
In stede of cote-armure over his harnais,
With nailes yelewe and brighte as any gold,
He hadde a beres skin, col-blak for old.
His longe heer was kembd bihinde his bak;
As any ravenes fethere it shoon for blak;
A wrethe of gold, arm-greet, of huge wighte,
Upon his heed, set ful of stones brighte,
Of fine rubies and of diamauntz.
Aboute his chaar ther wenten white alauntz,   1290
Twenty and mo, as grete as any steer,
To hunten at the leoun or the deer,
And folwed him with mosel faste ybounde,
Colered of gold, and tourettes filed rounde.
An hundred lordes hadde he in his route,
Armed ful wel, with hertes stierne and stoute.
    With Arcita, in stories as men finde,
The grete Emetreus, the king of Inde,
Upon a steede bay trapped in steel,
Covered in clooth of gold, diapred weel,   1300
Cam ridinge lyk the god of armes, Mars.
His cote-armure was of clooth of Tars

Couched with perles white and rounde and grete;
His sadel was of brend gold newe ybete;
A mantelet upon his shulder hanginge,
Bret-ful of rubies rede as fyr sparklinge;
His crispe heer lyk ringes was yronne,
And that was yelow, and glitered as the sonne.
His nose was heigh, his eyen bright citrin,
His lippes rounde, his colour was sangwin;
A fewe frakenes in his face yspreynd,
Bitwixen yelow and somdel blak ymeynd;
And as a leon he his looking caste.
Of five and twenty yeer his age I caste.
His berd was wel bigonne for to springe;
His vois was as a trompe thonderinge.
Upon his heed he wered of laurer grene
A gerland, fressh and lusty for to sene.
Upon his hand he bar for his deduyt
An egle tame, as any lilye whyt.
An hundred lordes hadde he with him there,
Al armed, save hir heddes, in al hir gere,
Ful richely in alle maner thinges.
For trusteth wel that dukes, erles, kinges
Were gadered in this noble compaignye,
For love and for encrees of chivalrye.
Aboute this king ther ran on every part
Ful many a tame leon and leopart.
And in this wise thise lordes, alle and some,
Been on the Sonday to the citee come
Aboute prime, and in the toun alight.
    This Theseus, this duc, this worthy knight,
Whan he had broght hem into his citee,
And inned hem, everich at his degree,

1310

1320

1330

He festeth hem, and dooth so greet labour
To esen hem and doon hem al honour,
That yet men wenen that no mannes wit
Of noon estaat ne koude amenden it.

    The minstralcye, the service at the feeste,
The grete yiftes to the meeste and leeste,   1340
The riche array of Theseus paleys,
Ne who sat first ne last upon the deys,
What ladies fairest been or best daunsinge,
Or which of hem kan dauncen best and singe,
Ne who moost felingly speketh of love;
What haukes sitten on the perche above,
What houndes liggen on the floor adoun—
Of al this make I now no mencioun,
But al th'effect, that thinketh me the beste.
Now cometh the point, and herkneth if yow leste. 1350

    The Sonday night, er day bigan to springe,
Whan Palamon the larke herde singe,
(Although it nere nat day by houres two,
Yet song the larke) and Palamon right tho
With hooly herte and with an heigh corage,
He roos to wenden on his pilgrimage
Unto the blisful Citherea benigne—
I mene Venus, honurable and digne.
And in hir houre he walketh forth a pas
Unto the listes ther hire temple was,   1360
And doun he kneleth, and with humble cheere
And herte soor he seyde as ye shal heere:

    'Faireste of faire, O lady myn, Venus,
Doughter to Jove, and spouse of Vulcanus,
Thow gladere of the mount of Citheron,
For thilke love thow haddest to Adoon,

Have pitee of my bittre teeris smerte,
And taak myn humble preyere at thyn herte.
Allas! I ne have no langage to telle

1370 Th'effectes ne the tormentz of myn helle;
Myn herte may mine harmes nat biwreye;
I am so confus that I kan noght seye
But, "Mercy, lady bright, that knowest weele
My thought and seest what harmes that I feele!"
Considere al this and rewe upon my soore,
As wisly as I shal for everemoore,
Emforth my might, thy trewe servant be,
And holden werre alwey with chastitee.
That make I myn avow, so ye me helpe.

1380 I kepe noght of armes for to yelpe,
Ne I ne axe nat tomorwe to have victorie,
Ne renoun in this cas, ne veyne glorie
Of pris of armes blowen up and doun;
But I wolde have fully possessioun
Of Emelye, and die in thy servise.
Find thow the manere hou, and in what wise:
I recche nat but it may bettre be
To have victorie of hem, or they of me,
So that I have my lady in mine armes.

1390 For though so be that Mars is god of armes,
Youre vertu is so greet in hevene above
That if yow list I shal wel have my love.
Thy temple wol I worshipe everemo,
And on thyn auter, where I ride or go,
I wol doon sacrifice and fires beete.
And if ye wol nat so, my lady sweete,
Thanne preye I thee tomorwe with a spere
That Arcita me thurgh the herte bere.

Thanne rekke I noght, whan I have lost my lyf,
Though that Arcita winne hire to his wyf.   1400
This is th'effect and ende of my preyere:
Yif me my love, thow blisful lady deere.'

 Whan the orison was doon of Palamon,
His sacrifice he dide, and that anon,
Ful pitously, with alle circumstaunces,
Al telle I noght as now his observaunces;
But atte laste the statue of Venus shook,
And made a signe, wherby that he took
That his preyere accepted was that day.
For thogh the signe shewed a delay,   1410
Yet wiste he wel that graunted was his boone;
And with glad herte he wente him hoom ful soone.

 The thridde houre inequal that Palamon
Bigan to Venus temple for to gon,
Up roos the sonne, and up roos Emelye
And to the temple of Diane gan hie.
Hir maidens, that she thider with hire ladde,
Ful redily with hem the fyr they hadde,
Th'encens, the clothes, and the remenant al
That to the sacrifice longen shal;   1420
The hornes fulle of meeth, as was the gyse:
Ther lakked noght to doon hir sacrifise.
Smokinge the temple, ful of clothes faire,
This Emelye, with herte debonaire,
Hir body wessh with water of a welle.
But hou she dide hir rite I dar nat telle,
But it be any thing in general;
And yet it were a game to heeren al.
To him that meneth wel it were no charge;
But it is good a man been at his large.   1430

Hir brighte heer was kembd, untressed al;
A coroune of a grene ook cerial
Upon hir heed was set ful fair and meete.
Two fires on the auter gan she beete,
And dide hir thinges, as men may biholde
In Stace of Thebes and thise bookes olde.
Whan kindled was the fyr, with pitous cheere
Unto Diane she spak as ye may heere:
  'O chaste goddesse of the wodes grene,
To whom bothe hevene and erthe and see is sene,
Queene of the regne of Pluto derk and lowe,
Goddesse of maidens, that myn herte hast knowe
Ful many a yeer, and woost what I desire,
As keepe me fro thy vengeaunce and thyn ire,
That Attheon aboughte cruelly.
Chaste goddesse, wel wostow that I
Desire to ben a maiden al my lyf,
Ne nevere wol I be no love ne wyf.
I am, thow woost, yet of thy compaignye,
A maide, and love huntinge and venerye,
And for to walken in the wodes wilde,
And noght to ben a wyf and be with childe.
Noght wol I knowe compaignye of man.
Now help me, lady, sith ye may and kan,
For tho thre formes that thou hast in thee.
And Palamon, that hath swich love to me,
And eek Arcite, that loveth me so soore,
(This grace I preye thee withoute moore)
As sende love and pees bitwixe hem two,
And fro me turne awey hir hertes so
That al hire hoote love and hir desir,
And al hir bisy torment, and hir fir

1440

1450

1460

Be queynt, or turned in another place.
And if so be thou wolt nat do me grace,
Or if my destinee be shapen so
That I shal nedes have oon of hem two,
As sende me him that moost desireth me.
Bihoold, goddesse of clene chastitee,
The bittre teeris that on my chekes falle.
Sin thou art maide and kepere of us alle,   1470
My maidenhede thou kepe and wel conserve,
And whil I live, a maide I wol thee serve.'

    The fires brenne upon the auter cleere,
Whil Emelye was thus in hir preyere.
But sodeynly she saugh a sighte queynte,
For right anon oon of the fires queynte,
And quiked again, and after that anon
That oother fyr was queynt and al agon;
And as it queynte it made a whistelinge,
As doon thise wete brondes in hir brenninge,   1480
And at the brondes ende out ran anon
As it were blody dropes many oon;
For which so soorc agast was Emelye
That she was wel ny mad, and gan to crye,
For she ne wiste what it signified;
But oonly for the feere thus hath she cried,
And weep that it was pitee for to heere.
And therwithal Diane gan appeere,
With bowe in honde, right as an hunteresse,
And seyde, 'Doghter, stynt thyn hevinesse.   1490
Among the goddes hye it is affermed,
And by eterne word writen and confermed,
Thou shalt ben wedded unto oon of tho
That han for thee so muchel care and wo;

But unto which of hem I may nat telle.
Farwel, for I ne may no lenger dwelle.
The fires which that on myn auter brenne
Shulle thee declaren, er that thou go henne,
Thyn aventure of love, as in this cas.'
1500 And with that word, the arwes in the caas
Of the goddesse clateren faste and ringe,
And forth she wente, and made a vanisshinge;
For which this Emelye astoned was,
And seyde, 'What amounteth this, allas?
I putte me in thy proteccioun,
Diane, and in thy disposicioun.'
And hoom she goth anon the nexte weye.
This is th'effect; ther is namoore to seye.

The nexte houre of Mars folwinge this,
1510 Arcite unto the temple walked is
Of fierse Mars to doon his sacrifise,
With alle the rites of his payen wise.
With pitous herte and heigh devocioun
Right thus to Mars he seyde his orisoun:
'O stronge god, that in the regnes colde
Of Trace honoured art and lord yholde,
And hast in every regne and every lond
Of armes al the bridel in thyn hond,
And hem fortunest as thee list devyse,
1520 Accepte of me my pitous sacrifise.
If so be that my youthe may deserve,
And that my might be worthy for to serve
Thy godhede, that I may been oon of thine,
Thanne preye I thee to rewe upon my pine.
For thilke peyne and thilke hoote fir
In which thow whilom brendest for desir,

Whan that thow usedest the beautee
Of faire, yonge, fresshe Venus free,
And haddest hire in armes at thy wille—
Although thee oncs on a time misfille,   1530
Whan Vulcanus hadde caught thee in his las,
And foond thee ligginge by his wyf, allas!—
For thilke sorwe that was in thyn herte,
Have routhe as wel upon my peynes smerte.
I am yong and unkonninge, as thow woost,
And, as I trowe, with love offended moost
That evere was any lives creature;
For she that dooth me al this wo endure
Ne reccheth nevere wher I sinke or fleete.
And wel I woot, er she me mercy heete,   1540
I moot with strengthe winne hire in the place,
And, wel I woot, withouten help or grace
Of thee, ne may my strengthe noght availle.
Thanne help me, lord, tomorwe in my bataille,
For thilke fyr that whilom brente thee,
As wel as thilke fyr now brenneth me,
And do that I tomorwe have victorie.
Myn be the travaille and thyn be the glorie!
Thy soverein temple wol I moost honouren
Of any place, and alwey moost labouren   1550
In thy plesaunce and in thy craftes stronge,
And in thy temple I wol my baner honge
And alle the armes of my compaignye;
And everemo, unto that day I die,
Eterne fir I wol bifore thee finde.
And eek to this avow I wol me binde:
My beerd, myn heer, that hongeth long adoun,
That nevere yet ne felte offensioun

Of rasour nor of shere, I wol thee yive,
1560 And ben thy trewe servant whil I live.
Now, lord, have routhe upon my sorwes soore;
Yif me victorie, I aske thee namoore.'
    The preyere stynt of Arcita the stronge,
The ringes on the temple dore that honge,
And eek the dores, clatereden ful faste,
Of which Arcita somwhat him agaste.
The fires brenden upon the auter brighte,
That it gan al the temple for to lighte;
A sweete smel the ground anon up yaf,
1570 And Arcita anon his hand up haf
And moore encens into the fyr he caste,
With othere rites mo; and atte laste
The statue of Mars bigan his hauberk ringe;
And with that soun he herde a murmuringe
Ful lowe and dim, and seyde thus, 'Victorie!'
For which he yaf to Mars honour and glorie.
And thus with joye and hope wel to fare
Arcite anon unto his in is fare,
As fain as fowel is of the brighte sonne.
1580   And right anon swich strif ther is bigonne,
For thilke graunting, in the hevene above,
Bitwixe Venus, the goddesse of love,
And Mars, the stierne god armipotente,
That Juppiter was bisy it to stente;
Til that the pale Saturnus the colde,
That knew so manye of aventures olde,
Foond in his olde experience an art
That he ful soone hath plesed every part.
As sooth is seyd, elde hath greet avantage;
1590 In elde is bothe wisdom and usage;

Men may the olde atrenne, and noght atrede.
Saturne anon, to stynten strif and drede,
Al be it that it is again his kinde,
Of al this strif he gan remedie finde.
  'My deere doghter Venus,' quod Saturne,
'My cours, that hath so wide for to turne,
Hath moore power than woot any man.
Myn is the drenching in the see so wan;
Myn is the prison in the derke cote;
Myn is the strangling and hanging by the throte,   1600
The murmure and the cherles rebelling,
The groininge, and the privee empoisoning;
I do vengeance and pleyn correccioun,
Whil I dwelle in the signe of the leoun.
Myn is the ruine of the hye halles,
The fallinge of the toures and of the walles
Upon the minour or the carpenter.
I slow Sampsoun, shakinge the piler;
And mine be the maladies colde,
The derke tresons, and the castes olde;   1610
My looking is the fader of pestilence.
Now weep namoore, I shal doon diligence
That Palamon, that is thyn owene knight,
Shal have his lady, as thou hast him hight.
Though Mars shal helpe his knight, yet nathelees
Bitwixe yow ther moot be som time pees,
Al be ye noght of o compleccioun,
That causeth al day swich divisioun.
I am thyn aiel, redy at thy wille;
Weep now namoore, I wol thy lust fulfille.'   1620
  Now wol I stynten of the goddes above,
Of Mars, and of Venus, goddesse of love,

And telle yow as pleynly as I kan
The grete effect, for which that I bigan.

PART IV

Greet was the feeste in Atthenes that day,
And eek the lusty seson of that May
Made every wight to been in swich plesaunce
That al that Monday justen they and daunce,
And spenden it in Venus heigh servise.
1630 But by the cause that they sholde rise
Eerly, for to seen the grete fight,
Unto hir reste wenten they at night.
And on the morwe, whan that day gan springe,
Of hors and harneys noise and clateringe
Ther was in hostelries al aboute;
And to the paleys rood ther many a route
Of lordes upon steedes and palfreys.
Ther maystow seen devisinge of harneys
So unkouth and so riche, and wroght so weel
1640 Of goldsmithrye, of browdinge, and of steel;
The sheeldes brighte, testeres, and trappures,
Gold-hewen helmes, hauberkes, cote-armures;
Lordes in parementz on hir courseres,
Knightes of retenue, and eek squieres
Nailinge the speres, and helmes bokelinge;
Gigginge of sheeldes, with layneres lacinge
(There as nede is they weren no thing idel);
The fomy steedes on the golden bridel
Gnawinge, and faste the armurers also
1650 With file and hamer prikinge to and fro;
Yemen on foote, and communes many oon

With shorte staves, thikke as they may goon;
Pipes, trompes, nakers, clariounes,
That in the bataille blowen blody sounes;
The paleys ful of peple up and doun,
Heere thre, ther ten, holdinge hir questioun,
Dividinge of thise Thebane knightes two.
Somme seyden thus, somme seyde 'it shal be so';
Somme helden with him with the blake berd,
Somme with the balled, somme with the thikke herd; 1660
Somme seyde he looked grimme, and he wolde fighte;
'He hath a sparth of twenty pound of wighte.'
Thus was the halle ful of divininge,
Longe after that the sonne gan to springe.

   The grete Theseus, that of his sleep awaked
With minstralcie and noise that was maked,
Heeld yet the chambre of his paleys riche,
Til that the Thebane knightes, bothe yliche
Honured, were into the paleys fet.
Duc Theseus was at a window set,   1670
Arrayed right as he were a god in trone.
The peple preesseth thiderward ful soone
Him for to seen, and doon heigh reverence,
And eek to herkne his heste and his sentence.
An heraud on a scaffold made an 'Oo!'
Til al the noise of peple was ydo,
And whan he saugh the peple of noise al stille,
Tho shewed he the mighty dukes wille.

   'The lord hath of his heigh discrecioun
Considered that it were destruccioun   1680
To gentil blood to fighten in the gyse
Of mortal bataille now in this emprise.
Wherfore, to shapen that they shal nat die,

He wol his firste purpos modifye.
No man therfore, up peyne of los of lyf,
No maner shot, ne polax, ne short knyf
Into the listes sende or thider bringe;
Ne short swerd, for to stoke with point bitinge,
No man ne drawe ne bere it by his side.
1690 Ne no man shal unto his felawe ride
But o cours, with a sharpe ygrounde spere;
Foyne, if him list, on foote, himself to were.
And he that is at meschief shal be take
And noght slain, but be broght unto the stake
That shal ben ordeyned on either side;
But thider he shal by force, and there abide.
And if so falle the chieftain be take
On outher side, or elles sleen his make,
No lenger shal the turneyinge laste.
1700 God spede you! gooth forth, and ley on faste!
With long swerd and with maces fighteth youre fille.
Gooth now youre wey, this is the lordes wille.'
    The vois of peple touchede the hevene,
So loude cride they with murie stevene,
'God save swich a lord, that is so good,
He wilneth no destruccion of blood!'
Up goon the trompes and the melodye,
And to the listes rit the compaignye,
By ordinance, thurghout the citee large,
1710 Hanged with clooth of gold, and nat with sarge.
    Ful lik a lord this noble duc gan ride,
Thise two Thebans upon either side;
And after rood the queene, and Emelye,
And after that another compaignye
Of oon and oother, after hir degree.

And thus they passen thurghout the citee,
And to the listes come they by time.
It nas nat of the day yet fully prime
Whan set was Theseus ful riche and hye,
Ypolita the queene, and Emelye,   1720
And othere ladys in degrees aboute.
Unto the seetes preesseth al the route.
And westward, thurgh the gates under Marte,
Arcite, and eek the hondred of his parte,
With baner reed is entred right anon;
And in that selve moment Palamon
Is under Venus, estward in the place,
With baner whyt, and hardy chiere and face.
In al the world, to seken up and doun,
So evene, withouten variacioun,   1730
Ther nere swiche compaignies tweye;
For ther was noon so wys that koude seye
That any hadde of oother avauntage
Of worthinesse, ne of estaat, ne age,
So evene were they chosen, for to gesse.
And in two renges faire they hem dresse.
Whan that hir names rad were everichon,
That in hir nombre gyle were ther noon,
Tho were the gates shet, and cried was loude:
'Do now youre devoir, yonge knightes proude!'   1740
   The heraudes lefte hir priking up and doun;
Now ringen trompes loude and clarioun.
Ther is namoore to seyn, but west and est
In goon the speres ful sadly in arrest;
In gooth the sharpe spore into the side.
Ther seen men who kan juste and who kan ride;
Ther shiveren shaftes upon sheeldes thikke:

He feeleth thurgh the herte-spoon the prikke;
Up springen speres twenty foot on highte.
1750 Out goon the swerdes as the silver brighte;
The helmes they tohewen and toshrede;
Out brest the blood with stierne stremes rede;
With mighty maces the bones they tobreste.
He thurgh the thikkeste of the throng gan threste;
Ther stomblen steedes stronge, and doun gooth al;
He rolleth under foot as dooth a bal;
He foyneth on his feet with his tronchoun,
And he him hurtleth with his hors adoun;
He thurgh the body is hurt and sithen take,
1760 Maugree his heed, and broght unto the stake:
As forward was, right there he moste abide.
Another lad is on that oother side.
And some time dooth hem Theseus to reste,
Hem to refresshe and drinken, if hem leste.
Ful ofte a day han thise Thebanes two
Togidre ymet, and wroght his felawe wo;
Unhorsed hath ech oother of hem tweye.
Ther nas no tigre in the vale of Galgopheye,
Whan that hir whelp is stole whan it is lite,
1770 So crueel on the hunte as is Arcite
For jelous herte upon this Palamon.
Ne in Belmarye ther nis so fel leon,
That hunted is, or for his hunger wood,
Ne of his praye desireth so the blood,
As Palamon to sleen his foo Arcite.
The jelous strokes on hir helmes bite;
Out renneth blood on bothe hir sides rede.

  Som time an ende ther is of every dede.
For er the sonne unto the reste wente,

The stronge king Emetreus gan hente   1780
This Palamon, as he faught with Arcite,
And made his swerd depe in his flessh to bite;
And by the force of twenty is he take
Unyolden, and ydrawe unto the stake.
And in the rescus of this Palamoun
The stronge king Lygurge is born adoun,
And king Emetreus, for al his strengthe,
Is born out of his sadel a swerdes lengthe,
So hitte him Palamoun er he were take;
But al for noght, he was broght to the stake.   1790
His hardy hertc mighte him helpe naught:
He moste abide whan that he was caught,
By force and eek by composicioun.

Who sorweth now but woful Palamoun,
That moot namoore goon again to fighte?
And whan that Theseus hadde seyn this sighte,
Unto the folk that foghten thus echon
He cryde, 'Hoo! namoore, for it is doon.
I wol be trewe juge, and no partie.
Arcite of Thebes shal have Emelie,   1800
That by his fortune hath hire faire ywonne.'
Anon ther is a noise of peple bigonne
For joye of this, so loude and heighe withalle,
It semed that the listes sholde falle.

What kan now faire Venus doon above?
What seith she now? What dooth this queene of love,
But wepeth so, for wantinge of hir wille,
Til that hir teeres in the listes fille?
She seyde, 'I am ashamed, doutelees.'

Saturnus seyde, 'Doghter, hoold thy pees!   1810
Mars hath his wille, his knight hath al his boone,

173

And, by myn heed, thow shalt been esed soone.'

The trompours, with the loude minstralcie,
The heraudes, that ful loude yelle and crie,
Been in hire wele for joye of daun Arcite.
But herkneth me, and stynteth noise a lite,
Which a miracle ther bifel anon.

This fierse Arcite hath of his helm ydon,
And on a courser, for to shewe his face,
1820 He priketh endelong the large place
Lokinge upward upon this Emelye;
And she again him caste a freendlich ye
(For wommen, as to speken in comune,
They folwen alle the favour of Fortune)
And was al his chiere, as in his herte.

Out of the ground a furie infernal sterte,
From Pluto sent at requeste of Saturne,
For which his hors for fere gan to turne,
And leep aside, and foundred as he leep;
1830 And er that Arcite may taken keep,
He pighte him on the pomel of his heed,
That in the place he lay as he were deed,
His brest tobrosten with his sadel-bowe.
As blak he lay as any cole or crowe,
So was the blood yronnen in his face.
Anon he was yborn out of the place,
With herte soor, to Theseus paleys.
Tho was he korven out of his harneys,
And in a bed ybrought ful faire and blyve;
1840 For he was yet in memorie and alive,
And alwey cryinge after Emelye.

Duc Theseus, with al his compaignye,
Is comen hoom to Atthenes his citee

With alle blisse and greet solempnitee.
Al be it that this aventure was falle,
He nolde noght disconforten hem alle.
Men seyde eek that Arcite shal nat die;
He shal been heeled of his maladye.
And of another thing they weren as fain,
That of hem alle was ther noon yslain,   1850
Al were they soore yhurt, and namely oon,
That with a spere was thirled his brest boon.
To othere woundes and to broken armes
Somme hadden salves and somme hadden charmes;
Fermacies of herbes and eek save
They dronken, for they wolde hir lymes have.
For which this noble duc, as he wel kan,
Conforteth and honoureth every man,
And made revel al the longe night
Unto the straunge lordes, as was right.   1860
Ne ther was holden no disconfitinge
But as a justes or a tourneyinge;
For soothly ther was no disconfiture.
For falling nis nat but an aventure,
Ne to be lad by force unto the stake
Unyolden, and with twenty knightes take,
O persone allone, withouten mo,
And haried forth by arme, foot, and too,
And eke his steede driven forth with staves
With footmen, bothe yemen and eek knaves—   1870
It nas arretted him no vileynye;
Ther may no man clepen it cowardye.
For which anon duc Theseus leet crye,
To stynten alle rancour and envye,
The gree as wel of o side as of oother,

And either side ylik as ootheres brother;
And yaf hem yiftes after hir degree,
And fully heeld a feeste dayes three,
And conveyed the kinges worthily
1880   Out of his toun a journee largely.
And hoom wente every man the righte way.
Ther was namoore but 'Fare wel, have good day!'
Of this bataille I wol namoore endite,
But speke of Palamon and of Arcite.

    Swelleth the brest of Arcite, and the soore
Encreesseth at his herte moore and moore.
The clothered blood, for any lechecraft,
Corrupteth and is in his bouk ylaft,
That neither veine-blood, ne ventusinge,
1890   Ne drinke of herbes may ben his helpinge.
The vertu expulsif, or animal,
Fro thilke vertu cleped natural
Ne may the venym voiden ne expelle.
The pipes of his longes gonne to swelle,
And every lacerte in his brest adoun
Is shent with venym and corrupcioun.
Him gaineth neither, for to gete his lif,
Vomit upward, ne dounward laxatif.
Al is tobrosten thilke regioun;
1900   Nature hath now no dominacioun.
And certeinly, ther Nature wol nat wirche,
Fare wel phisik! go ber the man to chirche!
This al and som, that Arcita moot die;
For which he sendeth after Emelye,
And Palamon, that was his cosin deere.
Thanne seyde he thus, as ye shal after heere:
'Naught may the woful spirit in myn herte

Declare o point of alle my sorwes smerte
To yow, my lady, that I love moost;
But I biquethe the service of my goost   1910
To yow aboven every creature,
Sin that my lyf may no lenger dure.
Allas, the wo! allas, the peynes stronge,
That I for yow have suffred, and so longe!
Allas, the deeth! allas, myn Emelye!
Allas, departinge of oure compaignye!
Allas, myn hertes queene! allas, my wyf!
Myn hertes lady, endere of my lyf!
What is this world? what asketh men to have?
Now with his love, now in his colde grave   1920
Allone, withouten any compaignye.
Fare wel, my sweete foo, myn Emelye!
And softe taak me in youre armes tweye,
For love of God, and herkneth what I seye.

   I have heer with my cosin Palamon
Had strif and rancour many a day agon
For love of yow, and for my jalousye.
And Juppiter so wis my soule gye,
To speken of a servaunt proprely,
With alle circumstances trewely—   1930
That is to seyen, trouthe, honour, knighthede,
Wisdom, humblesse, estaat, and heigh kinrede,
Fredom, and al that longeth to that art—
So Juppiter have of my soule part,
As in this world right now ne knowe I non
So worthy to ben loved as Palamon,
That serveth yow, and wol doon al his lyf.
And if that evere ye shul ben a wyf,
Foryet nat Palamon, the gentil man.'

1940 And with that word his speche faille gan,
For from his feet up to his brest was come
The coold of deeth, that hadde him overcome,
And yet mooreover for in his armes two
The vital strengthe is lost and al ago.
Oonly the intellect, withouten moore,
That dwelled in his herte syk and soore,
Gan faillen whan the herte felte deeth.
Dusked his eyen two and failled breeth,
But on his lady yet caste he his ye;
1950 His laste word was, 'Mercy, Emelye!'
His spirit chaunged hous and wente ther,
As I cam nevere, I kan nat tellen wher.
Therfore I stynte, I nam no divinistre;
Of soules finde I nat in this registre,
Ne me ne list thilke opinions to telle
Of hem, though that they writen wher they dwelle.
Arcite is coold, ther Mars his soule gye!
Now wol I speken forth of Emelye.

Shrighte Emelye and howleth Palamon,
1960 And Theseus his suster took anon
Swowninge, and baar hire fro the corps away.
What helpeth it to tarien forth the day
To tellen how she weep bothe eve and morwe?
For in swich cas wommen have swich sorwe,
Whan that hir housbondes ben from hem ago,
That for the moore part they sorwen so,
Or ellis fallen in swich maladye,
That at the laste certeinly they die.

Infinite been the sorwes and the teeres
1970 Of olde folk, and folk of tendre yeeres,
In al the toun for deeth of this Theban.

For him ther wepeth bothe child and man;
So greet weping was ther noon, certain,
Whan Ector was ybroght, al fressh yslain,
To Troye. Allas, the pitee that was ther,
Cracchinge of chekes, rentinge eek of heer.
'Why woldestow be deed,' thise wommen crye,
'And haddest gold ynough, and Emelye?'
No man mighte gladen Theseus,
Savinge his olde fader Egeus,   1980
That knew this worldes transmutacioun,
As he hadde seyn it chaunge bothe up and doun,
Joye after wo, and wo after gladnesse,
And shewed hem ensamples and liknesse.

  'Right as ther died nevere man,' quod he,
'That he ne livede in erthe in some degree,
Right so ther livede never man,' he seyde,
'In al this world, that som time he ne deyde.
This world nis but a thurghfare ful of wo,
And we been pilgrimes, passinge to and fro.   1990
Deeth is an ende of every worldly soore.'
And over al this yet seyde he muchel moore
To this effect, ful wisely to enhorte
The peple that they sholde hem reconforte.
Duc Theseus, with al his bisy cure,
Caste now wher that the sepulture
Of goode Arcite may best ymaked be,
And eek moost honurable in his degree.
And at the laste he took conclusioun
That ther as first Arcite and Palamoun   2000
Hadden for love the bataille hem bitwene,
That in that selve grove swoote and grene,
Ther as he hadde his amorouse desires,

179

His compleynte, and for love his hoote fires,
He wolde make a fyr in which the office
Funeral he mighte al accomplice.
And leet comande anon to hakke and hewe
The okes olde, and leye hem on a rewe
In colpons wel arrayed for to brenne.
His officers with swifte feet they renne
And ride anon at his comandement.
And after this, Theseus hath ysent
After a beere, and it al over spradde
With clooth of gold, the richeste that he hadde.
And of the same suite he cladde Arcite;
Upon his hondes hadde he gloves white,
Eek on his heed a coroune of laurer grene,
And in his hond a swerd ful bright and kene.
He leyde him, bare the visage, on the beere;
Therwith he weep that pitee was to heere.
And for the peple sholde seen him alle,
Whan it was day he broghte him to the halle,
That roreth of the crying and the soun.

Tho cam this woful Theban Palamoun,
With flotery berd and ruggy, asshy heeres,
In clothes blake, ydropped al with teeres;
And, passinge othere of wepinge, Emelye,
The rewefulleste of al the compaignye.
In as muche as the service sholde be
The moore noble and riche in his degree,
Duc Theseus leet forth thre steedes bringe,
That trapped were in steel al gliteringe,
And covered with the armes of daun Arcite.
Upon thise steedes, that weren grete and white,
Ther seten folk, of whiche oon baar his sheeld,

Another his spere up on his hondes heeld,
The thridde baar with him his bowe Turkeys
(Of brend gold was the caas and eek the harneys);
And riden forth a paas with sorweful cheere
Toward the grove, as ye shul after heere.   2040
The nobleste of the Grekes that ther were
Upon hir shuldres carieden the beere,
With slakke paas, and eyen rede and wete,
Thurghout the citee by the maister strete,
That sprad was al with blak, and wonder hye
Right of the same is the strete ywrye.
Upon the right hond wente olde Egeus,
And on that oother side duc Theseus,
With vessels in hir hand of gold ful fyn,
Al ful of hony, milk, and blood, and wyn;   2050
Eek Palamon, with ful greet compaignye;
And after that cam woful Emelye,
With fyr in honde, as was that time the gyse,
To do the office of funeral servise.

    Heigh labour and ful greet apparaillinge
Was at the service and the fyr-makinge,
That with his grene top the hevene raughte;
And twenty fadme of brede the armes straughte—
This is to seyn, the bowes weren so brode.
Of stree first ther was leyd ful many a lode.   2060
But how the fyr was maked upon highte,
Ne eek the names that the trees highte,
As ook, firre, birch, aspe, alder, holm, popler,
Wilugh, elm, plane, assh, box, chasteyn, linde, laurer,
Mapul, thorn, bech, hasel, ew, whippeltree—
How they weren feld, shal nat be toold for me;
Ne hou the goddes ronnen up and doun,

Disherited of hire habitacioun,
In which they woneden in reste and pees,
2070 Nymphes, fawnes and amadrides;
Ne hou the beestes and the briddes alle
Fledden for fere, whan the wode was falle;
Ne how the ground agast was of the light,
That was nat wont to seen the sonne bright;
Ne how the fyr was couched first with stree,
And thanne with drye stikkes cloven a thre,
And thanne with grene wode and spicerye,
And thanne with clooth of gold and with perrye,
And gerlandes, hanginge with ful many a flour;
2080 The mirre, th'encens, with al so greet odour;
Ne how Arcite lay among al this,
Ne what richesse aboute his body is;
Ne how that Emelye, as was the gyse,
Putte in the fyr of funeral servise;
Ne how she swowned whan men made the fyr,
Ne what she spak, ne what was hir desir;
Ne what jeweles men in the fire caste,
Whan that the fyr was greet and brente faste;
Ne how somme caste hir sheeld, and somme hir spere,
2090 And of hire vestimentz, whiche that they were,
And coppes fulle of wyn, and milk, and blood,
Into the fyr, that brente as it were wood;
Ne how the Grekes, with an huge route,
Thries riden al the fyr aboute
Upon the left hand, with a loud shoutinge,
And thries with hir speres clateringe;
And thries how the ladies gonne crye;
Ne how that lad was homward Emelye;
Ne how Arcite is brent to asshen colde;

Ne how that lyche-wake was yholde 2100
Al thilke night; ne how the Grekes pleye
The wake-pleyes, ne kepe I nat to seye;
Who wrastleth best naked with oille enoint,
Ne who that baar him best, in no disjoint.
I wol nat tellen eek how that they goon
Hoom til Atthenes, whan the pley is doon;
But shortly to the point thanne wol I wende,
And maken of my longe tale an ende.

By processe and by lengthe of certeyn yeres,
Al stynted is the moorninge and the teres 2110
Of Grekes, by oon general assent.
Thanne semed me ther was a parlement
At Atthenes upon certein pointz and caas;
Among the whiche pointz yspoken was
To have with certein contrees alliaunce,
And have fully of Thebans obeisaunce.
For which this noble Theseus anon
Leet senden after gentil Palamon,
Unwist of him what was the cause and why;
But in his blake clothes sorwefully 2120
He cam at his comandement in hye.
Tho sente Theseus for Emelye.
Whan they were set, and hust was al the place,
And Theseus abiden hadde a space
Er any word cam fram his wise brest,
His eyen sette he ther as was his lest.
And with a sad visage he siked stille,
And after that right thus he seyde his wille:
'The Firste Moevere of the cause above,
Whan he first made the faire cheyne of love, 2130
Greet was th'effect, and heigh was his entente.

Wel wiste he why, and what thereof he mente;
For with that faire cheyne of love he bond
The fyr, the eyr, the water, and the lond
In certeyn boundes, that they may nat flee.
That same Prince and that Moevere,' quod he,
'Hath stablissed in this wrecched world adoun
Certeyne dayes and duracioun
To al that is engendred in this place,
Over the whiche day they may nat pace,
Al mowe they yet tho dayes wel abregge.
Ther nedeth noght noon auctoritee t'allegge,
For it is preeved by experience,
But that me list declaren my sentence.
Thanne may men by this ordre wel discerne
That thilke Moevere stable is and eterne.
Wel may men knowe, but it be a fool,
That every part dirriveth from his hool;
For nature hath nat taken his biginning
Of no partie or cantel of a thing,
But of a thing that parfit is and stable,
Descendinge so til it be corrumpable.
And therfore, of his wise purveiaunce,
He hath so wel biset his ordinaunce
That speces of thinges and progressiouns
Shullen enduren by successiouns,
And nat eterne, withouten any lie.
This maystow understonde and seen at ye.
  Loo the ook, that hath so long a norisshinge
From time that it first biginneth to springe,
And hath so long a lif, as we may see,
Yet at the laste wasted is the tree.
Considereth eek how that the harde stoon

2140

2150

2160

Under oure feet, on which we trede and goon,
Yet wasteth it as it lyth by the weye.
The brode river somtime wexeth dreye;
The grete tounes se we wane and wende.
Thanne may ye se that al this thing hath ende.
Of man and womman seen we wel also
That nedes, in oon of thise termes two,   2170
This is to seyn, in youthe or elles age,
He moot be deed, the king as shal a page;
Som in his bed, som in the depe see,
Som in the large feeld, as men may see;
Ther helpeth noght, al goth that ilke weye.
Thanne may I seyn that al this thing moot deye.
What maketh this but Juppiter, the king,
That is prince and cause of alle thing,
Convertinge al unto his propre welle
From which it is dirrived, sooth to telle?   2180
And heer-agains no creature on live,
Of no degree, availleth for to strive.
Thanne is it wisdom, as it thinketh me,
To maken vertu of necessitee,
And take it weel that we may nat eschue,
And namely that to us alle is due.
And whoso gruccheth ought, he dooth folye,
And rebel is to him that al may gye.
And certeinly a man hath moost honour
To dien in his excellence and flour,   2190
Whan he is siker of his goode name;
Thanne hath he doon his freend ne him no shame.
And gladder oghte his freend been of his deeth,
Whan with honour up yolden is his breeth,
Than whan his name apalled is for age,

For al forgeten is his vassellage.
Thanne is it best, as for a worthy fame,
To dien whan that he is best of name.
    The contrarie of al this is wilfulnesse.
Why grucchen we, why have we hevinesse,
That goode Arcite, of chivalrie the flour,
Departed is with duetee and honour
Out of this foule prisoun of this lyf?
Why grucchen heere his cosin and his wyf
Of his welfare, that loved hem so weel?
Kan he hem thank? Nay, God woot, never a deel,
That both his soule and eek hemself offende,
And yet they mowe hir lustes nat amende.
    What may I conclude of this longe serye,
But after wo I rede us to be merye,
And thanken Juppiter of al his grace?
And er that we departen from this place
I rede that we make of sorwes two
O parfit joye, lastinge everemo.
And looketh now, wher moost sorwe is herinne,
Ther wol we first amenden and biginne.
    Suster,' quod he, 'this is my fulle assent,
With al th'avis heere of my parlement,
That gentil Palamon, youre owene knight,
That serveth yow with wille, herte, and might,
And ever hath doon sin ye first him knewe,
That ye shul of youre grace upon him rewe,
And taken him for housbonde and for lord.
Lene me youre hond, for this is oure accord.
Lat se now of youre wommanly pitee.
He is a kinges brother sone, pardee;
And though he were a povre bacheler,

Sin he hath served yow so many a yeer,
And had for yow so greet adversitee,
It moste been considered, leeveth me;   2230
For gentil mercy oghte to passen right.'

Thanne seyde he thus to Palamon the knight:
'I trowe ther nedeth litel sermoning
To make yow assente to this thing.

Com neer, and taak youre lady by the hond.'
Bitwixen hem was maad anon the bond
That highte matrimoigne or mariage,
By al the conseil and the baronage.
And thus with alle blisse and melodye
Hath Palamon ywedded Emelye.   2240
And God, that al this wide world hath wroght,
Sende him his love that hath it deere aboght;
For now is Palamon in alle wele,
Livinge in blisse, in richesse, and in heele,
And Emelye him loveth so tendrely,
And he hire serveth al so gentilly,
That nevere was ther no word hem bitwene
Of jalousie or any oother teene.
Thus endeth Palamon and Emclye;
And God save al this faire compaignye! Amen.   2250

NOTES

1. *olde stories* It is characteristic of medieval writers to take pride not in their originality but in the authority conferred by ancient sources. Sometimes indeed they refer to sources which we may suspect never existed. In this case Chaucer's main source is the *Teseida* of Boccaccio, but since Boccaccio was a contemporary it cannot fairly be described as 'old'. Chaucer probably wished his audience to think that his source was classical Latin, not modern Italian, just as in *Troilus and Criseyde*, also translated from Boccaccio, he speaks of his authority as being a Latin author called Lollius (who never existed).

2. *duc* Like other medieval authors, Chaucer 'medievalized' the past, and gave great men titles of nobility current in his own time. There was a 'Duke of Athens' in the fourteenth century.

7. *What with* 'by means of'.

8. *regne of Femenye* 'realm of the Amazons'. *Femenye* is a name invented in the Middle Ages (from Latin *femina*, 'woman') for a mythical country inhabited entirely by warlike women.

12. *solempnitee* 'ceremony' or 'festivity'. In Middle English this word did not possess its modern suggestions of seriousness.

15. 'I leave this noble ruler riding to Athens.'

17–27. An example of the rhetorical figure called *occupatio* or *praeteritio*, by which a writer explains what he is *not* going to say. The figure may be used as a means of surreptitiously mentioning something while pretending not to mention it; but here it is a quite genuine indication of an omission of source-material, since the events summarized by Chaucer in twenty lines are narrated at length in over a thousand lines in the *Teseida*.

18–19. *manere How* 'way in which'.

20. *chivalrye* This word may either mean the accomplishments of knighthood (as in line 7 above) or a company of knights (as probably here).

21. *for the nones* 'particularly'. The phrase is one of the many tags available in the idiom of Middle English poetry as rhymes or fillers of metrical space. Here clearly the phrase is used for the rhyme with *Amazones*. Such tags are natural in the style of a poetry written with listeners in mind, since they give the audience time to catch up with the narrative.

22. *Atthenes* (here) 'Athenians'.

27. *as* This word is often used by Chaucer redundantly in adverbial phrases.

27–8. This metaphor, of ploughing for writing, is not uncommon in medieval literature. Agricultural imagery would be familiar to medieval people, living in a society of small towns based on agriculture.

31. 'Also I do not wish to hinder any of this company.'

33. *lat se now* 'then let us see'.

31–3. The pilgrims had agreed before setting out that they would tell tales in turn to pass away the time on the journey to and from Canterbury, and that the one who was considered to have told the best tale would be given a supper by the whole company when they returned to the Tabard Inn.

39. *that* Often used redundantly in relative constructions in Middle English.

40. *tweye and tweye* 'two by two'—a first indication of the symmetrical order which is characteristic of the poem's action.

41. *Ech after oother* 'one behind another'.

42–4. It is typical of medieval poetry, and particularly of romances, to present a fictional world in which everything is superlative—the best or the worst, the richest, the loudest, the sweetest of its kind. The extreme thus becomes a quality of the world itself rather than of any particular incident within it.

57–8. The first of many indications that the world of the poem, like the world as seen by Boethius (see p. 97 above), is governed by Fortune, the fickle goddess. The lady seems to hint that even Theseus's seemingly complete triumph is unstable; and Theseus is the one stable point in the poem.

65. *That she ne hath* 'who has not'.

66. *as it is wel seene* 'as is perfectly clear'.

67. *Thanked be* 'thanks to'. Fortune was regularly pictured with a moving wheel, which raised people to prosperity and dropped them to misery.

68. 'Who (i.e. Fortune) gives secure prosperity to no condition of life.' This reference to the universality of Fortune's fickleness again seems to glance at Theseus himself: as the ladies used to be, so he is; as they are, so he may be.

70. *Clemence* Like Fortune, a deified abstraction such as actually became part of Roman religion (Clementia's temple is mentioned by Statius), and was passed on as a way of thinking to the Middle Ages.

Notes

74. *Cappaneus* One of the seven who besieged Thebes (see Introduction, p. 7).

84. 'To do dishonour to the corpses.'

89. A horrifyingly blunt and concrete picture as the climax to a brilliantly constructed speech. The picture of dogs eating human bodies is physically disgusting, but also represents an offence against religious practice, whether pagan or Christian.

97–8. 'When he saw those who had formerly been of such high rank now so pitiful and so downcast.' This fall from high position to wretchedness precisely corresponds to the medieval conception of tragedy, which Chaucer learned from Boethius and states explicitly in *The Monk's Tale*.

102–3. 'He would do everything in his power to avenge them on the tyrant Creon.'

105–6. *of Theseus yserved As he that* 'treated by Theseus like someone who'.

109. *To Thebes-ward* 'towards Thebes'.

110. *go ne ride* 'walk or ride', a tag used for emphasis, not to be taken literally.

112. 'But he camped that night on his journey towards Thebes.'

117–22. These details are added by Chaucer. He evokes the pageantry of medieval warfare, and at the same time, in the reference to Mars, hints at the sinister supernatural forces at work behind the human action.

119. 'That the fields all about glittered with its brilliance.'

122. The Minotaur was a monster, half bull and half man, which lived in Crete and devoured Athenian boys and girls sent to it as tribute, until Theseus killed it. For further comment, see Introduction, p. 93.

126. *Faire* 'satisfactorily, as planned'. A term of praise with little precise meaning, but helping to provide the alliteration that tends to accompany battles in this poem.

127–42. *But shortly for to speken of this thing . . . But it were al to longe for to devyse . . . But shortly for to telle is myn entente* Expressions of a wish to be brief are common in medieval narrative poetry, though sometimes as substitutes for brevity itself.

135. 'To carry out funeral ceremonies according to the custom of the time.' The bodies were burnt, whereas the medieval practice was burial.

136. 'But it would take very much too long to describe.'

146. The lack of explicitness sounds sinister: a hint of the

savagery involved in Theseus's chivalrous response to the ladies' request.

149. 'The pillagers worked with diligence and care.'

153–4. Amidst the confusion of the battlefield the two knights are arranged as symmetrically as the company of ladies. Symmetry will be a persistent quality in their story.

154. *in oon armes* 'in the same armour'.

158–61. Over their armour, medieval knights wore jackets (*cote-armures*) bearing their heraldic devices. The heralds would be able to identify them by these, and thus would be able to tell that they were of noble family and might therefore bring in a ransom if captured.

159–60. *knewe hem best in special As they that weren* 'recognized them distinctly as being'.

166. *he nolde no raunsoun* 'he would not accept any ransom'.

171. *Terme of his lyf* 'for the duration of his life'.

what nedeth wordes mo? A casual remark, little more than a tag; but already we are being conditioned to expect a world in which, as a matter of course, opposite extremes of the human condition will co-exist—Theseus 'in joye and in honour' for ever, the two knights 'in angwissh and in wo' for ever—with no comment either necessary or possible.

177–81. The effect of the three comparisons—with the lily, the rose, and May itself—is to make Emelye almost a personification of the season, rather than a person in her own right. Belonging to a long convention in medieval poetry, this May morning setting has become almost symbolic by Chaucer's time: the youth and beauty of the lady and the freshness of the season have become the expression of feelings rather than the objective description of facts. The references were added by Chaucer.

187. *Arys and do thyn observaunce* 'rise up and perform the rites of May'. On May Day it was the custom to get up early in the morning, walk in the fields or woods, and make garlands of may-flowers.

193. *at the sonne upriste* 'at sunrise'.

195. *party white and rede* May-blossom is mixed white and red in colour; on the other hand, the branches are prickly, and hence not very suitable for a garland to be worn.

198. *The grete tour* The part of a medieval castle that was used as a place of refuge, not the part that was lived in.

202. *evene joinant* 'right next to'.

203. *hadde hir pleyinge* 'went for relaxation'.

215. 'He often said, "Alas that I was born".'

216. *by aventure or cas* 'by accident or chance'. The two are not really

alternatives, but serve as an emphatic way of saying that what happened happened accidentally, not by anyone's choice—part of the contingency of a world governed by Fortune.

217–18. 'That through a window, thickly barred with pieces of iron as solid and strong as beams.'

224. *on to see* 'to look at'.

226–7. 'For the love of God, endure our prison with complete patience, for it cannot be altered.' Here Arcite produces spontaneously the same philosophy of despairing endurance that emerges from Theseus's reflexions at the end of the poem: 'take it weel that we may nat eschue' (2185).

228–33. Here once again Fortune is referred to, and, to judge from the abrupt transition, is identified by Arcite with the influence of the planetary deities.

229–30. *aspect . . . disposicioun . . . constellacioun* In astrology, the *aspect* of planets was their position relative to one another and to the earth, their *disposicioun* was simply their position, and their *constellacioun* was their position at the time when someone was born, which might influence his whole life. Arcite seems to be using the words rather vaguely, much as a modern person might loosely employ technical psycho-analytic terms ('complex', 'neurosis', etc.). Saturn was normally a planet of evil influence, as he himself explains later; see lines 1595–1611.

231. *although we hadde it sworn* 'although we had sworn to the contrary', cf. lines 808–9.

233. *this is the short and plain* 'that is the long and short of it'.

235–6. *of this opinioun Thow hast a veyn imaginacioun* 'this belief of yours is an empty fantasy'.

239. *that wol my bane be* 'and it will be the death of me'. Arcite had supposed that Palamon was crying out in misery at the thought of their imprisonment; in fact, his 'wound' was caused by love.

243–4. In Virgil's *Aeneid*, Aeneas, meeting a beautiful maiden, had asked whether she was a mortal or a goddess; it was in fact Venus in disguise. Here the idea is taken up again, though Emelye is *not* Venus; and this explains the use of the word *transfigure* in line 247.

246–53. This reverent attitude of Palamon's towards Venus is in keeping with his later prayer to Venus (lines 1363–1402). The present speech was added by Chaucer; in Boccaccio it is Arcite who sees Emelye first.

250–1. 'And if it should be that it is my fate, fixed by an eternal decree, to die in prison.'

252. *oure linage* i.e. the royal house of Thebes.

262. *hir mercy and hir grace* Like the idea of wounds and death caused by love, these terms belong to the specialized language of love in medieval courtly literature. The beloved lady is thought of as a goddess (cf. lines 243–4 above), and any reciprocal feelings she may have are a matter of mercy on her part.

263. 'So that I may at least see her.'

264. *I nam but deed* 'it will simply be the death of me'.

269. 'May God help me, I feel very little like joking.'

271–82. The structure of this long sentence is rather confused, though it would be clear enough in practice when read aloud. There is a kind of stammer in the syntax which expresses Palamon's incoherence under the pressure of emotion.

273–4. *thy brother Ysworn ful depe* They are 'sworn brothers', that is, they have taken an oath to regard each other as brothers.

275. *for to dyen in the peyne* 'though we were to die by torture'.

285. In Palamon's calling Emelye, of whom he has had only a glimpse, 'my lady', and in the disputation that follows about their right to a woman who knows nothing of their existence, there is clearly an extravagance that touches on absurdity. The absurdity is indeed hinted at in the curt dismissal of lines 329–31.

286. *til that myn herte sterve* 'till my heart ceases to beat'.

288–9. *tolde thee my wo As to my conseil* 'discussed my misery with you as with someone in my confidence'.

293. *I dar wel seyn* 'I can confidently say'.

295–301. '"It is more likely", he said, "that you are false than that I am; and indeed I tell you outright that you *are* false. For I loved her first, before you did, as a man loves a woman. What will you answer to that? You don't know even now whether she is a woman or a goddess. Your feeling is one of religious devotion, and mine is one of human love".' A clever piece of quibbling on Arcite's part, though some scholars have seen it as indicating a fundamental difference of character between Palamon and Arcite.

305. The *olde clerk* is Boethius, in the *De consolatione philosophiae*, where the *sawe* is applied to Orpheus and Eurydice. Orpheus's inability to resist looking back at Eurydice as he was rescuing her from the underworld caused him to lose her again.

306–11. The interlocking repetitions 'lovere . . . lawe . . . love . . . lawe . . . lawe . . . love . . . love' emphasize the two concepts played against each other in Arcite's argument.

309. *positif lawe and swich decree* 'human (as opposed to natural) law and all such mere enactments'.
312. *sholde be deed* 'were to die'.
313. *Al be she* 'whether the woman he loves is'.
314–15. *it is nat . . . hir grace* 'you are not likely at any time in your life to receive her favour'.
318. *us gaineth no raunsoun* 'no ransom will help us'.
319–22. A variant of a fable in Aesop, in which a fox runs off with a titbit while a lion and a tiger are quarrelling over it.
320. *hir part was noon* 'neither got a share of it'.
324. 'Every man for himself, that's all there is for it.' The saying was evidently proverbial, but Chaucer was familiar with court life.
339. 'And Theseus loved Pirithous as tenderly in return.'
340. *as olde bookes sayn* Vague references of this kind to ancient written authorities are common in medieval literature. In this case the 'old book' is probably the *Roman de la Rose*, where the story is told in the form given here. In classical literature the story is that Pirithous accompanied Theseus to hell to carry off Proserpina, not that Theseus sought Pirithous there.
352. *him Arcite* 'this Arcite'. A common Middle English idiom.
353. *if so were* 'if it should happen'.
359. *taketh* 'he (Arcite) takes'.
363. A characteristic Chaucerian formula for extreme grief. Compare the note on lines 42–4 above.
364. 'He looks out for a chance to commit suicide secretly.' In Chaucer, the intention to commit suicide tends to be another formula for intense grief; it is rarely put into practice. Suicide was associated with pagans, for whom such a death could be admirable rather than sinful. In *The Franklin's Tale* the pagan heroine, after listing twenty-two examples of ladies who have killed themselves rather than be dishonoured, does *not* kill herself.
366. Arcite is released from a physical prison into a metaphysical prison that is no less real; the prison becomes an image for human life itself.
367. *is me shape* 'I am destined'.
368. *purgatorie . . . helle* According to Catholic theology, souls in purgatory were being punished for a finite time before being allowed into heaven, while those in hell were punished eternally. Throughout this speech, Arcite implies a 'theology' of secular love which parodies Christian theology: note also *eternally* (line

367), *blisse* (line 372), *grace* (line 374), and the idea in lines 373–5 that the mere sight of Emelye would have been reward enough for him, just as the chief reward of the blessed souls is the sight of God. Similarly, the chief punishment of the damned is being deprived of the sight of God, just as Arcite is deprived of the sight of Emelye.

378–9. *blisfully . . . paradys* The theological language is continued.

380–1. 'Fortune has cast the dice well for you, who are in sight of her, while I am absent from her.'

387. *dispeir* Another theological term (identical in meaning with *wanhope* in line 391 below), meaning despair of God's mercy, the ultimate sin, which makes salvation impossible.

388–9. According to medieval physics, all created substances were made from the four elements of earth, water, fire, and air.

393–409. These lines, dealing philosophically with man's ignorance of what he wishes for in life, are based on Boethius. For comment on them, see Introduction, pp. 102–3.

393–4. 'Alas, why do people so commonly complain about the providence of God or of Fortune.'

397–9. *Som . . . som* 'one . . . another'.

399. 'And another man would willingly leave his prison.'

403–6. The image of the drunkard is all the more effective for being more familiar and immediate than we should expect in philosophical discourse; it comes from Boethius, typically Chaucerian though it sounds, but 'as a mous' is Chaucer's colloquial expansion.

416. *I nam but deed* 'I am as good as dead'.

421. 'The great fetters themselves on his shins'.

431. *to lady and to wyf* 'as your lady and as your wife'.

436. *that sterve here in a cage* 'who am dying here behind bars'.

443. *he lyk was to biholde* 'to look at he was like'.

444. *boxtree* The wood of this tree is very pale, and was traditionally used as an image for human pallor both in English and in Latin.

445–75. For comment on this speech, see Introduction, pp. 103–4.

447. *table of atthamaunt* The decrees of the gods being eternal, they are thought of as being inscribed on a tablet made from adamant, an indestructible stone.

449. 'Why is mankind under any greater obligation to you.'

455–6. 'What order is there in this foreknowledge by which the innocent are causelessly tormented?' Chaucer returns again and again in his poetry to the problem raised by the doctrine of divine foreknowledge: does it deprive human beings of their freewill, and, where the foreknowledge of disasters is concerned, does it imply callousness in God (or the gods)? Such problems were discussed by Boethius, but they were still living issues in the Christian philosophy of Chaucer's own time.

457–60. 'And my suffering is increased still further by the thought that man is bound by his duty to God to refrain from doing what he wishes, whereas a beast may fulfil all its desires.'

460–1. *his . . . he* We should use 'its' and 'it'.

463. *have* Subjunctive: 'may have had'.

464. *it may stonden so* 'that may be how things happen'.

465–6. 'I leave the solution of this problem to theologians, but I know well that there is great suffering in this world.' The contrast between the theory of the authorities and the knowledge that one derives from one's own experience is a common one in Chaucer.

467–9. 'Alas, one can see serpents or thieves, who have done harm to many good men, going about at liberty and wandering where they choose.'

470–1. Arcite has earlier (line 230) suggested that Saturn is to blame for the imprisonment of the two knights; here the planet Saturn merges into the pagan god. The anger of the goddess Juno (not a planet) is mentioned by both Statius and Boccaccio as the cause for the destruction of Thebes and the persecution of the Thebans.

474. The planetary goddess Venus is here used to refer to the human motive for which she was supposed to be responsible—sexual love.

475. *him Arcite* We might colloquially say 'that Arcite'.

482. *mester* 'occupation'. Chaucer is writing as though 'lover' and 'prisoner' were trades or professions.

486. *upon his heed* 'on pain of death'.

487. *as out of that contree* 'so far as that country was concerned'.

489–94. Medieval courtly poetry often leads up to an explicit question concerning love, a *demande d'amour*, which is to be answered not by the poet but by his audience.

493. *wher him list* 'wherever he pleases'.

497–521. Love-sickness is here presented in terms of the

psychological and physical symptoms defined in medieval medical treatises (see Introduction, pp. 20–1).

503. 'He lost his ability to sleep, eat, and drink.'

510. *he* 'to such an extent that he'. Compare line 616.

511–18. In the Middle Ages, psychology was very closely related to a traditional (though completely unscientific) physiology. This fact is particularly relevant to the interpretation of line 511: for us, to say of someone that his or her spirits are low is to speak metaphorically; in the Middle Ages, the statement had a literal sense. Human life was supposed to be dependent on three 'virtues' or 'spirits', which were conceived of as fluids carried about the body by the blood. The 'loveris maladye of Hereos' (derived from the Greek word *eros*, meaning 'love') was thought of as an actual disease from which lovers suffered, with the symptoms described in this passage. If it was not cured, according to some authorities, it led to mania (the *manie* of line 516). The brain was divided into three cells, the front one concerned with 'phantasy' (i.e. perception), the middle one with reason, the back one with memory. Mania was thought of as a disease of the *celle fantastik*, caused by an excess of the humour of melancholy, one of the four liquids that governed the whole condition of the body.

512. *chaunged so* 'he was so changed'.

518. 'At the front of his head, in the cell of perception.'

520. *habit* Lovers are traditionally careless in their dress.

521. *daun* A title of respect, which can variously be translated 'lord', 'master', 'sir', etc.

527–34. This vision of Mercury was added by Chaucer, who generally makes the gods influence the human actions of the story more directly than Boccaccio does. Mercury, another planetary deity, was the messenger of the gods in classical mythology, the god of sleep and dreams, and also the god with whom oracles were particularly associated. He was generally described as wearing a winged cap (*hat*, line 530) and bearing a magic staff or 'caduceus' which was capable of sending people to sleep (*slepy yerde*, line 529). The incident of Argus is referred to by Ovid, from whom Chaucer may have taken his description: Argus was a monster with a hundred eyes who was set as a guard over Io by Juno, but was sent to sleep and then killed by Mercury.

534. The end of Arcite's misery will indeed come in Athens, but

only through his death. The irony is cruel, and this is in keeping with the way the gods are presented in this story.

536. *hou soore that me smerte* 'however much it hurts me'.

538–9. *Ne for . . . To se* 'And the fear of death will not cause me to give up seeing.'

540. 'I do not care if I die, so long as I am with her.' Another case of dramatic irony: he does eventually die in her presence.

554. *Which* 'who'.

560. *chamberleyn* The official of a large household who was in charge of the lodging arrangements.

562–3. 'For he was prudent, and was soon able to discover which among the servants served her.'

565. *for the nones* See note on line 21.

567. 'Enough to do whatever anyone could order him.'

569–82. In being first *page of the chambre* to the duke's sister-in-law and then *squier* of the duke's chamber, Arcite is going through a normal course for any young man rising in the court world. Chaucer's own early career had followed a similar pattern though he had risen less rapidly. *Philostrate* was probably intended by Chaucer to mean 'overthrown by love'.

574. 'That his reputation spread all through the court.'

575–6. *were a charitee That Theseus wolde* 'would be a kindness for Theseus to'.

580. *his goode tonge* The ability to speak well was highly valued in medieval courtly society, where one of the main social activities was conversation.

581–2. The ruler was the physical as well as the metaphorical centre of the medieval court, and Arcite, becoming intimate in friendship with Theseus, is given a position which brings him close to his person.

586. *honestly and slyly* 'suitably and discreetly'.

596–8. This form of question, to which the answer ('no one') is obvious, is a means of emphasis recommended by the medieval *artes poeticae*.

601–3. Another rhetorical question, to which an answer is immediately supplied. To a modern reader, the lines may sound somewhat deflating, as though Chaucer were less impressed than he might be by Palamon's misery. But the assertion of modesty (*diminutio*) and the promise to be brief are both familiar devices of the *artes poeticae*. Moreover, the idea of love as a martyrdom is a common one in medieval courtly literature, so that there is no need to read it as ironic.

604–5. We do not know of any source from which Chaucer could have got the date 3 May, and so the reference to *olde bookes* is presumably only a convention. It seems likely that the date was invented by Chaucer, and this has led some scholars to find a special significance in it, particularly since it is a date he mentions elsewhere in his poetry. There is some evidence to suggest that in medieval times it was considered an unlucky day, but its exact significance, if any, is uncertain.

609. After a series of parentheses, Chaucer resumes the construction begun in line 604 by repeating the *that* of that line.

614. *opie of Thebes* This may be not the Thebes in Greece from which the two knights come but another Thebes in Egypt, which was famous for its opium. But Chaucer very likely did not distinguish between the two. In the *Teseida* Palamon was helped to escape by a Theban doctor. Chaucer makes the whole episode of the escape less complicated, and thus the repeated *fleeth . . . faste* of lines 611 and 617 becomes more convincing and dramatic.

616. *he* 'so fast that he'.

621. A most effective line, in conveying stealthy haste by transferring Palamon's dread to his feet, which are seen as though in close-up, stalking (with its associations with hunting) through the grove.

640. *squier principal* He has evidently been further promoted in the interim.

642–54. A second Maytime scene, paralleling the one of seven years before, and also added by Chaucer.

646. *were it* 'perhaps'.

654. Part of the courtly game of love in the Middle Ages was a division of the participants into two orders, those devoted to the flower and those devoted to the leaf; and it may be that Arcite's reference to *grene* alludes to this division, for we have just been told that his garland is of leaves, not flowers. But he may simply mean that he hopes to receive a garland from his beloved, or even in a vaguer sense, that he hopes for some possibility of growth, some favourable change in his situation.

658. *by aventure* The phrase has already been used in line 648 of Arcite's happening to come to this particular place. Throughout, Chaucer stresses the operation of chance, which is in effect the same as Fortune.

663–6. Chaucer is fond of such proverbial expansions of his material. They were recommended by the *artes poeticae*, which called them *sententiae*. The particular event is moralized and generalized, and thus made relevant to his audience's experience of life.

663. 'But for many years it has truly been said.'

665–6. 'It is a very good thing for a man to be on his guard, for people are always meeting unexpectedly.'

671. *roundel* A short poem with a refrain, originally sung to accompany a dance. Some lines from it are quoted above, lines 652–4.

673–81. The amplification of a single idea by varied expression was admired by medieval readers, and here the apparent diffuseness serves a specific purpose—to assert the power and unpredictability of one of the gods who control a story of which one of the points is its very randomness.

673. *thise loveres* Lovers in general.

674. A pleasantly rural way of saying 'in high spirits at one minute, in low spirits the next'. Chaucer lived in a predominantly agricultural society, where even the largest towns were small, and though he himself was a Londoner, his images frequently recall the countryside.

676–81. Friday was assigned to Venus (Latin *veneris dies*, French *vendredi*), and it was a proverbial saying that Fridays were changeable, or at least, as line 681 suggests, that they tended to be different in weather from the rest of the week.

680. *array* Either 'condition' in a general sense or, more specifically, 'dress': Venus's changefulness can be presented as the feminine trait of enjoying frequent changes of clothes.

684–713. These lines make up a formal lamentation (called *exclamatio* by the *artes poeticae*). They are not intended to represent what a real person would actually have said on such an occasion, but to provide an expression of grief more noble and more moving than any 'spontaneous overflow of powerful feeling' could be. They are composed in a 'high style' which is clearly distinguishable from the surrounding verse by such characteristics as a Latinate vocabulary, syntax, and word-order, and a tendency to parallelisms like those found in the Psalms (e.g. 'Of his linage am I and his ofspring', 'so caytyf and so thral'). The speech is as formal, and as capable of moving us, as an operatic aria. The sitting posture was conventional for a melancholy lover.

685–6. *Juno* See note on lines 470–1.

688. Cadmus was the founder of Thebes, and Amphion

afterwards ruled it and built a wall round it.

708. 'That (I now see that) my death was destined before my first
clothes were made (i.e. before I was born).'

711–12. 'I don't care a jot for all my other sorrows.'

734. *by grace* 'By the grace of God', and hence, when used
casually, 'by luck'. Here it must mean something like 'by fate':
it falls into place as one of many references to the destiny,
fortune, or blind chance that governs the poem's human actions.

745. *That thou ne sholdest dyen* 'without dying'.

754. *as a knight* 'equipped with knightly armour'.

761. *as for me* 'as far as I am concerned'.

764. *leyd his feith to borwe* 'pledged his honour (to keep the
agreement)'.

765–9. Another *exclamatio*, followed by a *sententia* ('Ful sooth is
seyd . . .'—compare the *sententia* beginning with 'But sooth is
seyd . . .' in line 663), and then by a line explicitly linking the
generalizing *sententia* with the particular situation.

765. 'O Cupid, lacking in all kindness.' Cupid is the son of Venus
and god of love; he is the god of the courtly religion of love, and
here his narrower kind of love, based on sexual desire, is
contrasted with *charitee*, the altruistic love of the true religion.

766. 'O rule, that will permit no companion to share you.' This
compressed line is expanded and explained by the couplet
following.

767–8. 'It is said with great truth that neither sovereignty nor love
will willingly accept any companionship'—the ruler insists on
ruling alone and the lover on loving alone. The triple negative
('ne . . . noght . . . no') is used as a means of emphasis.

769. 'Arcite and Palamon certainly find that to be true.'

775. *allone as he was born* 'as alone as when he was born'.

780–8. An extended simile of the kind originally used by Homer
and traditionally belonging to epic poetry. This one originates in
Statius, is adapted for a different purpose by Boccaccio, and for
a third purpose by Chaucer.

780. *hunters* Genitive singular.

784. *breketh* Though this word is syntactically parallel with *hereth*
and *thinketh*, it would more naturally be used not of the hunter
but of the animal as it crashes through the undergrowth.

790. Meaning uncertain: perhaps 'Well as each of them knew the
other'.

791–802. The way in which this incident is presented makes it a
perfect example of how, in the world of *The Knight's Tale*,

chivalric courtesy and humanity are the fine trappings of brutal violence. The touching brotherliness with which they arm each other is succeeded by the images of savage animals describing their attack on each other. The whole scene is of course exaggerated, if judged by realistic standards; but the exaggeration serves not just to excite but to make a serious point about the nature of the chivalric life.

792. *rehersing* 'repetition (of their agreement)'.

797–8. *mightest wene . . . were* 'might have supposed . . . was'.

802. Their metal shoes were full of blood, which had run down inside their armour.

803. *I lete hem fighting dwelle* Literally, 'I leave them remaining fighting', i.e. 'I leave them still fighting'.

805–14. This philosophical digression is based on Boccaccio but is stiffened with reminiscences of Boethius's more comprehensive philosophy, in which the pagan conception of Destiny is subordinated to a conception of divine Providence compatible with Christianity, so that Destiny becomes the *ministre general* of Providence.

809. *by ye or nay* 'definitely'.

810–11. 'Yet sometimes an event will happen on a certain day that does not happen again in a thousand years.'

814. *sighte* 'Providence'.

815. *This mene I now by* 'I say this with reference to'.

817. *namely at the grete hert* 'especially (to hunt) the great hart'. A 'great hart' was thought of as especially noble game for the hunt. The season for hunting it began in England on 3 May.

818–19. *in his bed ther daweth him no day That he nis clad* A mixture of two different constructions. 'No dawn finds him still in bed, but he is dressed.'

824. Mars is the god of war, Diana the goddess of hunting. We are constantly reminded, even in such casual and apparently decorative ways, of the powers that rule the world of the poem.

833. *rideth him* 'rides'. *Him* is a redundant reflexive pronoun.

836. *cours* 'pursuit' or 'chase', a technical hunting term.

839. *Under the sonne* 'shading his eyes against the sun'.

841. *as it were bores two* 'like two wild boars'. The preceding picture of Theseus as a hunter redoubles the effect of the beast-imagery applied to Palamon and Arcite. Their brutality is underlined, and his role comes to seem that of a tamer of the savagery of men as well as wild animals.

853. *for to* 'as to'.

860. 'Whose lives are a burden to us.'

878. *it am I* The usual Middle English idiom for 'It is I'.

888. *pine yow with the corde* One medieval torture, used to force a suspect to confess, was to tie his wrists behind his back and haul him up and down by them. This is perhaps what Theseus is referring to.

889. *by mighty Mars the rede* The planet Mars is red in colour.

890–2. A. E. Housman, the poet and distinguished classical scholar, wrote of these lines, 'If Homer or Dante had the same thing to say, would he wish to say it otherwise?'

895–6. Lines which embody characteristically medieval assumptions about society and the way people behave. They are *gentil* both in their nobility of character and in their high social rank: *gentillesse* is simultaneously an ethical and a social concept. And *love*, for courtly ladies, is necessarily the most admirable and deserving of motives for a fight.

897. *saugh* The subject of this verb is *the ladies* of line 892.

898. *bothe lasse and moore* Literally, 'of lower and higher rank', a common tag in Middle English verse used as an emphatic way of saying 'all'.

903. 'Pity flows readily in the noble heart.' This line is used by Chaucer in three other places in his work.

908. *in his resoun* 'when he considered it rationally'.

920. *that he first bigan* 'the offence he originally committed'.

921. *of discrecioun* 'power of discrimination'.

922. *kan no divisioun* 'recognizes no distinction'.

927–67. This long speech by Theseus, which was largely invented by Chaucer, begins with praise of the power of the god of love, and as such became famous among later poets in the courtly tradition; indeed its opening lines are sometimes quoted word for word. But the speech develops later in a way that reveals its irony; for the power it attributes to love is a power to make his followers behave like fools; and this disrespectful attitude towards love, emphasized particularly in the animal images of line 952, was not always noticed.

933. *Lo heere* A normal phrase for calling attention to a particular example illustrating some general point.

941. 'There are no true fools but lovers.'

942. *for Goddes sake that sit above* 'for the sake of God, who dwells above'.

943. *be they noght wel arrayed?* 'don't they look splendid?' The question is of course ironic.

946–7. 'And yet those who serve love whatever happens fancy themselves very wise.'

949. *jolitee* 'fun' (again ironic).

950. 'Shows them as much gratitude as she does me (i.e. none)'.

952. *a cokkow or an hare* Both traditionally silly creatures.

953. 'But everything has to be tried once, whatever it is.' *Hoot and coold* is probably just an emphatic way of saying 'everything, no matter what' (compare *lasse and moore* in line 898); but it is possible that it refers to the warmth (or the lack of it) of the love that is being discussed.

955. *myself* 'my own experience'.

956. *a servant was I oon* 'I was one of the god of love's followers'. For *servant* in this sense, compare *servise* and *serven* in lines 945 and 947. The god of love was conceived of as a feudal lord, and all lovers were in his service.

965. *night ne day* Another phrase on the pattern of *hoot and coold*, meaning 'at any time'.

966. *in all that ye may* 'in every way you can'.

968. 'And they promised him faithfully to do as he asked.'

969. 'And begged him for protection and mercy.' They have put themselves outside the law by their actions, and so they beg him to become their feudal lord and grant them his protection.

975. *as for* 'on behalf of'.

979–80. 'One of you, whether he likes it or not, may go and blow on an ivy leaf, for all the good it will do him.' *Pipen in an ivy leef* is a proverbial expression (with the country air of most of Chaucer's proverbs) meaning to do something pointless. The rhyming of words of identical sound but different meaning (like *lief* and *leef*) was permitted in Middle English, as it is in classical French verse.

982. 'However jealous or angry you may be.'

986. *youre ende of that* 'the result for you of what'.

987. *for plat conclusioun* 'to make a plain end of the matter'.

989. 'If you find it acceptable, take it as meant for the best.'

992. 'And in a year from today, neither more nor less.'

1002. *to wyve* 'as a wife'. *Wyve* is the inflected dative form of *wyf*.

1003. Again Fortune is asserted to be the overruling power of the action; indeed, Theseus is deliberately abandoning his power of choice, even while acting so decisively, and is throwing the event into the hands of Fortune.

1005–8. 'And as sure as I hope God will have pity on my soul, I will be an impartial and true judge. The only settlement I will accept will be the death or capture of one of you.'

1009. *yow thinketh* 'it seems to you'. In Middle English, the two verbs 'to seem' and 'to think', which in Old English had had the distinct forms *thynkan* and *thencan*, fell together as *thinken*.

1011. *youre ende* 'the end of your quarrel'.

1047. *Doon make* 'had made'. *Oratorie* i.e. a place for prayers.

1054. Diana is the goddess of chastity as well as of hunting.

1055. *doon wroght* 'had made'.

1060. *maystow se* In this section the poem is taking on the characteristically medieval (and particularly late-medieval) form of a description of emblematic painting, sculpture, etc. We are taken on a conducted tour of the temples, having their salient features pointed out to us; and because the reality seen is emblematic, what is conveyed is not merely decorative beauty or grandeur, but thought about the meaning of the gods and the human passions they stand for. For Chaucer this meaning is more important and more sombre than for Boccaccio; he adds lines 1060–6, where we are invited to 'see' unhappy consequences of passionate love which it would be hard to render pictorially, and lines 1089–94, where the destructive power of love is asserted in a way that does not even pretend to be pictorial.

1066. 'The oaths with which they support their promises.'

1067–9. Venus, or passionate love, being itself a non-moral impulse, leads to good and bad consequences at random.

1071. In matters connected with love, yellow symbolized jealousy.

1072. The cuckoo symbolizes the cuckoldry which gives cause for jealousy.

1073. *caroles* Ring dances accompanied by song.

1077. *make of mencioun* 'make mention of'.

1078. *Citheroun* Venus was called Cytherea because she was supposed to live in the island of Cythera, but Chaucer, in common with many medieval writers, wrongly associated her with Mount Cithaeron, the home of the Muses.

1082. Idleness keeps the gate of the garden of love in the *Roman de la Rose*. Now begins a catalogue of figures from scriptural and classical legend who were especially associated with love.

1083. *Narcisus* Narcissus fell in love with his own reflexion in a pool, and died as a result. The pool of Narcissus is also found in the garden of the *Roman de la Rose*.

1084. *Salomon* Solomon had many wives and concubines, and was led by them into idolatry in his old age, for which his kingdom was punished.

1085. *Ercules* Hercules was famous for his strength, but he also suffered through love, being killed by a poisoned shirt sent to him out of jealousy by his wife.

1086. *Medea and Circes* Both were enchantresses; Medea used her spells to help Jason, with whom she was in love, to capture the golden fleece, and later murdered their children through jealousy; Circe, with whom Ulysses fell in love, used hers to turn his companions into animals.

1087. *Turnus* Turnus, in Virgil's *Aeneid*, fought Aeneas for the sake of Lavinia, and was killed by him.

1088. *Cresus* Croesus, like the figures mentioned in the few lines preceding, came to a bad end, being overthrown by Cyrus; but why Chaucer thought this had something to do with Venus is not clear.

1089–96. Having gone through the list, Chaucer explicitly draws the moral it implies; the explicit moralizing is as typical of medieval poetry as the encyclopaedic list itself.

1097–1104. Venus was born of the sea, and one of the poses in which she is traditionally presented in medieval and Renaissance art is rising from the sea (Botticelli's *Birth of Venus* is probably the most familiar example nowadays). The pose and her attributes, such as the musical instrument, the roses, and the doves, were formalized in mythological treatises; it was through these, as much as through actual pictures, that the traditional description descended.

1114. This actual temple is described at length by Statius, and the description is repeated and elaborated by Boccaccio both in the *Teseida* and in the *De genealogia deorum*. Chaucer manages to get it in only by making it a picture on the wall of the temple erected by Theseus; but the lack of probability of this device does not matter, for once again description is made the vehicle for the exposition of ideas.

1116. *mansioun* 'dwelling'; but the word also has an astrological significance, meaning the 'house' or sign of the zodiac which specially belongs to the planet Mars.

1129. *The northren light* The temple is in the cold north (see line 1115), and so the light shining into it will be cold and dim.

1137. *Ther saugh I* Chaucer may have been influenced by the *Teseida*, in which the temple is actually seen by a personified prayer, and also by the tradition of dream-poetry, the commonest framework for visions of allegorical buildings.

1137–8. *the derke imagining* of treachery is its obscure conception in the mind; *the compassing* of it is its bringing to pass in action.

1159. *shippes hoppesteres* Statius has *bellatrices carinae* and Boccaccio *navi bellatrici*, both meaning 'warships', but Chaucer appears to have read the imaginary word *ballatrices* or *ballatrici*, meaning 'dancing' (as ships may be said to dance on the waves). There may have been an error in his manuscript of the *Teseida*.

1161. *freten* 'devour'. This is the infinitive following from *saugh I* two lines back; literally, 'I saw . . . the sow to eat the child'.

1163. *by the infortune of Marte* 'with reference to the ill-fortune caused by Mars'.

1164. *cartere . . . carte* Probably 'charioteer . . . chariot'. *Carte* was used both for 'cart' and for 'chariot', and indeed the very idea of a chariot seems not to have been understood in the Middle Ages, since pictures based on descriptions of people riding chariots (including pictures of Mars himself) tend to show them riding in farm wagons.

1166. *of Martes divisioun* 'belonging to the clan of Mars'.

1167. The barber comes under Mars's influence because medieval barbers also acted as blood-letters and surgeons. The place of the butcher as a shedder of blood is more obvious, and that of the smith is stated in the next line.

1170–2. Conquest is depicted like Damocles, with a symbolic sword hanging over his head, ready at any moment to deprive him of his glory.

1173–4. Julius Caesar was murdered, Nero and Mark Antony committed suicide.

1177. *right by figure* 'exactly in the diagram', i.e. the astrological diagram or horoscope showing how the stars foretold their deaths.

1187. One method of divination, called geomancy, began by making at random four rows of dots, which were taken as figures symbolic of the positions of the stars. *Puella* and *Rubeus* were the names of two such figures signifying respectively fortunate and unfortunate aspects of Mars.

1189–90. This detail, which was added by Chaucer, is part of a traditional symbolism, for an early etymology of Mars derives it from *mares vorans*, 'eating males'.

1198–1216. The temple of Diana is not described by Boccaccio, and these examples of transformations connected with Diana and chastity are taken partly from elsewhere in the *Teseida*, partly from Ovid's *Metamorphoses*.

1198–1201. Callisto was transformed by Diana into a bear, and the bear was transformed by Jupiter into the constellation called the

Great Bear. The pole-star, however, is in the Little Bear, and Chaucer may not fully have understood the legend.

1203. Callisto's son, Arcas, was transformed into the constellation Boötes.

1204–6. Daphne, the daughter of Peneus, a river-god, was transformed into a laurel tree when being pursued by Apollo, who loved her.

1207–10. Actaeon was turned into a stag for having seen Diana bathing naked, and was then killed by his own hounds.

1212–13. Atalanta and Meleager hunted and killed a wild boar sent by Diana to ravage Calydon. There are various accounts of the bad end Meleager came to as a result.

1217–28. Once again the details of the description are symbolic rather than evocative. The hart, dogs, bow, and arrows represent Diana's function as goddess of hunting. The moon is there because Diana was also Luna, the moon-goddess. She is looking down to the underworld because she had a third identity as Hecate, goddess of Hades. And the woman in labour is present because Diana had yet another identity as Lucina, goddess of childbirth.

1224. Pluto was ruler of the underworld of classical paganism.

1230. In Chaucer's time colours for painting were very expensive, and were often the subject of contracts between artists and patrons. Medieval conceptions of art emphasize the value of the materials as well as the skill of its craftsmanship.

1232. *his grete cost* 'great expense to himself'.

1246–7. 'Was there such a noble company for its size throughout the whole world God created.'

1257. *benedicitee* This common exclamation ('Praise the Lord!', 'God bless us!', etc.) was often slurred in pronunciation: *ben'citee* or *ben'dis'tee*.

1261–6. *Som* in each of these lines is singular, not plural: 'one'.

1263. *paire plates* 'Pair' is not followed by 'of' in Middle English. *Plates* are steel plates worn one over each breast.

1270–1323. In Boccaccio the whole of one book is occupied with descriptions of the various champions on each side. Chaucer reduces these to two, Lygurge and Emetreus, and borrows details from different portraits in Boccaccio in order to build up his own descriptions. They are arranged with careful symmetry, each being given twenty-seven lines, and the selection of details is highly significant. His descriptive method is that of medieval poetry in general—the exhaustive accumulation of detail rather than the selection of salient points to give a general impression. Here it is seen at its best, for the details combine to create a coherent effect. He lays great stress on the bestial qualities of the two champions: they are like savage animals in their appearance, their dress, and their attendants. Thus the chivalric pageantry orders without concealing or transforming the savage and destructive elements in human life, which are so prominent in the world of the poem. Similar as they are in this respect, the two champions are also clearly differentiated; and it has been suggested that they have an astrological significance, as being types of the man dominated by Saturn and by Mars. Contemporary accounts of the Saturnian and Martian types do indeed share many details of appearance with Lygurge and Emetreus, and their savage qualities would be appropriate as amplifications of the ferocity attributed to the planetary gods in *The Knight's Tale*.

1275. A griffin is a fabulous animal, part lion and part eagle.

1297–8. Emetreus seems to have been invented by Chaucer, and the reference to authority in *in stories as men finde* is presumably intended to distract our attention from this fact.

1301. This line supports the astrological interpretation mentioned above.

1302. *clooth of Tars* Rich silk from Turkestan.

1329. *alle and some* 'one and all'—another emphatic way of saying 'all'.

1339–48. Another instance of *occupatio*, in which the writer refuses to describe or discuss some particular subject. Here it is used not merely functionally, as a means of abbreviation, but as a way of evoking the atmosphere of medieval courtly revelry.

1342. At a medieval feast, as in some Oxford and Cambridge colleges today, the guests would be seated at the high table on the dais in order of seniority.

1350. As usual, the rhetorical devices of Chaucer's style are directed specifically at his audience: he draws their attention to the fact that now something important is going to happen.

1356–7. The language of Christian devotion is applied to the pagan goddess.

1357. *Citherea* See note on line 1078.

1359. *in hir houre* That is, in the hour belonging to Venus. For astrological purposes, day and night were each divided into twelve 'hours' (which would actually only have been an hour long when the days and nights were of equal length), and the first hour after sunrise on each day was dedicated to the planet after whom the day was named. Each following 'unequal' hour was dedicated to another planet according to the order of the distance of the seven planets from the earth. The first hour of Sunday would belong to the sun, and the second to Venus; the ninth, sixteenth and twenty-third hours would also belong to Venus. Palamon rose two hours before sunrise, which would be in the twenty-third hour.

1364. Venus was the daughter of Jove (Jupiter), the ruler of the gods, and was married to Vulcan, the deformed smith of the gods.

1365. *Citheron* See note on line 1078.

1366. Venus loved Adonis, and when he was killed by a boar she fell into intense grief.

1378. The descent in this line from the dignified language used earlier in his prayer is no doubt deliberate: we are to be reminded of what devotion to Venus would mean in practice.

1384–5. *Die in thy servise* is a significantly vague phrase: does it mean simply to die peacefully, married to Emelye rather than in battle, or does it mean to die while actually making love to Emelye?

1390. *so be* 'it may be true'.

1394. *where I ride or go* 'whether I ride or walk', i.e. at all times.

1413. For *houre inequal*, see note on line 1359.
that 'from the time when'. Palamon rose on the twenty-third hour of Sunday; the third 'unequal hour' from that, counting inclusively, would be the first 'unequal hour' of Monday. This would be dedicated to the god after whom Monday was named—that is, Diana, the moon-goddess, to whom Emelye prays.

1419. *clothes* In Boccaccio Emilia puts on a splendid purple robe after washing herself, and this is presumably what is referred to, although it might be the hangings mentioned in line 1423.

1424–30. 'This Emelye, with modest heart, washed her body with water from a well. But how she performed her rite I dare not tell, unless it were in somewhat general terms; and yet it would be fun to hear everything. It would be no burden to any man who means well; but it is a good thing for one to be free to imagine it.' For comment, see Introduction, pp.80–1.

1436. *Stace of Thebes* 'the *Thebaid* of Statius'. Statius does not in fact describe Emelye's sacrifice, but he does describe other pagan rites.

1441. See note on lines 1217–28 and 1224.

1444. *As keepe* 'keep'. The *as* is a normal way of introducing a request. See lines 1459–67.

1445. See note on lines 1207–10.

1455. Horace calls Diana *diva triformis*, 'three-natured goddess', the three natures being Diana on earth, Luna in heaven, and Hecate in Hades. See note on lines 1217–28.

1464. *do me grace* 'grant me favour'.

1470. 'Since thou art a virgin and guardian of all of us virgins.'

1472. *a maide* 'as a virgin'.

1482. *As it were* 'something like'. The bloody drops no doubt symbolize the loss of virginity.

1497–9. This has in fact already happened. In Boccaccio Diana's speech comes first and the omen afterwards, and Chaucer seems to have forgotten that he has reversed the order of events.

1509. See note on line 1359. Mars's next hour would have been the fourth after sunrise.

1518. 'Complete control of all warfare.'

1527–32. Mars had a secret love affair with Venus, but Vulcan, her husband, trapped them together in a net.

1530. 'Although on one occasion it went amiss with you.'

1536–7. 'And as I believe, more assailed by love than ever any creature alive has been.'

1551. 'To do your will and act according to your powerful skills.'

1575. *seyde* 'it said'.

1579. His delight is expressed in the jaunty rhythm and alliteration of the line; and it contrasts with the dolefulness with which the promise of victory is given.

1588. 'By which he soon satisfied each party.'

1593. 'Although it is against his nature', Saturn's nature being to produce disasters, as was suggested by Arcite in lines 229–31, and as Saturn himself goes on to indicate in detail.

1595. Venus was Saturn's granddaughter. *Doghter* was in any case used as a term of address to a younger woman.

1596. Of the seven 'planets' known in the Middle Ages, Saturn had the widest orbit.

1598. *wan* Like many medieval colour-adjectives, *wan* expresses emotional intensity rather than a precise tint. It means something like 'gloomy'—at once pale and dark, like lead. Here it seems to be applied to the sea, and appropriately, since drowning would be most likely to take place in a storm. But *wan* would also fit the appearance of the drowned man himself.

1599. In the Middle Ages (and in Shakespeare's time—see *Twelfth Night*) madmen were imprisoned in a dark house, and this may be referred to here.

1601. Chaucer and his audience would no doubt have had in mind the Peasants' Revolt of 1381.

1604. Leo is the sign of the zodiac opposite to Saturn's own house of Aquarius; in it he is as malignant as in his own house, and his strength is increased by that of the lion.

1608. Samson destroyed the Philistines, who had imprisoned him, by pulling down the supports of the temple where he was displayed, but in doing so killed himself too.

1610. 'The secret acts of treachery and the long-laid plots.'

1611. The recurrent plagues of the fourteenth century, from the Black Death of 1348–9 onwards, were associated with Saturn's influence.

1617–18. 'Although you are not of the same disposition, which is what causes such constant disagreement.'

1633–64. For comment on this scene, see Introduction, pp. 55–6.

1643–5. Here three ranks are distinguished among the participants: *lordes* who are independent, *knightes of retenue* who are in the service of the *lordes*, and *squieres* who serve both.

1645. *Nailinge the speres* Fastening the heads to the shafts.

1652. *thikke as they may goon* 'clustered as densely as possible'.

1654. *blody sounes* 'calls to bloodshed'.

1655–62. In these lines Chaucer gives the impression of a crowd made up of different groups all expressing their opinions at the same time.

1658. 'Some said one thing, some said another.'

1659. *him* 'the one'.

1661. *he . . . he* 'this one . . . that one'.

1677. *the peple of noise al stille* 'that the noise of the people was completely silenced'.

1694. *stake* A palisade, within which the prisoners on each side are to be kept.

1705–6. There is perhaps implied a contrast between this 'lord', who has previously been described as sitting like *a god in trone* (line 1671), and the actual gods of the poem, who do seem to desire bloodshed. There is at least a general contrast, which these lines help to build up, between Theseus, the human ruler who attempts to control the savage elements in human life, and the gods, who are the very expression of those savage elements.

1710. *and nat with sarge* Serge was a cheap woollen cloth used for hangings, far less valuable than cloth of gold.

1721. *in degrees* 'on the steps'. As described in lines 1032–4, the lists were constructed with stepped seats round them, so that the watchers could see over each other's heads.

1723. *Marte* i.e. the statue of Mars, before which Arcite had made his prayer.

1729. 'If one were to search up and down throughout the whole world.'

1735. *for to gesse* 'to judge by conjecture'—without actually counting and examining them.

1738. 'So that there should be no deception as to their numbers.' It had been agreed that there should be exactly a hundred on each side.

1744. *in arrest* The spears were very long, and were held steady in a rest attached to the saddle.

1748. *He* 'one man'.

1749. This and the preceding line mention the two consequences of the line before them: the spears splinter on the shields, one man is stabbed in the stomach by a spear, and pieces of broken spears fly twenty feet into the air. Then in the next line, having used their spears, they go on to the next stage of the battle, with swords. A general mêlée ensues.

1754. *He* 'one man'.

1756–9. *He . . . He . . . he him . . . He* 'one knight . . . a second . . . a third . . . a fourth . . . one'.

1762. 'Another is also led to the "stake" on the other side.'

1766. *his felawe* 'each other'.

1768–71. This comparison was added by Chaucer. *Galgopheye* (Gargaphia in Boeotia, a wild and remote place) was where Actaeon was turned into a stag, and was therefore associated by Chaucer with hunting—hence the hunter is mentioned as the tiger's prey. Together with the comparison of the lion, which follows, and was also added by Chaucer, it forms a deliberately symmetrical pair, recalling lines 797–801, in which Arcite was also compared to a tiger and Palamon to a lion. The lion and the tiger are conventional symbols of savage cruelty, ungoverned by reason, and they are part of a whole train of wild beast imagery in the poem, whose function is to suggest the savage element which lies close beneath the surface of human life.

1772. *Belmarye* Benmarin, in North Africa. In *The General Prologue* we are told that the Knight had been there.

1793. 'Because they were too strong for him and also because it was part of the agreement.'

1808. In the form of rain.

1816. Suggested by the noise of the trumpeters and heralds, but addressed to the imagined audience of the poem—'*You* be quiet too.'

1823–4. These antifeminist lines do not occur in the best manuscripts, but they may be Chaucerian. They are at least in keeping with the patriarchal nature of the world represented in the Tale.

1825. Probably 'And was all his delight, so far as his heart was concerned.' But the reading of the line is doubtful, and so is its interpretation. Some manuscripts have *and* for *as*.

1838. By cutting the straps that held the armour together.

1852. 'Who had his breast-bone pierced with a spear.'

1854. *charmes* 'incantations'. Medieval medicine, though elaborately developed as a theory (see lines 1885–1900 below), was by modern standards a pseudo-science, employing some of the methods of magic.

1856. *wolde hir lymes have* 'wanted not to lose a limb'.

1865–7. 'Nor (is it more than an accident) for one single person, without help, to be taken prisoner by twenty knights and, without surrendering, to be led by force to the "stake".'

1871. 'It was not imputed as any dishonour to him.' *Vileynye* is the behaviour or qualities of character to be expected of a *vileyn*, a person of the lower classes.

1873. *leet crye* 'had proclaimed'.

1875. This proclamation of the equal success of both sides, together with his earlier refusal to worry people by abandoning the festivities, helps to establish Theseus as a symbol of rational rule, struggling against the passions that turn men into beasts.

1885–1900. Most of these medical details were added by Chaucer, partly no doubt because he was interested in the sciences, but also because they increase the horror and inevitability of Arcite's death.

1887. *for any lechecraft* 'for all that medical skill can do'.

1889. *veine-blood* ('blood-letting') was a favourite remedy for almost any illness in medieval times and later. A vein was opened and the blood allowed to flow out.

ventusinge ('cupping') was a way of removing blood from some part of the body by applying a vacuum to a nearby part.

1891–3. The animal virtue, one of the three virtues mentioned in the note on lines 511–18, controlled the action of the muscles, including those that govern breathing. One of its functions was to expel impurities from the natural virtue through the lungs;

but in Arcite's case the lungs were damaged, and so the impurities collected in them and caused his death.

1901–2. No doubt this was a proverb: where the forces of the body itself will not help, medical treatment is of so little use that you might as well bury the sick person at once.

1903. *This* 'this is'—common abbreviated form in Middle English.

al and som 'the long and short of it'.

1908. *o point* 'a single part'.

1917. *wyf* In Boccaccio Arcite had gone through a form of marriage with Emelye immediately after the tournament; in Chaucer's version it is particularly moving that Arcite should call her wife for the first time when death makes it impossible to hope that he will marry her. Similarly in Shakespeare's play, Cleopatra calls Antony husband for the first time as she is about to die.

1918. *Endere of my lyf* 'cause of my death'.

1922. *Sweete foo* This and other oxymorons are commonly used in medieval literature to describe the paradoxical effect of love. Here the phrase takes on new meaning, for Emelye is his enemy in causing not the metaphorical 'death' of the lover but his real death.

1928. Compare line 1005 and note.

1929–30. 'So far as true lovers are concerned, with all the attributes proper to them.' *Servaunt* is here used in the specialized sense of line 956, to mean a follower of the god of love. *Service* in line 1910 above may have an undertone of the same meaning.

1931–3. These are the qualities traditionally attributed to the lover in medieval literature. *Heigh kinrede*, 'noble relations'; *that art*, 'the art of love'.

1934. 'May Jupiter protect my soul'—a repetition of the asseveration of line 1928, after the parenthesis.

1943. *And yet mooreover for* 'and all the more because'.

1945. *withouten moore* 'and that alone'.

1946. According to medieval physiology, the heart, and not the brain, was the seat of the intellect.

1951–78. After the pathos of Arcite's death, Chaucer seems to retreat from seriousness into something almost like burlesque. This is observable first in the Knight's refusal of theological speculation about the destination of Arcite's soul—a dangerously topical subject, given that Arcite is a pagan, and one on which Chaucer has sly remarks elsewhere in his works, usually making the point that those who argue so knowingly about the after-life are necessarily arguing from a total lack of experience. Next there seems to be some deliberate exaggeration in the shrieking and howling of Emelye and Palamon; though it is difficult to be certain about this, since emotions are generally presented in a conventionally intensified form in this poem, and the word 'howl' may have sounded less undignified in Chaucer's time than it does now. There is surely some Chaucerian slyness, though, in lines 1964–8: we are not necessarily to accept the generalization about women, especially since Emelye does not die of grief, but lives to marry Palamon. And finally the sorrow of the women is again debased by their linking of gold and Emelye in line 1978, in a way that makes Emelye sound almost an after-thought.

1952. 'Whose whereabouts, since I have never been there, I cannot tell.' In Boccaccio, Arcite's soul ascends to the eighth sphere of the heavens—a passage which Chaucer had used in describing the end of Troilus in *Troilus and Criseyde*. It is not only for this reason, though, that he does not use it again here; for in *The Knight's Tale* he wishes to draw a sharper distinction between the dark uncertainty of paganism and the Christian faith of his audience and himself.

1954–6 'I find nothing about souls in the contents of my book, nor do I wish to report opinions concerning them, even if they (*divinistres*, theologians) do write where they dwell (after death).'

1957. 'May Mars direct his soul!' Boccaccio had referred to Mercury, but Chaucer inserts a last reminder of Arcite's dedication to Mars, which has caused his death.

1960–1. *Theseus his suster took anon Swowninge* 'Theseus immediately seized his sister-in-law as she fainted'.

1974–5. When Hector, the greatest warrior of the Trojans, and son of King Priam, was killed in battle by the Greek Achilles, there was great sorrow at his death. The story of the Trojan war provided a universal standard of judgement for medieval poets and their audiences.

1977. *woldestow be deed* 'wouldst thou die'—as we should say, 'why did you have to die'.

1990. A line especially appropriate to the inclusion of the story in the Canterbury pilgrimage.

1997–8. *may best ymaked be, And eek moost honurable in his degree* 'might be arranged best and most suitably to his rank'.

2003–6. The fire of destructive passion appropriately receives its last expression in the funeral pyre.

2007. *leet comande* 'had orders given'.

2012–13. *ysent After* 'sent for'.

2019. *bare the visage* 'with his face bare'.

2027. *passinge othere of wepinge* 'weeping more than the others'.

2030. *in his degree* 'in accordance with Arcite's rank'.

2031. *leet forth thre steedes bringe* 'had three war-horses brought out'.

2037. *bowe Turkeys* 'Turkish bow'—distinctively curved and richly ornamented.

2056. *fyr-makinge* 'making of the pyre'.

2057–9. Chaucer personifies the pyre as a giant whose head reaches the heaven.

2061–2104. An extraordinarily long *occupatio*, forming the longest sentence in Chaucer's poetry. It does indeed abbreviate Boccaccio's description, but calls attention to itself as a piece of rhetorical virtuosity.

2063–5. Lists of trees are a common convention of medieval (and classical) poetry. Chaucer would have found lists both in the *Teseida* and in the *Thebaid*, as well as in Ovid and other poets, and he gives another list himself in *The Parliament of Fowls*.

2067. *the goddes* The spirits who in classical mythology were supposed to live in the woods, and who are enumerated in line 2070.

2070. Nymphs is strictly the generic name for local deities; fauns are half men, half goats; and hamadryads are tree-gods.

2100. It was the custom in Chaucer's time (as in some places now) to stay up at night with the dead body.

2102. *wake-pleyes* In classical times a funeral was celebrated with games. In medieval England too the *lyche-wake* was sometimes interrupted with games, but the naked, oiled wrestlers evoke pagan antiquity.

2118. 'Had the noble Palamon sent for.'

2119. *Unwist of him* 'without his knowing'.

2129–58. The first thirty lines of Theseus's speech are not found in Boccaccio. They are largely made up of ideas and phrases taken from Boethius, as can be illustrated by quotation from Chaucer's own translation of the *De consolatione*. It is argued in the Introduction (pp. 104–10), however, that the speech cannot be taken simply as an exposition of Boethian philosophy, explaining the principle of order in the universe in answer to

Palamon's arraignment of divine providence at the end of Book 1, and fitting all the events of the Tale into a philosophical pattern. The speech expresses the difficulty philosophy has in ordering the universe: it begins confidently, but gradually loses itself in embarrassedly over-assertive repetitions, and eventually moves away from metaphysics altogether, turning to 'philosophy' of another kind—practical wisdom about how to live in *this wrecched world*. In view of the difficulty of the Boethian part of the speech, I give a modern version of these lines. It should be understood that in medieval philosophy God is conceived of both as the 'First Mover' of the universe, who sets the spheres in motion, and as its 'First Cause', on which it depends for its existence. Boethius sees the universe as governed and held together by a bond of love; in the *Roman de la Rose* this is imagined as a golden chain binding together the four elements (the basic units of matter), kept by Nature, who rules the world on God's behalf.

'When the First Mover of the heavenly first cause originally created the beautiful chain of love, his purpose was exalted and the consequence was great. He well knew why he did this and what he intended the outcome to be; for with that beautiful chain of love he bound fire, air, water, and earth within certain limits, so that they cannot escape. That same Prince and Mover (Theseus said) has ordained in this wretched world below, for all things that come into being here, a fixed duration and number of days, beyond which they may not pass, though they may indeed cut those days short. There is no need to adduce any authority for this statement, for it is proved by experience, except that I wish to explain my meaning. From this order, then, it can easily be recognized that the Mover from whom it originated is unchanging and eternal. Anyone but a fool can easily understand that each part derives from the whole of which it is a part; for the natural order does not draw its origin from a part or portion of anything, but from something that is perfect and unchanging, moving downwards from that until it becomes corruptible. And therefore, in his wise providence, the First Mover has so firmly established his decree that the patterns and processes of things must survive in succession to one another and not each eternally. You can understand this and see it by looking around you.'

2142–3. Compare with the note on lines 465–6.

2159. Here Chaucer returns from Boethius to Boccaccio.

2168. *al this thing* 'everything' (also in line 2176).

2169. *Of man and womman* 'so far as men and women are concerned'.

2172. *He moot be deed* 'they must die'. The reference to medieval society was added by Chaucer.

2174. *large feeld* Perhaps 'field of battle', in which case *as men may see* would imply 'as we have seen'.

2177. Here Theseus identifies the First Mover with the planetary god Jupiter, disregarding Saturn, whose sphere encloses Jupiter's. We have seen how ineffectual the benevolent Jupiter is compared with the more sinister god Saturn.

2183–5. Here is the turning-point of the speech, at which it abandons the attempt to make the universe rational, and turns to an attempt to give advice about how to live in an irrational universe.

2186. 'And especially what is due to all of us'—that is, death.

2188. *him that al may gye* 'him who has power to control everything'—that is, Jupiter.

2192. *him* 'himself'.

2203. Life as a prison is a familiar conception of medieval and earlier philosophy, but here it takes on a more specific meaning from the material prison in which both knights have earlier been kept, and from which they have been released. The release was only apparent; life itself is a prison.

2206. *Kan he hem thank?* 'does he show them any gratitude?'

2218. He has to bear in mind that the marriage of two persons of such high rank is of public importance.

2225. 'Let a proof of your feminine pity now be seen.'

2227. *bacheler* A probationer knight—a man who was training for knighthood but had not yet attained it.

2231. A final application of Christian theology to human love; just as God's mercy overcomes his justice in saving mankind, so the lady's mercy must offer the knight what he can never deserve by way of justice—herself.

2241–2. 'And may God, who created this whole wide world, send his love (Emelye) to Palamon, who paid dearly for it.' With these lines we are smoothly returned from the pagan world of the Tale to the Christian world of the pilgrimage.

GLOSSARY

a a; in

abide(n) wait for, remain
(l. 2124) waited

aboght (inf. *abyen*) paid for

abood delay

aboughte (inf. *abyen*) (l. 1445)
suffered

aboute (l. 32) in turn;
(l. 1029) around;
(l. 284) *been aboute* be
getting ready.

above (l. 1045) in the upper
part; (l. 2129) in the
heavens

aboven (l. 1911) before

abregge (inf. *abreggen*) cut
short

accomplice (inf. *accomplicen*)
accomplish

accord agreement

accused (inf. *accusen*) blamed

acorded (inf. *acorden*) agreed

Adoon Adonis

adoun down, down here

afered afraid

affermed (inf. *affermen*)
decreed

after afterwards, after,
according to

again, ageyn again, in return,
in reply; (l. 1593) against;
(l. 1822) upon

agast(e) (inf. *agasten*) terri-
fied; (l. 1566) *him agaste*
was frightened

ago(o)n gone (away); ago;
(l. 1926) *many a day agon*
for many days past

agreved (inf. *agreven*)
offended

aiel grandfather

al (adv.) all; very much

al (as conj. followed by subj.
verb) although

alauntz mastiffs

alight (inf. *alighten*) arrived

alighte (inf. *alighten*)
dismounted

alle and some one and all

als as

alwey always

amadrides hamadryads

amende(d) (inf. *amenden*)
(l. 52) put right; (l. 2208)
correct

amenden (l. 2216) reform
ourselves

amiddes in the middle

amorwe next day

amounteth (inf. *amounten*)
means

Amphioun Amphion

an on

a-night at night

animal see note on ll. 1891–3

ano(o)n at once

Antonius Mark Antony

apalled (inf. *apallen*) dimmed

apayd (inf. *apayen*) satisfied

apparaillinge preparation

appetites desires

Argus see note on ll. 527–34

armes arms, warfare; armour;
(l. 154) *in oon armes*, in the
same armour

arm-greet as thick as his arm

220

Glossary

armipotente powerful in arms

array condition; dress; decoration

arrayed (ll. 1188, 1232, 2009) arranged; (l. 948) *be they noght wel arrayed?* don't they look splendid?

arreest detention

arrest (l. 1744) rest

arretted (inf. *arretten*) imputed

ars-metrike arithmetic

art (l. 1587) device

artow (inf. *been*) art thou

arwes arrows

arys (inf. *arysen*) rise up

as as; as if; like

ashamed (inf. *ashamen*) humiliated

aside to one side

asketh (inf. *asken*) demands

aslaked (inf. *aslaken*) abated

aspect position of planets in relation to each other

assaut assault, direct attack

assayed (inf. *assayen*) tried

asseged (inf. *assegen*) besieged

assent (l. 2111) consent; (l. 2217) opinion; (l. 87) *by noon assent* on any terms

asshen ashes

asshy ash-covered

assuren (inf. *assuren*) (l. 1066) support

assureth (inf. *assuren*) (l. 68) makes secure

astert (inf. *asterten*) escaped

asterte (inf. *asterten*) escape

astoned dumbfounded

atones simultaneously

atrede (inf. *atreden*) outwit

atrenne (inf. *atrennen*) outrun

atte at the

atteyne (inf. *atteynen*) attain

Atthalante Atalanta

atthamaunt adamant

Atthenes Athens, Athenians

Attheon Actaeon

auctoritee authority

aught something, anything

aungel angel

auter altar

availleth (inf. *availlen*) it avails

ava(u)ntage advantage

aventure accident; chance; lot; event; (l. 302) *myn aventure* what had happened to me; (l. 328) *his aventure* what comes to him; (l. 1499) *thyn aventure of love* what will happen to you in love

avis opinion

avow vow

axe (inf. *axen*) ask

axing request

ay ever, always

ayeyn (l. 34) again; (l. 651) towards

ayeyns against

ba(a)r (inf. *beren*) carried; *bar him* conducted himself, acquitted himself; (l. 547) *bar him lowe* acted humbly

bacheler see note on l. 2227

bad (inf. *bidden*) told

balled bald (man)

bane (l. 239) death; (l. 823) killer

bar see *ba(a)r*

barbour barber

bareyne devoid, empty; barren

baronage assembly of barons

bataille battle

bauderie gaiety

bay bay-coloured (i.e. reddish-brown)

be (inf. *been*) are

be(e)n (inf. *been*) are, be

beere bier

— *beest* animal

beete (inf. *be(e)ten*) kindle

Belmarye Benmarin

— *benedicite* praise the Lord!

benigne kind

bente slope

berd beard

ber(e) (inf. *beren*) carry; (l. 1398) pierce; *bere him* behave

bere (noun) bear

bibledde covered with blood

bide (inf. *biden*) wait

— *bifel* (inf. *bifallen*) (it) happened

bifor(e)n before, at the front, in front of

bigonne (inf. *biginnen*) begun

bihoold (inf. *biholden*) look, behold

bihote (inf. *bihoten*) promise

biknowe (inf. *biknowen*) acknowledge

biraft (inf. *bireven*) taken away

biseken beseech

biside alongside

bisily diligently

bisy (l. 633) lively; (ll. 1462, 1584, 1995) anxious

bisynesse industry, diligence (l. 1070) anxiety

bitinge (inf. *biten*) piercing

bitwix(e)(n) between

biwreye (inf. *biwreyen*) disclose

blede (inf. *bleden*) bleed

bleynte (inf. *blenchen*) started back

blisful blessed

blisfully joyfully

blis(se) happiness, blessedness

blody bloody

blood (l. 160) family; (l. 472) race, people; (l. 725) kinsman

blowen (inf. *blowen*) proclaimed

blyve quickly

bocher butcher

bokeling buckling

boket bucket

boles bulls

bond (noun) agreement

bond (inf. *binden*) bound

boon bone

boone prayer, request

boor boar

bore (inf. *beren*) born

bores boars

born (inf. *beren*) borne, carried

borwe (l. 764) *leyd to borwe* pledged

bouk trunk

bounden (inf. *binden*) bound

boundes limits

bowes boughs

brak (inf. *breken*) broke out of

brawnes muscles

brede breadth

breke (inf. *breken*) break

breme furiously

brend burnished

brendest (inf. *brennen*) didst burn

brenninge burning

brenningly fiercely

brent(e) (inf. *brennen*) burnt
breres briars
brest (noun) breast
brest (inf. *bresten*) burst
bresten break
bret-ful brim-full
— *briddes* birds
bridel bridle
brighte beautiful
brode broad
broghte (inf. *bringen*) brought
broided braided
brondes logs; (l. 1481)
    brondes ende end of the
    piece of burning wood
browdinge embroidery
bulte (inf. *bilden*) built
burned burnished
busk(es) bush(es)
but but; unless; only;
    (l. 1387) if
— *by and by* side by side
byjaped (inf. *byjapen*) tricked
caas see *cas*
Cadme, Cadmus Cadmus
Callistope Callisto
cam (inf. *comen*) came
cantel portion
care sorrow
careful sorrowful
careyne corpse
carieden (inf. *carien*) carried
caroles ring dances
carte chariot
cartere charioteer
cas, caas chance, case,
    matter, event; (l. 553)
    affairs; (ll. 1222, 2038)
    quiver; (l. 1964) cases;
    (l. 2113) matters
caste (inf. *casten*) (l. 1313)
    reckon; (l. 1996) considered

castes plots
caughte (inf. *cacchen*)
    seized
cause (l. 1630) *by the cause
    that* because
caytyf wretched
caytyves wretches, miserable
    creatures
cerial evergreen
certes certainly
certeyn (l. 281) without
    doubt
chambre (small) room,
    bedroom
champartie (l. 1091) *holde
    champartie* share in
    power
char chariot
charge (l. 426) *thou yevest
    litel charge* you care very
    little; (l. 1429) *it were no
    charge* it would be no
    burden
charitee kindness; (l. 863)
    charity
charmes incantations
chasteyn chestnut
— *chaunce* accident
chaungen change
— *cheere* expression
che(e)s (inf. *chesen*) choose
— *cherles* of the lower classes
cheyne chain
chiere bearing; (l. 1825) see
    note
chirche church
chirking grating
chivalrie knightly
    accomplishments; company
    of knights
Circes Circe
circuit circumference

circumstances (ll. 1074, 1930)
  attributes; (l. 1405)
  ceremonies
citee city
Citherea Cytherea (see note
  on l. 1078)
Citheroun Cithaeron (but see
  note on l. 1078)
citole a musical instrument
  played by plucking its
  strings
citrin greenish-yellow
clariounis clarions (shrill,
  narrow-tubed trumpets)
clarree drink of sweetened
  wine
clause (l. 905) *shortly in a
  clause* in a short while
Clemence mercy
clene clean, pure
— *cleped* (inf. *clepen*) called
clepen call
~ *clerk* learned person, scholar
cloke cloak
clothered clotted
~ *clothes* (l. 1423) hangings
cloven (inf. *cleven*) split
cokkow cuckoo
~ *colde* cheerless
cole coal
colered with collars
colpons pieces
comen (inf. *comen*) come
commune in commune
  commonly, in general
communes common people
compaignye company; (l. 1453)
  intercourse; (l. 1916)
  intimacy
compas circle
compassing accomplishment
compleccioun disposition

compleyne (inf. *compleynen*)
  lament
compleyninge of lamenting
compleynte lamentation
composicioun agreement
concluden sum up
conclusioun judgement
condicioun character
confort comfort
conforteth (inf. *conforten*)
  comforts
confus distraught
confusioun destruction
conseil (l. 283) *of my conseil*
  in my confidence; (l. 289)
  confidant; (l. 725) *to my
  conseil sworn* sworn to keep
  my confidence; (l. 2238)
  council
conserve (inf. *conserven*)
  preserve
considered (inf. *consideren*)
  taken account of
— *constellacioun* position of
  planets at time of man's
  birth
contek strife
contenaunce appearance
contrarie opponent
contree country
convertinge (inf. *converten*)
  turning back
conveyed (inf. *conveyen*)
  escorted
coppes cups
⌐ *corage* heart, spirits
coroune crown
correccioun punishment
corrumpable corruptible
corrupcioun (l. 1896)
  putrefaction
— *cosin* friend

cote hut, cell
cote-armures jackets worn over armour to display heraldic devices
couched (l. 1308) studded; (l. 2075) laid
cours pursuit; (l. 1596) orbit; (l. 1691) charge
courser war-horse, charger
covenant(z) promise(s), agreement(s)
cowardye cowardice
cracchinge (inf. *cracchen*) scratching
craftes skills
Cresus Croesus
cridestow? (inf. *crien*) didst thou cry?
cri(e)de(n) (inf. *crien*) cried, shouted
crope treetop
cry outcry
Cupide, Cupido Cupid
cure care, attention
dampned condemned
Dane Daphne
dar (inf. *daren*) dare, venture
darreyne (inf. *darreynen*) settle (the right to)
darst (inf. *daren*) darest
dart arrow, spear
daun see note on l. 521
daunger obligation, resistance
daweth (inf. *dawen*) dawns
day (ll. 310, 1618) *al day* constantly; (l. 1763) *ofte a day* frequently
debaat conflict
debonaire meek, modest
declare (inf. *declaren*) express, explain

decree enactment
dede (noun) deed, action
deduyt pleasure
deed, dede (adj.) dead; (l. 720) deathly
deedly deathlike
deel (ll. 967, 1233) *every deel* completely; (l. 2206) *never a deel* not at all
deeth death
defye (inf. *defyen*) repudiate
degree rank, state of life; (l. 983) situation; (ll. 1032, 1033, 1721) step; (l. 1334) *at his degree* according to his rank; (l. 1721) *in degrees* on the steps
delit delight
deme(th) (inf. *demen*) judge, decide, consider
departe(d) (inf. *departen*) separate(d)
departinge splitting up
depe (l. 274) solemnly
depeynted (inf. *depeynten*) depicted
dere (inf. *deren*) trouble
derke dark, obscure
derknesse darkness
derre hath derre loves more
desiringe desire
despence extravagance
despit malice
despitous angry, contemptuous
desplayeth (inf. *desplayen*) unfurls
destreyneth (inf. *destreynen*) afflicts
deth death

devisinge provision

devoir duty

devyse, divyse (inf. *devysen*) (ll. 136, 1056) describe; (ll. 396, 932, 986, 1043) plan; (ll. 558, 567) order

deys dais

Diane Diana

diapred having diaper patterns

diched moated

dide(n) (inf. *doon*) did, made, performed

dight (inf. *dighten*) prepared

digne noble

diligence (l. 1612) *doon diligence* take special care

dim faint

dirriveth (inf. *dirriven*) derives

disconfitinge defeat

disconfiture defeat

disconfort grief

disconforten dishearten

disgised disguised

disherited disinherited

disjoint (l. 2104) *in no disjoint* without getting in difficulties

dispeir despair

dispence expenditure

dispitously scornfully

disposicioun (l. 229) position of planet; (l. 520) disposition

disserved (inf. *disserven*) deserved

distreyne (inf. *distreynen*) afflict

divininge (inf. *divinen*) guessing (what will happen to)

divinis theologians

divinistre theologian

divisioun (l. 922) distinction; (l. 1166) company, clan; (l. 1618) disagreement

divyse see *devyse*

doghter daughter

dominacioun power

dongeoun keep

do(o)n cause, show, do, perform; done

dooth (inf. *doon*) does, causes, makes

dore(s) door(s)

doun down; (l. 519) *up so doun* upside down

doute doubt; (l. 283) *out of doute* without doubt

doutelees without doubt

dowves doves

drawe (inf. *drawen*) carry

drawen (l. 1216) recall

drede (noun) fear

drede (inf. *dreden*) fear, doubt

dredeful full of dread

drenching drowning

dresse (inf. *dressen*) (l. 1736) *hem dresse* draw themselves up

dreye dry

dronk drunk

dronken (inf. *drinken*) drank

drugge (inf. *druggen*) (l. 558) *drugge and drawe* fetch and carry

duc ruler

duetee reverence

dure (inf. *duren*) remain, last

dusked (inf. *dusken*) grew dim

dwelleth (inf. *dwellen*) stay(s), remain(s)

dyen die

dys dice

ech(on) each, every

Ector Hector

eek also

eet (inf. *eten*) ate, was eating

effect conclusion, outcome, substance

eft again

Egeus Egeus

eir air

elde old age

elles, ellis else, otherwise

emforth according to

empoisoning poisoning

emprise undertaking

encens incense

enchauntementz magic spells

encombred (inf. *encombren*) burdened

encrees increase

encreeseth (inf. *encressen*) increases

encressen (inf. *encressen*) increase

ende end; (l. 986) result; (l. 1007) settlement

endelong lengthways, the length of

endite write

engendred (inf. *engendren*) produced

enhauncen advance

enhorte (inf. *enhorten*) exhort

enoint (inf. *enointen*) anointed

ensample(s) example(s), illustration(s)

entente intention; (l. 100) *in ful good entente* with good will

entree way in

er before

Ercules Hercules

ere (inf. *eren*) plough

eres ears

ernest earnest

erst than before

erthely earthly, on earth

eschue (inf. *eschuen*) avoid

ese ease

esed (inf. *esen*) comforted

esen (l. 1336) entertain

espye (inf. *espyen*) notice, discover

estaat high rank, condition of life

estres inner rooms

estward to the east

eterne eternal

eve (l. 1963) *bothe eve and morne* all the time

evene (adj.) impartial, equal

evene (adv.) exactly; steadily

evere ever, always; (l. 913) *evere in oon* continually

everemo (for) ever

everich each, every

ew yew

excercise (inf. *excercisen*) display

executeth (inf. *executen*) carries out

expulsif expulsive (see note on ll. 1891–3)

eyen eyes

eyleth (inf. *eylen*) is the matter with

eyr air

fader father

fadme fathoms

faille(n) fail

fain glad(ly)

fair (l. 665) desirable

faire (l. 126) satisfactorily; (l. 1736) properly; (l. 1838) deftly; (l. 968) *faire and weel* faithfully *falle* (inf. *fallen*) fallen, occurred

fallen occur

falle(th) (inf. *fallen*) occur(s)

falow grey

fals(e) false, deceptive, unreliable, untrustworthy

fantastik (l. 518) *celle fantastik* cell of perception

fare (noun) (l. 951) goings on

— *fare* (inf. *faren*) travel; (l. 1577) *wel to fare* to get on well; (l. 1578) gone

faren behave

— *faste* (a general intensifier) (l. 408) eagerly; (ll. 618, 620, 830) close; (ll. 1501, 1565) loudly; (l. 1700) hard

faught (inf. *fighten*) fought

feeld(es) field(s)

feere fear

fe(e)ste festivity

feith faith, honour

fel (inf. *fallen*) (l. 604) happened

felawe member of the company; companion, comrade

felaweshipe companionship

feld (inf. *fellen*) felled

felicitee (true) happiness

felingly with understanding

— *fel(le)* fierce

felonye treachery

Femenye the country of the Amazons

fer far; (l. 790) *as fer as* inasmuch as; (l. 992) *fer ne ner* neither more nor less

ferde(n) (inf. *faren*) acted

fere fear

ferforthly completely

fermacies medicines

ferre further

feste see *feeste*

fet (inf. *fecchen*) fetched

fewe (l. 1247) *of so fewe* for its size

fey faith; (l. 265) *by my fey* on my honour

fiers fierce

figure (l. 1177) diagram; (l. 1185) arrangements

fil(le) (inf. *fallen*) (ll. 176, 1252) happened; (ll. 245, 714) fell

fille (noun) (l. 670) *al his fille* as much as he wanted

fillen (inf. *fallen*) fell

finde (inf. *finden*) (l. 1555) provide

fir fire; (l. 1462) passion

firy fiery

fledden (inf. *fleen*) fled

fleen flee, escape from

fleete (inf. *fleten*) float

fletinge (inf. *fleten*) floating

flikeringe (inf. *flikeren*) fluttering

florin coin worth one-third of a pound

flotery disordered

flour(es) flower(s)

foghte(n) (inf. *fighten*) fought

folwen (inf. *folwen*) follow

folye folly

fomy foam-flecked

foo enemy

foom foam

foond (inf. *finden*) found

footmen men on foot

for for; out of; so that; *for to* to; (ll. 302, 1873) *for which* therefore

forbere (inf. *forberen*) let alone

fordo (inf. *fordon*) destroyed

formes natures

forpined wasting away

forther (l. 1211) *forther moor*
further on

forthre(n) help

forthy so, therefore

fortunest (inf. *fortunen*) give
good or bad fortune

forward agreement

foryet(e) (inf. *foryeten*)
forget

foryeten (inf. *foryeten*)
forgotten

foryeve (inf. *foryeven*)
forgive

fother cart-load

founden (inf. *finden*) found

foundred (inf. *foundren*)
stumbled

fourtenight fortnight

fowel bird

foyne (inf. *foynen*) (l. 1692)
let him thrust

foynen (inf. *foynen*) thrust

frakenes freckles

fredom generosity

free noble

freend(es) friend(s)

freendlich friendly

freeten (inf. *freten*) devoured

frely freely

fressh newly

fressh(e) fresh, gay, bright;
(l. 190) brightly

freten devour

fro from

frothen froth

fruit benefit

ful very

fulfild completely full

fulfille (inf. *fulfillen*) satisfy

fully completely; (l. 111) even

furie spirit from hell

fy fie

fyn fine, pure

fyr fire; pyre

gadereth (inf. *gad(e)ren*)
gathers

gaf (inf. *given*) gave

gaineth (inf. *gainen*) (l. 318)
us gaineth helps us;
(l. 929) *ther gaineth none
obstacles* no obstacles
avail; (l. 1897) *him gaineth*
there avails him

game joke, entertainment

Galgopheye Gargaphia

gan (inf. *ginnen*) began; often
used as an auxiliary to
indicate past tense (e.g.
gan knitte in l. 270,
'knitted')

gardyn garden

gastly ghastly

gaude bright

gayler gaoler

geere behaviour

geery moody, fickle

general (l. 805) universal

gentil noble, magnanimous

gentillesse nobility,
magnanimity

gere (ll. 158, 1322) equipment

gereful changeable

geres moods

gerland garland

gesse (inf. *gessen*) suppose,
conjecture

gete (inf. *getten*) (l. 1897)
save

gigginge (inf. *giggen*) fitting
straps to

gilt offence

giltelees (l. 454) innocent;
(l. 457) causelessly
gladen comfort
gladere one who makes glad
gleede burning coal
godhede godhead, divinity
gold-hewen made of gold
goldsmithrye goldsmith's work
gonne (inf. *ginnen*) began (to)
gooldes marigolds
go(o)(n) go, walk; *go sithen*
see note on l. 663
goon (inf. *goon*) gone
goost spirit
gooth (inf. *goon*) go(es)
goth (inf. *goon*) goes, walks
governaunce order
governour ruler
grace mercy, favour; (l. 734)
see note
graunte (inf. *graunten*) agree to
graunteth (inf. *graunten*)
grants
graunting grant
Grece Greece
gree excellence
gre(e)t(e) great; (l. 218) solid
grene green
gretter greater
greves (ll. 637, 783) thickets;
(l. 649) branches
greveth (inf. *greven*) vexes
grevous severe
grifphon griffin (see note on
l. 1275)
grisly horrible
groininge discontent
gruccheth (inf. *grucchen*)
complains
gruf face-down
gye (inf. *gyen*) rule, guide
gyle deception

gypoun vest worn over mail
and breastplate
gyse custom; fashion; (l. 981)
at his owene gyse just as he
chooses
habit dress
habitacioun dwelling-place
hadde (inf. *ha(ve)n*) had,
should have, would have
haf (inf. *heven*) raised
hakke (inf. *hakken*) cut
han (inf. *ha(ve)n*) have
happed (inf. *happen*) came about
hardinesse daring
hardy daring
haried (inf. *harien*) dragged
by force
harneys equipment, armour
haubergeoun mail coat
hauberk mail coat
have (inf. *ha(ve)n*) (l. 1856)
preserve
heed head; *(up)on his heed*
on pain of death; *by myn*
heed I swear
heeld (inf. *holden*) kept
heele wellbeing
heeled (inf. *heelen*) cured
heer hair
heer-agains against this
heerbiforn before this
heer(e) here
he(e)re (inf. *he(e)ren*) hear
he(e)ris hair
heete (inf. *hoten*) promises
heigh(e) high, great, serious,
noble
helmes helmets
helpeth (inf. *helpen*) (l. 1962)
what helpeth it? what is the
use (of)?
hem them

Glossary

hemself themselves

henne away

hente(n) (inf. *henten*) seize(d), caught

heraud(es) herald(s)

herd (adj.) (l. 1660) *the thikke herd*, the one with thick hair

herde (inf. *he(e)ren*) heard

her(e) her

Hereos lovesickness (see note on ll. 511–18)

helden (*with*) (inf. *holden*) (l. 1659) supported

herknen listen to

herkneth (inf. *herknen*) listen

hert hart

herte heart

herte-spoon pit of the stomach

heste command

hevenisshly divinely

hevinesse grief

hewe (noun) complexion, colour

hewe (inf. *hewen*) chop

hider (to) here

hidouse terrifying

hidously terribly

hie (inf. *hien*) hasten

highte (noun) *on highte* (l. 926) aloud, (l. 1749) in the air; (l. 2061) *maked upon highte* built up

hight(e) (inf. *hoten*) was (were) called, be called; (l. 1614) promised

himselven himself

hir(e) her; their

his his; its

holde(n) (inf. *holden*) (l. 449) obliged; (l. 648) make; (l. 832) followed; (l. 1861) considered to be

holdeth (inf. *holden*) (l. 1010) consider

holm holm-oak

holwe sunken

hond hand; (l. 745) *of myn hond* at my hands

honestly suitably

honge(th) (inf. *hangen*) hang(s), hung

hool stop!

hool whole

hoolly completely

hoom home

hoost army

hoot(e) (adj.) hot, fervent; (l. 951) *this hoote fare* these heated goings on; (l. 953) *hoot and cold* see note

hoote (adv.) (l. 879) fervently

hoppesteres dancing

hostelries lodgings

hou how; *hou...that* however

houndes dogs

housbondes husbands

humblesse humility

hunte huntsman

hunteresse huntress

hurtleth (inf. *hurtlen*) hurls

hust hushed

hye (adj.) high

hye (noun) (l. 2121) haste

imaginacioun fantasy

imagining conception

in (noun) lodging

Inde India

infortune ill-fortune

iniquitee wickedness

inned lodged

ire anger

iren iron

jalous(e) jealous
jalousie jealousy
japed (inf. *japen*) tricked
joinant adjoining
jolitee fun
journee day's journey
Jove Jupiter
juge judge
Julius Julius Caesar
Juno Juno
juste(n) (inf. *justen*) joust
justes jousting match
— *juwise* sentence
kan (inf. *konnen*) can;
   know(s) how to; (l. 922)
   recognizes; (ll. 950, 2206)
   shows
kaytyf wretched
keep (l. 531) *took keep*
   observed
kembd (inf. *kemben*) combed
kempe coarse
kene sharp
kepe (inf. *kepen*) (ll. 1380,
   2102) care; (l. 2471)
   guard
kepere guardian
kervere carver
kerving sculpture
— *kinde* (l. 1593) nature;
   (l. 543) *al in another kinde*
   completely transformed
kinrede kindred
kist (inf. *kissen*) kissed
knarry gnarled
— *knaves* servants
knew (inf. *knowen*) (ll. 739,
   790) recognized
knighthod (l. 1245) *knighthod
   of hir hond* their skill in
   war
knowe (inf. *knowen*) known

knyf knife
korven (inf. *kerven*) cut
koude (inf. *konnen*) could;
   knew how to
kouthe (inf. *konnen*) could
la(a)s snare
lacerte muscle
lacinge (inf. *lacen*) fastening
lad(de) (inf. *leden*) led
laft (inf. *leven*) left
large large, broad, wide;
   at thy (his) large at liberty
largely fully
las see *laas*
lasse and moore see note on
   l. 898
lat (inf. *leten*) let
launde field
laurer laurel
lay (inf. *lyen*) (l. 112) camped
layneres straps
— *lechecraft* medical skill
leef (noun) leaf
leef (inf. *leven*) leave
leep (inf. *lepen*) leapt
leeste least, slightest
leet (inf. *leten*) let, allowed,
   caused
leeve dear
leeveth (inf. *le(e)ven*) believe
lefte (inf. *leven*) left, gave up
lene (adj.) lean
lene (inf. *lenen*) give
lenger longer
leo(u)n lion
lese (inf. *lesen*) lose
lesinge losing
lesinges lies
lest pleasure
leste see *liste*
lete (inf. *leten*) leave
letted (inf. *letten*) prevented

letten hinder; (l. 459) *letten of* refrain from

leve leave

ley (inf. *leyen*) (l. 1700) *ley on* attack

leyde (inf. *leyen*) (l. 526) *him leyde* lay

leye (inf. *leyen*) lay

leyser leisure

lief pleasing

lif see *lyf*

lifly in a life-like way

liggen lie

ligginge (inf. *liggen*) lying

lighte bright, shining

lightly cheerful(ly)

ligne descent

liketh (inf. *liken*) it pleases

liknesse simile(s)

linage family, descent

linde lime

list it pleases (e.g. *me list* or *list me* I like, I desire)

liste, leste it pleased (e.g. *him leste* it pleased him, he liked; *as hire liste* as she pleased)

listes tilting-ground

lite(l) small, little

lith (inf. *lyen*) lies

lives alive

lo behold (see note on l. 933)

lode load

lond land

long long, tall

longen be appropriate

longes lungs

longeth (inf. *longen*) belongs, is appropriate

loode-sterre pole-star

looking glance

looth see note on l. 979

lordshipe sovereignty; (l. 969) protection

lowe humbly

Lucina Lucina (see note on ll. 1217–28)

lust joy; desire(s)

lustily joyfully

lustinesse joy

lusty joyful, rigorous

lyche-wake watch over a corpse

lyf, lif life

Lygurge Lycurgus

lyk like

lymes limbs

maad (inf. *maken*) made

maat downcast

maide virgin

maidenhede virginity

maintaine (l. 583) maintain; (l. 920) stand by

maister (l. 2044) *maister strete* main street

maistow mayst thou

make (l. 1698) counterpart

maked (inf. *maken*) made, caused

maketh (inf. *maken*) (l. 2177) causes

malencolik melancholic

manace threat

manasinge threatening

maner(e) way; (l. 1017) *every maner* every kind of; (l. 1031) *in manere of* like

manhede courage

manie mania

manly courageously

mansioun dwelling (but see note on l. 1116)

mantelet short cloak

mapul maple

marbul marble

Mars, Marte Mars

martireth (inf. *martiren*) martyrs, punishes

matrimoigne matrimony

maugree despite; (ll. 311, 1760) *maugree his heed* despite all he can do; (l. 749) *maugree al thy might* despite all you can do; (l. 938) *maugree hir eyen two* despite all they can do

mayst mayst; art capable

maystow mayst thou

Medea Medea

meeste, and leeste highest and lowest

meete properly

meeth mead

Meleagre Meleager

memorie (l. 1840) *in memorie* conscious

men men, people; one

mencioun mention

mene (inf. *menen*) mean, intend; say

mente (inf. *menen*) intended

Mercurie Mercury

meschaunce misfortune

mescheef harm

meschief disadvantage

messager messenger

mester occupation

mete (adj.) fit

mete (noun) food

meynee servants

might power; (l. 1254) *hath his might* is in possession of his full strength

ministre executor

minour miner

mirour mirror

mirre myrrh

misboden (inf. *misboden*) ill-treated, threatened

misfille (inf. *misfallen*) it went amiss

mishappe (inf. *mishappen*) it goes badly (for)

mo more

mone lamentation

montance value

mood anger

moore more, greater; (l. 683) *withouten any moore* without more delay; (l. 1458) *withoute moore* as my only request

moost most

mooste greatest

moot (no inf.) must

mordre murder

mordringe murder

morwe(ninge) morning

mosel muzzle

moste must

mowe may

muche (l. 2029) *in as muche as* in order that

muchel much

murie cheerful, pleasant

murmure complaint, dissatisfaction

myn my, mine

myrie see *murie*

myster (l. 852) *what myster men* what kind of men

nailes claws

nailinge see note on l. 1645

nakers kettle-drums

nam (inf. *been*) am not

name name, reputation

namely especially

234

namo no others

namoore no more

Narcisus Narcissus

— *nas* (inf. *been*) was not

nat not

nathelees nevertheless

naught not

nay no

ne neither, nor, not

necligence negligence

nedes necessarily; (l. 619) *nedes cost* necessarily

nedeth is (are) necessary

neer nearer

nekke neck

ner see *fer*

nercotikes narcotics

— *nere* (inf. *been*) were not, would not be, was not

Nero Nero

newe newly

nexte nearest

nis (inf. *been*) (there) is not

no thing not at all

noght not

nolde (inf. *willen*) would not

nombre number

none no

nones for the nones (l. 21) particularly; (l. 565) indeed

noon no, none

noot (inf. *witen*) do not know

norisshinge period of growth

ny nearly; *wel ny* very nearly

obeisaunce obedience

obsequies funeral ceremonies

observaunce (ll. 187, 642, 1406) rite; (l. 458) duty

of of; off

offence injury

offende(d) (inf. *offenden*) assail(ed), injure(d)

offensioun hurt

office (l. 2005) rite; (l. 560) *fil in office* got a position

officere official

ofte often; (l. 454) *ofte times* frequently

okes oaks

on on, in

ones once; (l. 1530) *ones on a time* on one occasion

Oo! listen!

ook oak

oold old

o(o)(n) one; (l. 913) *evere in oon* continually; (l. 923) *after oon* alike; (l. 979) *that oon* one; (l. 1260) *many on* many; (l. 1715) *of oon and oother* in pairs

oonly only, merely

ooth oath

oother other, the other, another

opie opium

opinio(u)n belief; (l. 622) intention; (l. 1269) choice

ordeyned (inf. *ordeynen*) provided

ordina(u)nce (l. 2154) decree; *by ordinance* in procession

ordre (l. 1076) *by ordre* in order

— *orison* prayer

othes oaths

ought at all

out (l. 765) *out of* lacking in

outhees outcry

outher either

outrely outright

over over, beyond; *over al* everywhere, anywhere

overriden (inf. *overriden*) run
 over
overthwart across
owene own
pace (inf. *pacen*) pass
pacience patience
paleys palace
palfreys saddle-horses
pan head
paramour(s) (l. 297) as a man
 loves a woman; (l. 1254)
 devotedly
pardee indeed
parementz rich mantles
parfit perfect
parlement (l. 448) decree;
 (l. 2112) assembly
part share; side; (l. 1934)
 have . . .part (of) protect;
 (l. 1966) *the moore part*
 the most part
partie (l. 1799) partisan
party mixed
pas foot, feet; (l. 1032) yards; *a
 pas* at walking pace
passant pre-eminent
passeth (inf. *passen*) continues
passinge (inf. *passen*)
 surpassing
payen pagan
pees peace
penaunce suffering
pencel paintbrush
Penneus Peneus
pennon small pointed flag
peple people
perfit perfect
Perotheus Pirithous
perrye jewellery
perturben disturb
peyne pain, torture
peynted (inf. *peynten*) painted

phisik medical treatment
pighte (inf. *pichen*) (l. 1831)
 pighte him fell
piler pillar
pilours pillagers
pine (inf. *pinen*) torture
pine (noun) suffering
pipen (*in*) blow (on)
pipes pipes; (l. 1894) veins
pitee pity
pitous full of pity, pious,
 pitiful
pitously pitifully, piously
place (l. 1541) field
plain see *pleyn*
plat plain
plates see note on l. 1263
plesaunce pleasure, will
pley joke, game
pleye (inf. *pleyen*) joke,
 amuse (oneself)
pleyinge amusement, relaxation
pleyn, plain (l. 629) full;
 (l. 606) fully; (l. 1603)
 severe; (l. 130) *pleyn
 bataille* open battle; (l. 233)
 short and plain long and
 short of it
pleyne(n) (*on*) lament, complain (about)
pleynly plainly, openly
Pluto Pluto
point (l. 643) essence; (l. 1908)
 part
polax battle axe
pomel top
porter gatekeeper
portreiture(s) painting(s)
portreyinge painting
portreyour painter
pose (inf. *posen*) (l. 304)
 I pose let us suppose

positif (l. 309) *positif lawe* human law

povre poor

povrely poorly, in poverty, humbly

pray(e) prey

preesseth (inf. *pre(e)ssen*) crowd

preeved (inf. *preven*) proved

prescience foreknowledge

preyde (inf. *preyen*) begged

preye (inf. *preyen*) pray, beg

preyere prayer, supplication

priketh (inf. *priken*) urges, dashes

prikinge (inf. *priken*) rushing, riding

prikke stab

prime early morning

pris reputation

privee secret

prively secretly

privetee secret

profreth (inf. *profren*) offers

progressiouns processes

propre own

proprely (l. 1929) exactly

proudly (l. 294) haughtily

Pruce Prussian

Puella see note on l. 1187

pure very

purveiaunce providence

putte (inf. *putten*) put; (l. 2084) *putte in* thrust in

pykepurs pickpocket

pyne suffering

qualm plague

questioun discussion

queynt(e) (inf. *quenchen*) (ll. 1463, 1478) quenched; (ll. 1476, 1479) was extinguished

queynte (adj.) strange

quiked (inf. *quiken*) revived

quite (inf. *quiten*) ransom

quitly completely

quod (inf. *quethen*) said

quook (inf. *quaken*) trembled

quyke alive

rad (inf. *reden*) read over

rage (l. 1127) raging wind

ran (inf. *runnen*) (l. 544) *ran him in his minde* suddenly occurred to him

rancour ill-feeling

ransake (inf. *ransaken*) search

rasour razor

rather sooner

raughte (inf. *rechen*) reached

raunsoun ransom

rebelling rebellion

recche(th) (inf. *recchen*) care(s)

reconforte (inf. *reconforten*) (l. 1994) *hem reconforte* take new heart

recorde (inf. *recorden*) confirm

rede (adj.) red

rede (inf. *reden*) advise

redily in readiness

redoutinge reverence

redy ready

reed (help) for it

refuge shelter

regioun kingdom; (l. 1899) area of the body

registre contents of book (see note on l. 1954)

regne (ll. 8, 1441) realm; (l. 766) rule

rehersing repetition

rek(e)ne(d) (inf. *reknen*) list(ed)

remedie way out

remenant remainder

renges ranks

renne(th) (inf. *rennen*) run(s), flow(s)

renoun reputation

rente (noun) income

— *rente* (inf. *renden*) tore

rentinge (inf. *renden*) tearing

repplicacioun answering back

rescus rescue attempt

rese (inf. *resen*) shake

resoun reason

resouneth (inf. *resounen*) resounds

respit delay

retenue see note on ll. 1643–5

retourninge return

reuled (inf. *reulen*) governed

rewe (noun) row

— *rewe* (inf. *rewen*) have pity

rewefulleste most sorrowful

reyneth (inf. *reynen*) rains

richesse wealth

right (adv.) just, very, quite, directly

right (noun) (l. 2231) justice

righte (adj.) direct

rightes (ll. 994, 1242) *at alle rightes* in every respect

ringes ringlets

rit (inf. *riden*) ride(s)

rite religious ceremony

roially in royal state

romed (inf. *romen*) roamed

romen roam

ronnen (inf. *rennen*) ran

rood (inf. *riden*) rode

roos (inf. *risen*) rose

roreth (inf. *roren*) (l. 2023) *roreth of* resounds with

rouketh (inf. *rouken*) cowers

— *route* company

routhe (a) pity

Rubeus see note on l. 1187

ruggy rough

ruine collapse

rumbel rumbling

sad composed

sadel-bowe projection at front of saddle

sadly firmly

Salomon Solomon

salueth (inf. *saluen*) greets

saluing greeting

salves ointments

Sampsoun Samson

sanguin blood-red

sarge serge (see note on l. 1710)

Saturne, Saturnus Saturn

saugh (inf. *seen*) saw

— *save* (conj.) except for

save (noun) sage

savinge except

— *sawe* saying; (l. 668) *al his sawe* everything he said

sayn, sey(e)n say

scapen escape

Scithia Scythia, a district north of the Black Sea

scriptures learned writings

see (noun) sea

seege siege

se(en) see

seene (l. 66) apparent

seet (inf. *sitten*) sat

seide see *seyde*

seigh (inf. *seen*) saw

seinte holy

seistow (inf. *seyn*) saist thou

seith (inf. *seyn*) says

selde seldom

selve same

semed (inf. *semen*) (l. 2112) *semed me* it would appear

238

semely fitting
sene (adj.) (l. 1440) visible
sene (verb) see
sentence decision, opinion
sepulture funeral rites
sermoning discussion
servage servitude
servise service; (ll. 568, 577)
  position
serye argument
seso(u)n season
seten (inf. *sitten*) sat, remained
sette (inf. *sitten*) (l. 712) reckon;
  (l. 1670) seated; (l. 2126)
  fixed; (l. 683) *sette him doun*
  sat down
seurete pledge
seyde(n), seide(n) (inf. *sayn,*
  sey(e)n) said
seyen see *sayn*
seye(th) (inf. *sayn, sey(e)n*)
  say
seyn (inf. *seen*) seen; (l. 807)
  seyn biforn foreseen
shaft stick, spear
shal (inf. *shullen*) shall be;
  (ll. 1420, 1466) must;
  (l. 1696) shall go; (ll. 1847,
  1848) would
shaltou shalt thou
shamefast modest
shap (l. 1058) form
shape(n) (inf. *shapen*) con-
  trived, fixed, destined;
  (l. 1683) arrange
sharp fierce
she(e)ne beautiful, shining
shent (inf. *shenden*) injured
shepne stable
shere scissors
sherte shirt
shet (inf. *shetten*) shut

shewed (inf. *shewen*) declared
shiveren (inf. *shiveren*)
  splinter
shode crown of the head
sholde (inf. *shullen*) should,
  would; (l. 1630) must
sholdest (inf. *shullen*) shouldst
shoon (inf. *shinen*) shone
shortly briefly, in a short time
shot missile
shrighte (inf. *shryken*)
  shrieked
shul(len) shall
shuldres shoulders
shynes shins
sighte sight; (l. 814) Providence
sike(d) (inf. *siken*) sigh(e)d
siker certain; *siker of* secure
  in
sikerly truly, certainly
sikes sighs
sin since
sit (inf. *sitten*) (ll. 749, 942)
  dwells
sith(en) since
sithe (l. 1019) *often sithe*
  often
slakke slow
sle (inf. *sleen*) kill
sleen kill
sleep (inf. *slepen*) slept
sleere killer
sleeth (inf. *sleen*) kills,
  slays
sleighte cunning
slep(es) sleep(s)
slepy sleep-producing
slider slippery
slogardie laziness
slough, slow (inf. *sleen*) slew,
  killed

slyly discreetly

smerte (adj.) stinging, piercing

smerte (inf. *smerten*) (l. 536)
 me smerte it hurts me

smite(th) (inf. *smiten*) strike(s)

smokinge (inf. *smoken*)
 burning incense in

smoot (inf. *smiten*) struck

so (l. 1379) provided that;
 (l. 1389) *so that* so long as

socour assistance

sodeynliche, sodeynly suddenly

softe gently, quietly

solempnitee ceremony, festivity

som some; one; (l. 1903) *this
 al and som* this is the long
 and short of it

somdel somewhat

somer summer

sone son

song (inf. *singen*) sang

songe(n) (inf. *singen*) sung

so(o)ng (inf. *singen*) sang

soor(e) (adj.) aching; (l. 1946)
 wounded

soore (adv.) severe(ly),
 extremely, passionately

soor(e) (noun) pain

sooth(ly) truly

soper supper

sore severely

sorwe sorrow

sorweful sorrowful

sorwen (inf. *sorwen*) are
 miserable

sorweth (inf. *sorwen*) is
 miserable

sory wretched

sothe for sothe truly

soun(es) sounds

soutil (l. 1172) fine; (l. 1191)
 skilful

soverein principal

space space of time

spak (inf. *speken*) spoke

spare (inf. *sparen*) refrain,
 give up

sparre beam

sparth battle-axe

speces patterns

special (l. 159) *in special*
 distinctly

spedde (inf. *speden*) (l. 359)
 him spedde hurried

spede (inf. *speden*) (l. 1700)
 God spede you good luck
 to you

speke (inf. *speken*) speak;
 (ll. 971, 1245) (*as for*) to
 speke of in respect of

spere spear

spicerye mixture of spices

spores spurs

sprad(de) (inf. *spreden*) spread

springe (inf. *springen*) (l. 1633)
 break; (l. 1664) rise

spronge (inf. *springen*) sprung
 up

square strong

squier(es) squire(s)

stable unchanging

stablissed (inf. *stablissen*)
 established

Stace Statius

stake see note on l. 1694

starf (inf. *sterven*) died

startlinge leaping

statue image

staves sticks

steede(s) war-horses

stent(e) (inf. *stenten*) stop(ped)

stenten cease

sterres stars

stert spring

sterte, stirte (inf. *sterten*)
leapt; (l. 186) spring up;
(ll. 535, 1826) sprang up;
(l. 904) started

sterve die

stevene time; voice

stierne grim

stille quietly

stirte see *sterte*

stith anvil

stok family

stoke (inf. *stoken*) stab

stole (inf. *stelen*) stolen

stomblen (inf. *stomblen*)
stumble

stonden stands; (l. 315)
stonden in hir grace receive
her favour; (l. 464) occur

stondeth (inf. *stonden*) stands

stongen (inf. *stingen*) sting

stoon stone

stounde moment; (l. 354) *oo*
stounde for a single
moment

stoute strong

straughte (inf. *strechen*)
stretched

stree straw

streight(e) directly

streit narrow

strepe (inf. *strepen*) strip

strif strife, argument

stronge strong, severe

stroof (inf. *striven*) vied

strook blow

stubbes stumps

studie fit of meditation

stynten put a stop to

stynt(e)(th) (inf. *stynten*)
cease(d) (talking); put an
end to

subtil intricate

successiouns by successiouns
in succession to one
another

suffisaunt adequate

suffised (inf. *suffisen*) sufficed

suffiseth (inf. *suffisen*) (it) is
(are) enough

suffren (l. 87) permit

suite (l. 2015) *of the same*
suite to match

sustene (inf. *sustene*) hold
up

suster sister(-in-law)

sustren sisters

swelte (inf. *swelten*) fainted

swerd(es) sword(s)

swich such (a)

swoor (inf. *sweren*) swore

swoote sweet

sworen (inf. *sweren*) promised

swough murmuring (of wind)

swowned (inf. *swownen*)
fainted

swowninge (inf. *swownen*)
fainting

syk sick

taak (inf. *taken*) take; (l. 226)
endure

taas heap

table tablet

take(n) (inf. *taken*) taken;
(ll. 1008, 1693, 1750) taken
prisoner, captured

tare seed

targe light shield

tarien (l. 2962) *tarien forth*
the day spend the whole
day

Tars Turkestan

teene annoyance

teeres, teeris tears

telleth (inf. *tellen*) tell

terme duration

termes periods

testeres head-pieces (for horses)

thank gratitude

thankes his (hir) thankes willingly, gladly

than(ne) then

that that; so that; when

ther there; where; *ther as* whereas, where

ther-biforn beforehand

therto moreover

therwithal thereupon

Theseus Theseus

thider to there, to it

thiderwards towards there, towards it

thikke (l. 198) solid; (l. 1652) densely; *thikke of* (l. 217) thick with

thilke the same, that

thinges (l. 1485) rites

thinketh (inf. *thinken*) (l. 1009) it seems (see note)

thirled (inf. *thirlen*) pierced

thise these

tho (adv.) then

tho (pron.) those

thonked (inf. *thonken*) thanked

though though; (l. 1096) yet

thoughte (inf. *thinken*) (it) seemed (e.g. *him thoughte* it seemed to him)

thral enslaved

threed thread

threste (inf. *thresten*) push

thridde third

thries thrice

thurgh through; out of; because of

thurghfare passage

thurgh-girt pierced through

thurghout right through

thyn thy, thine

thyselven thyself

til to; *til that* (l. 286) until

time (l. 1717) *by time* early

tirannye tyranny, arbitrary attitude

tiraunt tyrant

to to; for; too

tobreste (inf. *tobresten*) break to pieces

tobrosten (inf. *tobrosten*) shattered

togidre together

tohewen (inf. *tohewen*) cut to pieces

tolde see *toold*

tomorwe tomorrow

tonge tongue, speech

tonne-greet wide as a barrel

too toe

took (inf. *taken*) (l. 1408) understood

toold, tolde (inf. *tellen*) said, told, recounted

torn (l. 162) dragged

toshrede (inf. *toshreden*) cut to shreds

tour tower

touret turret

to(u)rneyinge (inf. *tourneyen*) tournament

tourrettes swivel-rings (for attaching leads)

Trace Thrace

trais traces

transfigure (inf. *transfiguren*) (reflexive) appear in another form

transmutacioun changeability

trapped having trappings

trappures horse-trappings
travaille labour
travaillinge in labour
treso(u)n treachery
trespas offence
tretee negotiation
trewe true, faithful
trewely faithfully, indeed
trompe(s) trumpet(s)
trompours trumpeters
tronchoun broken shaft of
  spear
trone throne
trouthe promise, word;
  (l. 1951) fidelity
trowed (inf. *trowen*) believe(d)
Troye Troy
Turkeys Turkish
turneying see *tourneyinge*
Turnus Turnus
tweye two
unknowe unknown
unkonninge ignorant
unkouth curious
unset unappointed
unto (l. 1690) against;
  (l. 1860) for
untressed (inf. *untressen*) let
  down
unwist of unknown to
unyolden without surrendering
up up; (l. 849) on
upright face upwards
upriste uprising
usage practice
usedest (inf. *usen*) enjoyed
vale valley
vassellage prowess
veine-blod blood-letting
venerye hunting
ventusing cupping

venym poison
verraily truly
verray true
vertu (l. 578) excellence;
  (l. 1391) power; (ll. 1891,
  1892) see note
vestimentz vestments
veyn(e) empty, vain
veze blast
vileynye (ll. 84, 1871)
  dishonour
voiden discharge
vois voice
vomit emetic
Vulcanus Vulcan
waiteth (inf. *waiten*)
  watches
wake-pleyes funeral games
wan (adj.) gloomy (see note
  on l. 1598)
wan (inf. *winnen*) won,
  conquered
wane (inf. *wanen*) decline
wanhope despair
wantinge lacking
wanye (inf. *wanien*) (l. 1220)
  (of moon) wane
war (ll. 38, 840) *was war*
  noticed; (l. 360) *be war*
  be careful
waste devastated
wasted (inf. *wasten*) decayed
wasteth (inf. *wasten*) decays
wawes waves
wayke weak
waymentinge lamentation
wedde (l. 360) *lith to wedde*
  is at stake
wedden marry
wede clothing
weel (adj.) (l. 68) prosperous;
  (l. 968) see *faire*

we(e)l(e) well; very; certainly;
(l. 1251) *wel was him* he
was lucky; (l. 2185) *take it
weel* accept cheerfully
weep (inf. *wepen*) wept
wele (l. 37) success; (l. 414)
happiness; (l. 1815) *in hir
wele* at their happiest
— *welle* source
__ *wende* (inf. *wenden*) go,
vanish
— *wende* (inf. *wenen*)
believed
wene(n) (inf. *wenen*) suppose
wepe (inf. *wepen*) weep
wep(e)ne weapon
were (inf. *been*) were, would
be
were (inf. *weren*) (l. 2090)
wear
were (inf. *weren*) defend
wered(e) (inf. *weren*) wore
weren (inf. *been*) were, had
been
werre war
werreye(n) make war (on)
wessh (inf. *wasshen*) washed
wete wet
wex (inf. *waxen*) grew
wexeth (inf. *waxen*) becomes
wexinge (of moon) waxing
wey(e) road, way
weyeth (inf. *weyen*) weighs
weylaway alas
whan when
what what; why; who; *what
so* whatever; *what for*
what with
wheither (l. 267) which (of
two); (l. 997) whichever;
(l. 998) whether
whelp cub

wher(e) (ll. 243, 1394, 1539)
whether
which which; who; *which a*
what a
whil while
whilom formerly
whippeltree dogwood
whit white
— *wight* person
wighte weight
wikke evil
wilnen desire
wilnest (inf. *wilnen*) desirest
wilneth (inf. *wilnen*) desires
wilugh willow
wise manner; (l. 480) *double
wise* twofold
wis(ly) certainly, surely
wiste (inf. *witen*) knew
wit mind
— *witen* know
withoute(n) without; (l. 1050)
on the outside
withseyn deny
witing knowledge
wo misery, sorrow, harm;
(l. 42) lamentation
wode(s) wood(s)
wodebinde honeysuckle
wofuller more unhappy
wolde would
— *woldestow* (inf. *willen*) wouldst
thou
wol(e) will, intend to
wolt (inf. *willen*) wilt,
desirest
— *woltow* (inf. *willen*) wilt thou
wommanhede womanliness
wonder (adj.) wonderful
wonder (adv.) incredibly,
extremely
wone custom

woneden (inf. *wonen*) (had) dwelt

wonne (inf. *winnen*) conquered

wont accustomed

wood mad, enraged

woodly fiercely

woodnesse madness

wook (inf. *waken*) woke

woost (inf. *witen*) knowest

woot (inf. *witen*) knows

worshipe honour, worship

worshipful honourable

worthily suitably

worthinesse nobility

worthy noble; (ll. 973, 1522, 1936) worthy

wostow (inf. *witen*) dost thou know

wowke week

wrastleth (inf. *wrastlen*) wrestle

wrecched wretched

wreke (inf. *wreken*) avenge

wrethe wreath

wroghte (inf. *werchen*) fashioned, made; caused; done; created

wrothe angry, enraged

wyf wife

wykes weeks

wyn wine

wys prudent, skilful

wyve (l. 1002) *to wyve* as a wife

yaf (inf. *yeven*) gave

ybete embroidered, beaten

yborn born, carried

ybounde(n) (inf. *binden*) (l. 291) obliged; (l. 1293) bound

ybrent (inf. *brennen*) burnt

ybro(u)ght (inf. *bringen*) brought

yburied (inf. *burien*) buried

yclenched clamped

ycleped (inf. *clepen*) called

yclothed (inf. *clothen*) dressed

ycorve (inf. *curven*) cut

ydo(n) (inf. *do(o)n*) done, acted, taken

ydrawe (inf. *drawen*) dragged

ydriven (inf. *driven*) driven

ydropped (inf. *droppen*) sprinkled

ye you

ye (ll. 238, 1822) eye; *at ye* at a glance

ye(e)r year, years

yelewe yellow

yelpe (inf. *yelpen*) boast

yemen attendants

yerde yard; (l. 529) staff

yere year

yet yet, still; (l. 1159) moreover

yeve (inf. *yeven*) give

yeve(n) see *yiven*

yeveth (inf. *yeven*) gives

yfetered (inf. *feteren*) fettered

yground (inf. *grinden*) ground, sharpened

yholde (inf. *holden*) considered as

yhurt (inf. *hurten*) wounded

yif (inf. *yiven*) give

yiftes gifts

yive (inf. *yiven*) give

yiven, yeven (inf. *yiven*) given

ylaft (inf. *leven*) left

yliche alike

ylike like, alike, equally

ymaked (inf. *maken*) made (into); held

ymet (inf. *meten*) met (in battle)

ymeynd mingled

ynough enough

yolden (inf. *yelden*) *up yolden* given up

yond over there

yonge young

yore (l. 955) *yore agon* long ago

youling howling

yow you

ypayed (inf. *payen*) paid

Ypolita Hippolyta

yraft (inf. *reven*) snatched away

yronne (inf. *rennen*) arranged

yronnen (inf. *rennen*) run together

ysaid (inf. *say(e)n*) said

yscalded (inf. *scalden*) scalded

ysent (inf. *senden*) sent

yserved (inf. *serven*) treated

yset (inf. *setten*) appointed

yslain (inf. *sleen*) slain

yslawe (inf. *sleen*) slain

yspoken (inf. *speken*) proposed

yspreynd scattered

ystiken (inf. *stiken*) stabbed

ystorve (inf. *sterven*) killed

ysworn (inf. *sweren*) sworn

yturned (inf. *turnen*) (l. 380) cast; (l. 1204) transformed

yvele hardly

ywedded (inf. *wedden*) married

ywonne (inf. *winnen*) won

ywrye (inf. *wryen*) covered